THE ESSENTIAL MARATHI COOKBOOK

Kaumudi Marathé was born in Pune, Maharashtra but her childhood was spent on three continents. She studied journalism in Mumbai and worked there as a journalist, writing on subjects ranging from local conservation issues and art to business and risk management.

She now lives with her husband and daughter in California where she cooks, writes and researches Indian food history. In 2007 she started un-curry, a catering company and cooking school, which features regional Indian cuisines.

For amusement, she runs, does tai chi and eats out. She likes to explore new cuisines but when comfort food is required, for her nothing beats home-made varan-bhat-tup or a dish of steaming hot pohé.

The Essential Marathi Cookbook is her third book. Her first cookbook of Marathi food is titled *Maharashtrian Cuisine: A Family Treasury* (Mumbai: Zaika, BPI, 1999). She has written a guide to India's Hindu architecture, *Temples of India: Circles of Stone* (Mumbai: Eeshwar, BPI, 1998).

For more information, visit the author's website: www.un-curry.com or email her at kaumudi@un-curry.com

THE ESSENTIAL
MARATHI
COOKBOOK

Kaumudi Marathé

PENGUIN BOOKS

An imprint of Penguin Random House

PENGUIN BOOKS

USA | Canada | UK | Ireland | Australia
New Zealand | India | South Africa | China

Penguin Books is part of the Penguin Random House group of companies
whose addresses can be found at global.penguinrandomhouse.com

Published by Penguin Random House India Pvt. Ltd
7th Floor, Infinity Tower C, DLF Cyber City,
Gurgaon 122 002, Haryana, India

Penguin
Random House
India

First published by Penguin Books India 2009

Copyright © Kaumudi Marathé 2009

All rights reserved

12 11 10 9 8 7 6

ISBN 9780143068020

Typeset in Sabon by Mantra Virtual Services, New Delhi

Printed at Repro Knowledgecast Limited, India

www.penguin.co.in

MIX
Paper from
responsible sources
FSC® C047271

This one's for
Meera
who feeds me with love
and
for
Keya
whom I love to feed

Contents

Come, let's fall ill,
It'll be such a lark!

I'll feast on sanja, and sago;
Go, lump sugar, raisins, sultanas,
Oranges and sweet lime, bring;
Go, rush to the market!

from *Padu AjAri, mauj heecha vAte bhAri!*
Bhanudas, Translated by Sudhakar Marathe, 2009

Foreword

My memories of food are always intermingled with memories of people. When I see a ghadichi poli appetizingly roasted till the layers separate and the surface becomes crisp, with nicely browned bits, I recall their fabulous taste, the warmth off the griddle and my mother behind the stove.

As for the flavours of Marathi food, one can never say enough. And yet it is barely known outside Maharashtra. It is astonishing that a community so fiercely proud of everything else Marathi does not feel the need to share its cuisine with the world. A lethargy or native tendency to tacit pride must account for this lacuna.

To wish to acclimatize oneself to it, study the phenomenon, take pride in it and write about it in a medium available worldwide —these are necessary acts of belonging. My daughter Kaumudi was deprived of my kind of upbringing, living as we did in other parts of India and beyond. I consider it a very fair deal that she should want to perform this service for the community to which she belongs. She has already written a much-appreciated book on the cuisine of both sides of her family. So it is her right and duty to study and write on this subject, by way of recovery of her native culture.

No one can write a 'complete' or exhaustive book about any cuisine, hardly surprising in light of the cultural and historical diversity involved. But the present book attempts to offer an introductory sketch of some history and information about Marathi society, and represents a great variety of recipes across the state and social strata. It definitely attempts to fill the huge gap in English language publication on Marathi cuisine.

The book also attempts to hint at the human system that enriched it, and the crucial role of food in family and community life. Personal references take the reader to individuals who contributed recipes. Much more needs to be said about the transmission of this art from generation to generation, its binding force within families and its role in nutrition and cultural evolution. That would require several bulky volumes.

The food habits of a society are an important yet inexhaustible kind of material in culture study. Yet a beginning must be made somewhere. Kaumudi presents the subject in English, something that could not have been achieved by translating an existing book. The difficulties and uncertainties inherent in the exercise are obvious. That someone who has spent a good deal of her life outside Maharashtra yet enjoyed its cuisine, wishes to write about it can only be described as matru-bhakti (service of the motherland). This lends the book a certain piquancy.

If readers feel there are lacunae or inadequacies, they can make the necessary effort to fill them. However, if the book proves an effective Shri Ganesha (auspicious beginning) for the great and necessary task of bringing together the cuisine and culture of Maharashtra, it will have served its main purpose.

As many imaginative and brave women have shown before, writing with erudition on sociology or politics need not be the only service to one's culture. A practically useful cookbook is fundamentally valuable. The recipes will satisfy those with adventurous palates, those in search of a balanced and nutritious diet, and also those who watch with alarm Marathi culture being consigned bit by bit to the dead letter office of history in a world increasingly dominated by idli-dosa, tandoori chicken, Macdonald's hamburgers and Smith & Jones' jars of ginger-garlic paste.

While economic compulsions mean that in most homes daily meals are routine, it would be fair to claim that there is hardly another cuisine in the world so nutritious, versatile, satisfying, varied and attractive. Yet Marathi cuisine has never found due recognition. I believe this book will pave the way for it.

Hyderabad
November 2009

Sudhakar Marathe

Acknowledgements

The Essential Marathi Cookbook has been a *TRIP*! I have made new friends, eaten the most delicious food and discovered much about my roots.

Without the encouragement and help of my father, Sudhakar Marathe, this book would have remained forever on my hard drive. Despite his super-busy schedule, Dad spent much time over the last few years, sharing invaluable information and insights; procuring recipes; translating from Marathi to English; and editing and re-editing my manuscript. I am eternally grateful to him for this and many other things, especially for making me eat my greens!

I am forever grateful to my mother, Meera Marathe and my maternal grandmother, Surekha Sirsikar (née Shakuntala Manjrekar) who taught me to love food, cooking and sharing by feeding me superb food in an atmosphere of joy and generosity.

For this project, Mom tested recipes and answered my frequent, probably annoying, questions promptly and enthusiastically. What she does not know about cooking is not worth knowing. This should really have been *her* book.

Other contributors include my grandmother, my great-aunt, the late Susheela Marathe and my aunts Sushama Marathe, Medha (Mangal) Marathe, Maya Kale-Laud, Jyoti Joshi, Madhavi Sirsikar, Usha Marathe and Manisha Sirsikar. Medha Marathe and my parents also shared recipes from my father's mother,

Padmavati Marathe (née Veerbala Modak).

My dear friend Anuradha Samant shared recipes from the Konkan and Kolhapur regions. Aruna Karande and her mother Susheelabai generously sent contributions from western Maharashtra.

Jeanne D'Penha and her family—mother, Iris; brother, Keith (a chef in his own right); and sister, Elizabeth Pereira—contributed many East Indian recipes and information. Historian Mohsina Mukkadam big-heartedly shared her wealth of knowledge, contributed Hindu and Muslim recipes and put me in touch with women from various Marathi communities.

My brother Sameer and sister-in-law, Dhanashree, procured books, utensils, spices and other necessities. I appreciate their help and the contributions of my cousins Ashwini Marathe, Aditi Bhide, Sheetal Joglekar, Pramodan Marathe and Sudarshan-Deepti Marathe.

My heartfelt thanks to all the other contributors: Deepak and Ujwal Mankar, Meeheika Karekar, Mira Gokhale, Prabhavati Gopalrao and Pradeep Gopal Deshpande, Pragati Parkar, Sheela Pradhan, Shubhangi Vaze, Uma Dadegaonkar.

I acknowledge all the grandmothers, mothers, aunts, sisters, cousins, friends and neighbours, whose recipes my contributors generously sent.

My friends Jagruti Gala and Sameera Khan sustained me with encouragement and feedback. Sameera shared her research on East Indian cooking and provided some important sources.

Other friends enthusiastically tested recipes or read parts of my manuscript: Jayalalitha Venkatraman, Lela Nargi, Robert Basile and Danny Kon.

My husband Sanjiv Bajaj is wonderful to cook for and unfailingly complimentary. He helped format this book, dealt with computer eccentricities and relieved me of other responsibilities so I could write. He also shot the wonderful photograph of beetrootchi dahyatli koshimbir used on the front cover.

My friend David King generously offered his office to work in, away from the distractions of home. I am grateful for that 'quiet space' and for his sense of humour.

Thank you to everyone at Penguin India who helped bring this book to fruition, particularly to Sherna Wadia for her meticulous editing. Obviously it was a rewarding collaboration with many. But for any errors in it, I take sole responsibility.

When I was a rookie journalist, Sheila Shahani and the late Janardhan Thakur guided me; Sharada Dwivedi gave me my first opportunity to write a book. I am also grateful to my teachers, P. Sainath and Jeroo Mulla, some of whose passion, energy and dedication to work rubbed off.

Stacy Kon, Alicia Gold and many other friends provided encouragement, shoulders to lean on, a good laugh when most needed and help with play dates when time was of the essence!

I could not have accomplished much in my life without dear ones who shared in culinary adventures and nourished me with love, food and conversation. Here I acknowledge some of them:

Lt. Col. S. M. Sirsikar (Anna) for helping to create my history and Srikrishna Chintaman Marathe (Appa) for gifting his love of history to me; Jerry and Beth Bentley, whose presence in my life enriches it; Janie McLeod, who believes; Sameera, Jagruti and Leena Pandit who've shared half my life with me; Rajeev Lingam who has been there even longer; Melkon Khosrovian and Litty Mathew who help make California home; Irene Borromeo, Melissa Robertson and Uta Briesewitz who prop me up and keep me going; Lawson-Andrea Newman, our first 'family' in the USA and the first recipients of my cooking experiments; Rachel Mathew and Nadia Fakhreddine, 'adoptive' mothers; my mother-in-law, Madhu Bajaj and the clan; and Jayalalitha Venkatraman, Mathew K. F., Jerry Pinto, Reena Sirsikar, Reny Mathew and Nick Almond, Yadira Rojas, Rosemarie Klee and Garnet and Robert Basile.

Most importantly, I thank Keya: for being my biggest supporter and best helper, for *oohing* and *aahing* over everything I cook, for always saying, '*You* make it better!' and for the Post-It that reads: 'You can DO it, Mama!' You are a joy to cook for. This book is for you.

Contributors and the Region/Community They Represent

Aditi Bhide: Pune/Konkanastha Brahman
Anuradha Samant: Mumbai-Kolhapur/Maratha
Aruna Karande: Sangli/Maratha
Ashwini Marathe: Pune/Konkanastha Brahman
Deepak and Ujwal Mankar: Mumbai/Patharé Prabhu
Iris, Jeanne, Keith D'Penha and Elizabeth Pereira: Vasai/East Indian
    Christian
Jyoti Joshi: Pune/Konkanastha Brahman
Madhavi and Ramesh Sirsikar: Mumbai/Saraswat Brahman
Maya Kale-Laud: Mumbai/Saraswat Brahman
Medha (Mangal) Marathe: Pune/Konkanastha and Saraswat
    Brahman
Meera Marathe: Nagpur-Pune/Saraswat Brahman
Mira Gokhale: Western Maharashtra/Deshastha Brahman
Meeheika Karekar: Mumbai/Sonar
Mohsina Mukkadam: Malvan, Konkan/Muslim
Prabhavati Gopalrao Deshpande: Beed, Marathwada/Deshastha
    Brahman
Pragati Parkar: Malvan, Konkan/Hindu
Sameer and Dhanashree Marathe: Pune/Konkanastha and
    Deshastha Brahman
Sheela Pradhan: Mumbai/Chandraseniya Kayastha Prabhu (CKP)
Sheetal Joglekar: Pune/Konkanastha Brahman
Shubhangi Vaze: Kurundwad-Sangli/Brahman
Sudhakar Marathe: Pune/Konkanastha Brahman
Surekha Sirsikar: Chindwada-Nagpur/Saraswat Brahman
Sushama Marathe: Pune/Konkanastha Brahman
Susheela Marathe (late): Pune/Konkanastha Brahman
Uma Dadegaonkar: Varhad/Deshastha Brahman
Usha and Deepti Marathe: Pune/Konkanastha Brahman.

Introduction

Food is the heart of any culture. But in one mere generation, from that of my father who was born in 1944 to my own (I was born in 1968), much has been lost of the rich cooking traditions of my native state, Maharashtra.

Over the years, many people have asked me what exactly Marathi cuisine is or even, only half-jokingly, wondered whether there is such a cuisine at all! Perhaps the fact that so few people, even in Mumbai, knew about Marathi food should not have astonished me. Marathi people have not done enough to make their food accessible to others, either from a self-deprecatory stance, a lack of entrepreneurship or the fact that, till very recently, eating out was not prevalent among urban middle-class Marathi people. Good Marathi food was only available in private homes. Even today, Marathi restaurants are few and far between, focussing only on a few regions or specialities.

Soon after I was married, my maternal grandmother (Vahini Aji) came to visit me in Mumbai. I asked her to share her recipes for my favourite dishes (her fabulous tomato-coconut soup, appropriately named santosh or 'contentment', prawns and her crisp, crunchy chakli). She did, all the while pooh-poohing the idea that what she was sharing might be important. Jotting down her recipes, I thought, 'Is there a more flavourful way to learn about one's history and culture than by documenting its recipes?'

I spoke to people of my grandparents' and parents' generations. Many warmly shared parts of their lives and memories, with recipes for dishes I had never heard of or eaten till then: wafola (savoury cabbage cake), khatta (vegetables in a sour gravy), khadkhadi (prawn pickle). These now make frequent appearances at my table. They also helped me to get to know my extended family and learn about Maharashtra in relation to myself. For instance, my affinity to kokum, rice, coconut and fish is more than personal taste; it is a 'collective unconscious' of food. Since my roots are in the Konkan where these ingredients have been consumed for centuries, they are 'in my blood'.

For me, Marathi food is *comfort, family* and *history*. It is *essential* and very much worth sharing. Eager to do so, I wrote an English language cookbook of Marathi food in 1999.[1] In 2003, years after that book was published and sold out, I was astonished that there was still no other representative English language book of Marathi cooking in Indian bookstores. I suggested *The Essential Marathi Cookbook* to Penguin India and here we are.

An increasingly urban and global culture (and I write as a self-avowed city slicker and citizen of the world)[2] and a lack of documentation have exacerbated the loss of culinary traditions. Just as in other social arts, in cooking too, it is natural that over time, some foods, dishes, ingredients will be lost to us as others are revealed. However, because India as a society has traditionally not documented great parts of its heritage on paper, be that its legacy of music, dance or food, we lack the kind of record available to certain other cultures where cooking and food history are concerned.

Until recently, this lacuna was perhaps not much of an issue. Family was close at hand and oral history alive and well. But now recording food history is not only critical, it is essential. Our lives are much faster paced than our parents'. We live farther and farther away from older relatives, obvious and natural teachers of arts such as cooking.

I am the first to applaud the fact that liberation from the kitchen has been an important political statement for women.

Cooking should be a conscious personal choice. But today, both men and women are so busy multitasking that we often look for short cuts, unwilling to make food from scratch, choosing convenient, ready-made products over more 'time-consuming' home-made ones or even simply eating out instead of cooking for ourselves.

Yes, we have a *lot* to do—laundry, bills, spending quality time with our kids. But if the quality of our efforts in these realms matters, should it not matter what we put into our stomachs, what legacy we leave our children? Making a full-scale traditional meal every day may be unrealistic but once every few weeks, it can be a great trip down memory lane or a creative history project with the children.

In our speed-of-light lifestyles, smaller homes (often apartments rather than houses with extended outdoor kitchens, pantries, vegetable gardens, etc.) and nuclear family set-ups (less division of labour), our stockpile of recipes is dwindling and many ingredients and implements risk being lost or becoming obsolete within this generation.

In a small urban kitchen, there is little room to store and use traditional utensils like a large mortar and pestle or a pata-varvanta (grinding stone), with which to turn coconut, herbs and spices into fine, delicately nuanced seasonings and chutney pastes. We do have refrigerators, blenders and other convenient time-saving innovations and gadgets but funnily enough, these have irrevocably altered the taste of our food, limiting *what* we cook and *how* we cook it. For instance, though the blender grinds or blends up food satisfactorily enough, it cannot replicate the flavour and texture of patiently hand-ground pastes. The earthiness of the rough stone pata-varvanta and the ability of the hand to gauge texture and doneness are missing. I can never make with my blender the silky coconut-garlic chutney my grandmother made several times a month on her grinding stone.

The careful advance planning and enjoyable anticipation, the patience and care needed to prepare certain dishes have been replaced by hurry and lack of time. The language to express some of these culinary processes and ingredients is disappearing too. And who spends hours any more peeling dozens of tiny incipient bananas nestled in a banana flower, staining their hands purple in the process, to make kelphulachi bhaji (sautéed banana blossoms)? When I was fifteen, my father taught me how to peel the tiny fruit and gently remove the edible portion. The time it took to peel them all frustrated me. However, the dish my mother made with the blossoms was exquisite.

Most lamentable of all is the lost opportunity of learning by osmosis. I grew up watching Mom and my grandmothers plan the day's meals, shop for and prepare vegetables, knead dough, clean fish, do everything, really. So though I did not actually start cooking till I was twenty-three, as my husband puts it: 'The day after we were married, she went into the kitchen and made a meal as if she had been doing it all her life!' Obviously, I learnt something during my childhood without knowing I was in cooking school!

Now my own daughter, Keya, lives in the USA, 10,000 miles away from *her* grandmothers and great grandmother. Osmosis from them is impossible. To Keya, even common Marathi words like pata-varvanta or ladu require explanation just as gavhlé or dagad phul do for me (if they mean nothing to you either, don't worry, they are explained here).

In the days before TV, radio, the Internet, fast travel and even electricity, entertainment was a communal activity, a coming together of generations in moments of sharing and learning, including the making and sharing of food.

In an age when going to the movies or meeting friends for coffee was not the trend, life revolved around work, which happened all the time. While achieving some goal it was also an enjoyable social activity, rooting one to the community. In the introduction to her 1978 Marathi-language cookbook *Annapurna*, author Mangala Barve writes about the 'avdicha kam' (pleasurable work) of women (or men). A homemaker's life was full, even tough. Apart from daily chores and cooking, almost everything was prepared at home seasonally; pasta, papad, pickles, jams, herbal drinks, dried vegetables and fruits. In the evenings, women would carry dough in a bowl to the temple, shaping it into gavhlé (small pasta) as they listened to a kirtan (the narrative by a Haridas). They also collaborated on annual work, gathering to make pickles or papad. They even sang special songs on such occasions.

Weddings, 'baby showers', naming ceremonies, haldi-kunku[3] and festivals were extra-special occasions on which to gather and see loved ones. Part of the enjoyment and excitement was the preparation. Everyone pitched in, making sweets and snacks, cooking meals, decorating the house with flowers, lamps and rangoli (rice powder patterns drawn on the floor and yard). Out-of-town relatives often arrived weeks ahead of time to help: rolling ladus, sorting vegetables, chatting, singing, recalling the 'good old days'. Children watched their elders, helped, and learned, storing up a fund of experience, social knowledge and folklore. Today we are increasingly removed from such exchange and education.

In this age of instant gratification, we are also losing a sense of seasonality. A premium is being set on *availability* rather than on *anticipation*, eroding the connection between food and the natural and social occasions when it might be prepared or needed to sustain the body. Many ingredients are now available year round instead of seasonally, and thanks to modern methods of preservation, we rarely lack products we are in the mood for.

Not so long ago, many fruits and vegetables (green peas, cauliflower, sugarcane) were available only in the winter, others (mangoes, drumsticks) in the summer. People looked forward to using them in special dishes and recalled them with relish for the rest of the year.

I remember, about thirty years ago, helping my paternal grandmother (Ai Aji) shell harbhara (fresh gram) on her stoop. My cousins and I nibbled the sweet beans, then watched her make pastries with them, and devoured them fresh out of the wok. Often I watched Mom roll a batch of semolina ladus, eagerly waiting for one to bite into. These are qualitatively different experiences

Introduction   5

from quickly opening up a bag of frozen green peas or pulling chocolate out of a wrapper.

A related idea is *terroir* or what I consider respect for the origins of food. In the French language the word literally means land or soil. But in France, a nation famous the world over for its cuisine and its enlightened attitude to food, the term has a broader connotation. *Terroir* denotes the particular origins of a product like a wine or a cheese (now other foods or ingredients too): either the peculiarities of the land, soil and climate that the ingredients were grown or raised in *or* the particular traditional processes by which the product was made in its region of origin.

Each region has its own peculiar characteristics that make its products unique and these distinctive elements must be appreciated and preserved to protect diversity and quality of taste, the history of tradition and the artisanal method of production. In a world increasingly fed industrially mass-produced foods and food products, the concept fosters a high standard of local flavour and craftsmanship.

In India, people have long been aware of quality regional ingredients and products: jaggery (unrefined sugar) from Kolhapur, the fragrant saffron of Kashmir's hill slopes, fresh kokum (*Garcinia indica*) from Goa, milk products of the Punjab. Maharashtra itself is only a little smaller in size than France and boasts (dare I say it?) as much culinary variety or *more*. But do we protect our food products and those responsible for growing, making or processing them? To preserve regional culinary traditions, ingredients, craftsmanship and provenance, and to ensure the worth of such ingredients and foods in the eyes of consumers, Indians must emulate the French model. This includes preserving our regional cooking traditions.

By the mid-twentieth century, some Marathi women were already thinking about the consequences of neglecting our culinary and cultural heritage and blindly aping the West. These 'housewives' had vision and foresight. In an era before computers and the Internet, with typewriters not commonly used for Marathi writing, the likes of Laxmibai Vaidya (*Pakasiddhi*[4]), Kamalabai

Ogale (*Ruchira*[5]) and later, Mangala Barve did us a huge favour by painstakingly researching and collating priceless information about Maharashtra's foods, culinary traditions and social mores.

Their books are the Marathi equivalents of the American classic, *The Joy Of Cooking*,[6] providing recipes from every region in Maharashtra. They also share valuable information: from why we eat certain foods at certain times of the year to which foods are suitable for fasts and festivals; from how to serve a meal on a banana leaf or taat (diagrams included) to what pans to cook certain foods in.

And their outlook towards nutrition is surprisingly modern. Barve, writing nearly 30 years ago, encourages eating locally and seasonally, combining different groups of ingredients (like lentils with grain) for an overall nutritional package, and making food enjoyable and interesting for children.

These books were aimed at women, chiefly young brides and new housewives. They are somewhat outdated and they take for granted a certain prerequisite of culinary knowledge in their users. But their essence is noteworthy: how to provide tasty, nutritious, efficiently and affordably cooked food for your loved ones in the context of your environment.

Since then, others have written niche, Marathi-language cookbooks. Their inexpensive, locally published work definitely makes the state's food accessible to literate Marathi users. It includes collections by writers focussing on their own communities or regions or specific dishes.[7] Many share my fear of 'loss'. But again, they assume Marathi language and culinary enculturation in their audience. They are not accessible to non-Marathis or to those who lack the vocabulary or grounding to make sense of laconic instructions like 'make a syrup' or 'add the *usual* seasoning ingredients'.

My book aims at filling in the gaps. It is written for anyone who wants to learn about Maharashtra's culinary riches. I don't take their knowledge for granted. *The Essential Marathi Cookbook* provides cooking basics: processes, ingredients and spices, and recipes for the principal elements of a middle-class Marathi meal.

Most recipes are middle class, because for the majority, cooking is largely just a means of survival. The norm is a staple (bhakri or rice) with one accompaniment: a mess of besan (gram flour), salt and chillies; a chutney, lightly sautéed seasonal wild greens or a little lentil soup; an onion smashed open with the fist; or even just a green chilli and salt.

An exhaustive one-volume document on the subject is impossible but I hope these recipes (tested by their contributors and myself) give a sense of the diversity of Marathi peoples and cultures. There are recipes from Hindu communities across the socio-economic spectrum and a sampling of recipes from Marathi Muslims and East Indian Christians who share a language, ethnicity and many traditions with their Hindu compatriots but also have their own unique customs.

There are dishes that may be bywords of Marathi culture abroad: puranachi poli, jhunka-bhakar, pohé and sabudanyachi khichadi; and recipes for equally well-loved dishes unknown outside Maharashtra: gulachi poli, besnaché ladu, gavhlyachi kheer. There are regional and family variations. And I am proud to bring you regional specialties that you may not find in any other English-language publication on Marathi food, like kulthachi pithi (vetch pithla) from the Konkan, ukad shengulé (sorghum pasta) from Beed and sarolyachi kheer (home-made pasta-twist pudding) from Varhad. To include these, I have reluctantly foregone classics like jilebi or ghavan-ghatlé, which are either widely available or often written about. My apologies in advance to people who feel certain recipes should have been included or that others don't quite belong here.

Keya is my most recent reason for writing this book. She is eight and has been 'in the kitchen' since she was four months old. Living in the USA without extended family or the help many people in India are lucky to have, I wanted to engage and involve her while I cooked! She would sit in her baby seat, content to watch and listen intently as I explained what I was doing.

The older she gets, the more symbiotic our kitchen relationship becomes. We usually cook dinner together. She helps weigh ingredients, chops soft foods with a knife, stirs yogurt for raita. She also likes to hear stories of my childhood; how I sipped Vahini Aji's spiced buttermilk with my grandfather, Anna, or how occasionally a farmer would stop his cart and hop out to visit Anna, calling out, 'Namaskar, Colonel Saheb', bringing him a sack of onions, green peas or peanuts straight from the farm.

When my father recalls the foods and habits of his childhood, I am as captivated as Keya is with my stories. Dad told me tea, once always meant gulacha chaha (jaggery-sweetened tea) because refined sugar was neither common nor affordable. I had never drunk gulacha chaha but it sounded delicious, 'exotic'!

In the span of thirty-five years, the prosaic facts of my father's reality have become the wondrous tales of my family history. Change is inevitable and often welcome. However, remembering the past is to honour it and to learn from it. These recipes give us a glimpse into many personal histories, into stories of people's families, lives and loves told through their taste buds.

No one expresses it better than M.F.K. Fisher, a food writer I have long admired:

> ... like most other humans I am hungry . . . . Our three basic needs, for food and security and love, are so mixed and mingled and entwined that we cannot straightly [sic] think of one without the others ... When I write of hunger, I am writing about love and the hunger for it, and warmth and the love of it and the hunger for it ... and then the warmth and richness and fine reality of hungers satisfied ... it is all one.[8]

I hope *The Essential Marathi Cookbook* will satisfy some hungers, reconnect you to your history and lead to a greater understanding of the traditions that shape who you are.

THE BOOK

Read the introductory chapters before attempting the recipes. 'The State, the People, the Cuisine' gives a background of Maharashtra and Marathi people. 'The Marathi Kitchen' introduces important

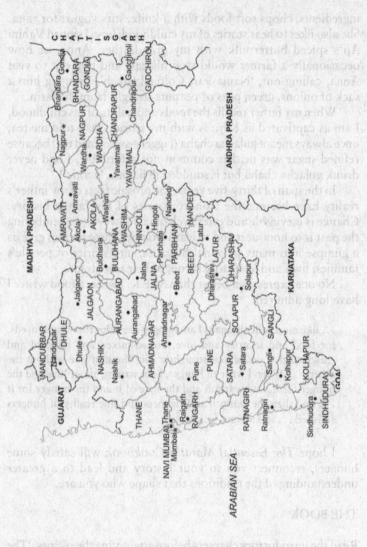

The Essential Marathi Cookbook

ingredients, tools, cooking methods. 'The Ingredient Primer' explains some of these in depth.

Over 240 recipes and 35 variations are divided into 11 chapters for easy reference. Recipes are categorized as snacks, breakfasts, grains, etc., but frequently cross over. You can eat a breakfast dish for lunch, desserts as snacks, salads as condiments, etc. Use the recipes to suit your tastes.

Chapter introductions and recipes themselves provide important cooking, storage and usage tips, menu suggestions and page references to similar recipes or related processes. Quotes in recipes come from their respective contributors.

A dish may specify main ingredients but I indicate when other ingredients may be cooked the same way. If ingredients are hard to locate, substitutions are suggested.

Important: Information about the therapeutic qualities of ingredients comes from *folklore* or *common knowledge*, not from a doctor. No medical claims are made. Before using ingredients that might be a health concern, *consult your physician*.

HOME STATE

Maharashtra lies along India's west coast, the third largest state in the nation[9] with the second largest population.[10] Important cities include the capitals: Mumbai on the west coast and Nagpur in the north-east, Pune (my home town), Solapur in the south-east, Aurangabad and Nashik in the north, and Kolhapur towards the south.

Maha-rashtra (great state) has the largest state economy—about 13 per cent of the national income.[11] The economy of this industrial and industrialized region (Mumbai is its commercial and financial heart) once hinged on agriculture. Even today, there is significant agricultural production, and fishing is an important industry.

A long, rugged coastline and lush coastal lowlands delineate Maharashtra's western border. Just east is the Western Ghat mountain range (640 km). Further east is the Deccan Plateau, with the Krishna, Bhima and Godavari river valleys.

Maharashtra's monsoon climate has four seasons: March–May (hot–dry), June–September (hot–wet), October–November (warm–dry), and December–February (cool–dry). Coastal regions are humid with heavy rainfall in parts of the Konkan (up to 6,350 mm per year). But the plateau, home to some of India's least fertile, most underprivileged regions,[12] can get as little as 635 mm annually.

Food crops—sorghum, millet, sugarcane and pulses (including peanuts)—make up a large part of the harvest (cotton and tobacco are major cash crops). Rice is grown in areas of high rainfall while wheat is the plateau's winter crop. Mangoes, bananas, oranges and cashew are widely grown as are many indigenous and 'imported' vegetables and fruit.

THE PEOPLE AND THE CUISINE

Maharashtra's many communities are varied by caste, religion, ethnicity and economic wherewithal. There has been much genetic exchange over the ages. Noteworthy are Marathi and other communities that inhabit either side of Maharashtra's borders: Gujarat (north), Madhya Pradesh (north-east), Orissa (east), Andhra Pradesh (south-east), Goa-Karnataka (south and west). Equally important are the culturally and linguistically somewhat distinct regions of the west coast (Konkan and Goa) and the Deccan Plateau ('Desh').

Regardless of its provenance, the essence of Marathi food stems from an often-harsh climate and the innovations of frugal people who made a little go a long way. Its success lies in subtle, complex tastes and healthy, flavourful dishes. Geographical, weather and soil differences also influenced the genesis of diverse culinary styles. Along the coast, seafood, rice, coconut and mango figure largely; inland, grains like wheat, millet and sorghum are the staple, complemented by lentils, jaggery, peanuts and tamarind.

The majority of people are Hindu, for millennia divided into

The Essential Marathi Cookbook

four major castes: Brahman (priests), Kshatriya (warriors), Vaishya (merchants) and Shudra (labourers), with many sub-castes. While the Konkanastha and some other Brahman communities traditionally ate no meat, the Saraswats ate seafood. Other castes generally ate meat and seafood when possible. Again, many Brahman communities considered onion and garlic taboo but people of other social groups consumed them.

Maharashtra's Kshatriyas, the Marathas, possibly the most widely recognized Marathi people outside the state, are traditionally soldiers, farmers or landowners. The most famous was Shivaji.

Other Hindu communities include the Chandraseniya Kayastha Prabhus (CKPs), a Kshatriya sub-caste whose roots are said to be in Kashmir, and the Patharé Prabhus, thought to have migrated to Mumbai from Rajasthan in the twelfth to thirteenth centuries. They are some of Mumbai's oldest residents. Its other ancient inhabitants are the Koli fisher folk[13] whose diet included seafood and rice-flour bread.

Of the many Muslim peoples across the state, some are native, like the coastal people, from Thane in the north to Sawantwadi in the south, frequently called Konkani Muslims. The term 'Malvani Muslim' refers specifically to Muslims from Malvan, the southern part of the Konkan. Marathi Muslims eat indigenous ingredients and regional dishes like jhunka-bhakar as well as pan-Indian Muslim dishes like biryani.

One Marathi Christian community is called 'East Indian'. Their ancestors took the name from Britain's East India Company (for whom many worked) to distinguish themselves from Goan Christians. East Indians, fisher folk and farmers from Bassein (Vasai), likely converted to Christianity en masse by the Portuguese before the British colonized the region, adopted Portuguese names (Fernandes, Viegas, etc.) and often learned and spoke Portuguese.

Many continued to speak Marathi and retained some pre-Christian traditions (the nau-vari/nine yard sari and kumkum/tikli). Their food had Marathi roots and British and Portuguese influences. They consumed more seafood and meat than Hindus and had their own characteristic spice blends.

Maharashtra's Bene Israeli Jews are a dwindling group, many members having emigrated to Israel. Said to be descendants of Jewish oil pressers who left Galilee to escape persecution in the second century BCE, they mixed with the native folk, adopting their language but retaining many original customs. Their cuisine was influenced by the tastes of their adopted home.[14]

Maharashtra is also home to many tribal peoples (Agaris, Warlis, Bhils, Gonds, etc.) with their own unique cultures and lifestyles. Unfortunately it is impossible to take stock of their cuisines here.

There is a minimal use of fat in Marathi cuisine. Foods are generally not overcooked or double-fried. Though deep-frying is important, especially on festive occasions and for snacks, it is not prominent in everyday cooking.

With its lack of preoccupation with meat, it is ideal for vegetarians. Lentils, providing 99 per cent of the proteins found in meat, are the major protein source. I doubt if such a plethora of legumes is used so diversely anywhere else. They are eaten raw, sprouted or cooked and used whole, split, powdered, and as flour.

Vegetables retain texture and flavour, and a large variety of cultivated and wild leafy green vegetables are popular.

The number, variety and richness of foods reduces as one descends the economic ladder but it is hard to match the range of Maharashtra's sweet, savoury and spicy snacks. Sweets particularly, play a crucial role as special occasions are observed by their preparation.

Before the advent of refrigeration and artificial preservatives, preserving vegetables, fruits and other ingredients against emergencies was critical. The sun's power was used creatively to preserve almost anything edible. Fresh fruits and vegetables were sun-dried and dehydrated, or preserved in pickles and jams. Other ingredients were converted to long-lasting papads.

Fasting is an age-old socio-religious tradition. Some days are personal fasting days while others, like Mahashivaratri, see the community fasting as a whole. Special weekly and monthly fasts celebrate ancient observances (the full moon, harvests, etc.). Muslims fast during the mourning month of Ramzan. Catholics observe strict dietary rules during the forty days of Lent.

India possesses a rich culture of foods with which to break fasts. Children, though not expected to fast, look forward to such days for delicious treats like sabudanyachi khichadi (p. 67) or batatyacha kees (p. 86).

THE MEAL

While many Marathi people eat three square meals a day, some are lucky to have even one. The traditional working-class meal consisted of a staple starch and side dish or condiment. The middle-class meal was a better-balanced mix of grains, pulses, vegetables, condiments and milk products.

The staple (bread or rice) provides the most calories, eaten in larger quantities than vegetables, meats or lentils, which supply other nutrients and add texture, flavour and contrast.

Traditionally, middle-class folk sat to eat on a paat (low wooden seat). Today most white-collar urban people reserve these for festivals or religious rites. Food was served in a taat (large metal plate) on the ground or on another paat in front of the seat. For special occasions, food was served on a banana leaf or patraval (a leaf plate) with several vati/dron (bowls) for gravied dishes, buttermilk and sometimes dessert. A phulpatra (tumbler) and tambya (a bulbous metal container of water) were placed next to the plate, on the left.

Meeth (salt) and every other item of food has a designated location. Salt, an essential, is served first (except at a meal following obsequies) at the farthest point on the taat from the eater. To the right are one or two bhajya (vegetables), and amti (gravied lentils). To the left are dishes requiring less replenishing: limbu (lime wedges), pickle or chutney, koshimbir or bharit (salad) and tondi lavna (appetizers).

Bhat (rice) is served in the centre of the plate, closest to the eater, topped with varan (yellow lentils) and tup (ghee or clarified butter). When the entire first course or meal has been served to the whole company, the Brahmans, at least, offer chitravati/chitrahuti (honorary morsels of food to the gods), before eating.

For those who could afford them, there might be as many as four courses in a meal served on the same plate:

The first course: As described above. More courses are offered after it is finished.

The second course: Special spiced rice, with the same accompaniments.

The main course: A sweet bread like puran poli, or special desserts like shrikhand, kheer, etc., possibly with bread. Side dishes are served throughout the meal, except during the last course. Special accompaniments might be offered.

The fourth course: Hot white rice with yogurt or buttermilk. People finish their side dishes to avoid waste.

Lunch and dinner menus differ, in that, people who can, generally eat smaller quantities and easily digestible food at night: hot white rice, sar or kadhi (soup) yogurt or buttermilk.

Dessert, not part of an everyday meal, is the focus on special occasions. It is served as the main course and eaten in large quantities. At his wedding feast, my skinny father surprised his in-laws by easily consuming twenty-five jilebis!

A digestive might conclude a meal: badishep (fennel seeds); dried, sweetened or salted avla (Indian gooseberries); supari (betel nut); or vida (betel leaf) with edible lime, catechu, spices and betel nut. A special vida might contain fresh coconut with sugar or gulkand (rose petal jam).

THE CALENDAR

Though the Gregorian calendar is widely used in India's secular life, Hindus consult a lunar calendar for socio-religious purposes. Muslims use a different lunar calendar.

Because of the lunar basis, most Hindu festivals are moveable feasts. Important celebrations are listed by month, along with major secular celebrations and some important holidays/

observances of other religions (in italics).

Chaitra (March–April): Gudhi Padva (Marathi New Year);
Ram Navmi.

Vaishakha (April–May): Akshay Truteeya; Hanuman Jayanti;
Mahavir Jayanti; *Buddha Jayanti*; *Eid E Milad*; *Easter*;
Maharashtra Day (1 May).

Jyeshtha (May–June): Vata Purnima.

Ashadh (June–July): Guru Purnima.

Shravan (July–August): Nag Panchami; Narali Purnima;
Raksha Bandhan; Gokulashtami.

Bhadrapad (August–September): Ganpati Utsav (10 days,
Ganesh Chaturthi to Anant Chaturdashi); Gauri Puja; *Indian
Independence Day (15 August)*.

Ashwin (September–October): Navratri-Dussehra (10 days);
Kojagiri Purnima.

Kartik (October–November): Diwali (up to 5 days:
Dhanatrayodashi, Narak Chaturdashi, Deepavali, Bali Pratipada,
Bhau Beej); *Eid-ul-Fitr (ends month-long Ramzan fast)*.

Margasheersha (November–December): Datta Jayanti.

Paush (December–January): Bhogi; Sankranti *(10/14 January)*;
*Christmas (25 December); New Year (1 January); Bakr-Eid; Indian
Republic Day (26 January)*.

Magh (January–February): Vasant Panchami; Mahashivaratri;
Moharram.

Falgun (February–March): Holi Purnima; Dhuli Vandan;
Ranga Panchami.

HINDU FESTIVALS

Maharashtra celebrates holidays and festivals with great
enthusiasm. There are four types of monthly observances: san
(holiday); utsav (festival); jayanti (the birth anniversary of a god,
saint or hero) and jatra (fair).[15] Every occasion is an opportunity
to celebrate with folk songs, dances, games and special foods.

Important auspicious days include Gudhi Padva (the New
Year); Sankranti (the Winter Solstice), generally celebrated on

14 January with sesame sweets; Holi and Ranga Panchami, observed in the spring with bonfires and boisterous games; and Dussehra, an autumn festival. Ganesh Utsav is celebrated for 10 days at the end of the monsoon.

Diwali, the year's most highly anticipated festival, celebrates the return of Ram, Sita and Lakshmana to Ayodhya after their exile. Homes are cleaned, quantities of pharal (sweets and snacks) are prepared, and the five festival days are celebrated with new clothes, fire crackers, feasts, exchanges of visits and religious rituals; the goddess of wealth, Lakshmi is honoured on Lakshmi Pujan day; husbands and wives are honoured on Dhanatrayodashi; and the bond between brothers and sisters is renewed on Bhau Beej.

THE MARATHI KITCHEN

Swayampak (cooking)
Marathi cuisine can satisfy virtually every taste, ingeniously combining salty, bland, sweet, sour, spicy and bitter flavours. It uses a vast number of ingredients in innovative and even improbable ways.

Cooking methods retain the nutritive value of food and recipes pair equally well with other Indian and Western foods. Many dishes can be made beforehand and reheated before serving, while others can be made very quickly.

Cooking *can* be labour-intensive, requiring chopping, mincing, grating, grinding, etc. but is also frequently quick and easy, since many traditional recipes are designed for quick cooking and instant gratification.

With a little planning, you can have a simple, nutritious and balanced meal (rice, lentils, vegetables and salad) on the table in under 60 minutes.

Kitchen Implements
Apart from basic implements, you may need: a cheesecloth; ceramic or glass jars; griddle; pressure cooker; rolling board and pin; slotted spoons; spice mill; and wok.

Optional Implements

Ganja/taakacha bhanda (buttermilk pan): A narrow, 6"-10" high butter and tup pan.

Katna (scallop-edged pastry crimper): To cut and shape the edges of karanjis, shankarpalis, etc.

Khalbatta (mortar and pestle): For grinding or pounding spices, etc.

Masalyacha daba (spice box): A round metal box, with 6-8 small cylindrical containers for storing basic spices and measuring spoon.

Modak patra (steamer): Used to steam modak or other foods.

Parat (mixing platter): A large multipurpose metal plate in several sizes, with distinctly raised sloping sides. It is used for making and kneading dough, shaping bhakri, cleaning lentils and grains, drying foods and prepping vegetables.

Pata-varvanta (grinding stone and pestle): A thick, flat, rough-hewn stone for grinding chutneys, pastes, etc. Placed on a counter or the floor, the long stone pestle is rolled back and forth to grind ingredients between the two surfaces. Some water or tamarind pulp helps in the process.

Phodnichi kadhai (seasoning wok): A small iron wok for making oil seasonings. Sometimes an iron ladle (pali) was used. The modern version has a heat-resistant handle.

Puranacha yantra (food mill): For grinding gram cooked with jaggery for puranachaya polya; or for other ingredients.

Ravi (butter churning stick): Used with a ganja to make butter and buttermilk, and to stir/smoothen cooked lentils.

Sorya (chakli and shev press): A wooden or brass press with various stencils to shape dough in different patterns and sizes for frying.

Sup (winnowing fan): To separate broken bits, chaff, etc. from grain. To keep ingredients from falling through, the very tightly woven surface was covered with an application of wet, antiseptic cow dung and thoroughly dried.

Vati (metal bowl): A multipurpose bowl (for serving liquid dishes, measuring ingredients, etc.), which holds about 100 gms solid ingredients.

Vili (board knife): The traditional Marathi knife, with its curved blade set obliquely in a wooden seat. Sit with one knee on the base facing the knife to cut ingredients or to grate coconut on the rounded, serrated top. Place a plate below its circular, serrated grater to collect the shavings.

WEIGHTS AND MEASURES

Recipes list ingredients by weight/quantity, as appropriate. There is generally a lot of 'andaaz' (experienced guesswork) involved in Indian cooking. I have tested my contributors' estimates and converted them into metric measures. For Imperial measures, use the table below. For recipes where ingredient volume matters, I retain cup measures.

Cooking times are as precise as possible but there are variables: altitude, heating methods, ingredients, stoves, water, weather, etc. Oven temperatures are provided where relevant. For ovens without a temperature gauge, the medium setting works best. For baking and pressure-cooking, I offer an alternative method where possible.

CONVERSION TABLE

Metric	Imperial
125 gms	4 oz
250 gms	8 oz
500 gms	16 oz (1 lb)
1 kg	32 oz (2 lb)

1 cup = 250 ml (8 fl oz)
1 tsp = 5 ml
1 tbsp = 3 tsp or 15 ml (½ fl oz)
A pinch = $\frac{1}{8}$ tsp (literally a pinch)
A dash = 1-2 drops
Scant cup/tbsp = a little less than the measure given
All spoon measures are level

PHODNI (SEASONING)

Most cuisines employ many universal cooking methods (stir-frying, sautéing, baking, etc.) but, to my knowledge, only Indian cooking uses the concept of a hot-oil-and-spice seasoning to flavour and infuse ingredients either before or after they have been prepared or cooked. This seasoning or phodni (tadka/vaghar) is definitely the essence of Marathi savoury cooking.

Over hundreds of years and countless influences, generations of cooks have worked out which spices and ingredients pair well together and every Indian region has its favourite flavourings.

For cooks daunted by this variety, it is helpful to understand that many of the same spices are used in various combinations and while there may be many spices in a single dish, the essential process is virtually the same every time. With a little practice and familiarity with the taste and property of spices, you will learn to combine or substitute them, to adjust quantities and cooking times, and to build menus based on their virtues.

The word phodni comes from the verb phodné, 'to break open'. What is broken open is either mustard or cumin seed. Seasonings can be raw or oil-based. For the first, raw or roasted spices are tossed, ground or whole, into a dish, like cumin seeds in a tomato-onion salad. For the second, spices are heated in oil, like mustard seeds and garlic for spinach in buttermilk sauces.

Oil seasonings are of two types: primary or finishing. For a primary seasoning, spices are added to hot oil. They pop and splutter, releasing their oils and flavours. The phodni is briskly stirred to release these. Then, if necessary, aromatics (onion, garlic and ginger) are added to the pan and sautéed. Now the main ingredient is mixed thoroughly with this seasoning before other ingredients or a cooking liquid are incorporated, and the dish cooked through.

A finishing seasoning is made separately and poured over a previously prepared or cooked dish. For more or less solid dishes, the seasoning is stirred in just before serving. For gravied dishes, it is poured in, stirred briskly and the pan immediately covered for several minutes, to infuse the dish with flavour.

Making a Phodni: Be careful when handling hot oil. Use dry pans and utensils because water and oil together mean splatters. Have your ingredients measured and *ready* by the stove or keep your spice box handy. Mind your hands, lower arms and face when making a seasoning. Use a lid or mesh, held 6" above the pan or cover it completely, to minimize splatter.

Follow these basic guidelines:

- One classic Marathi seasoning consists of mustard seeds, asafoetida and turmeric added to hot peanut or sesame seed oil (nowadays refined vegetable oil) in that order. Omit asafoetida if you dislike it.

- Cumin, another important spice, is frequently used with mustard seeds or on its own, often in clarified butter. Fat should be less hot for cumin than for mustard.

- Coriander and cumin seed powders are used together in a ratio of 2:1, added during the cooking process *after* the main ingredients are partially cooked.

- Mango powder, red chilli powder and garam or goda masala are also often added *after* the main ingredient is partly cooked.

- Red chillies/powder can be used with green vegetables and lentils to be clearly visible. They are added after spices have popped. Red chilli powder may be added later on in the process.

- Reduce heat and add curry leaves *after* the spices have popped.

- Bay leaves are used with cumin but usually not with mustard. Add bay to the oil before other seasoning ingredients.

- Some spices (cardamom, cinnamon, cloves, nutmeg, mace and saffron) are considered 'sweet' and used in both sweet and savoury dishes. They may be powdered (except saffron, which is soaked in warm milk) but are not heated in oil before use in desserts and sweets.

- For savoury dishes, cardamom, cinnamon and cloves may be seasoned in oil. Nutmeg, mace and saffron are usually added towards the end of the cooking to retain their delicate fragrance and flavours.

THE USE OF SALT

Generously and judiciously used, salt brings out the inherent flavours of ingredients. It is usually mixed in towards the end of the cooking process, not over the top of a dish. However, note that:

- Legumes will *not* become tender if salt is added to the cooking water. Salt them after cooking.

- Greens wilt and reduce extensively in volume during cooking, so salt them when the heat is off but the greens are still hot.

- Do not salt raw, chopped vegetables like cucumber and tomato till serving time. They will exude too much liquid.

PREPARATION AND PROCESSES

Kapna/chirna (cutting, dicing, mincing): Cut, chop or mince ingredients evenly for uniform cooking and appearance. Chop or mince onions very fine. Where onion is a flavouring agent, omit it if you like.

When chopping potatoes, have handy a bowl filled halfway with water. Put the chopped potatoes into it to prevent oxidation. Drain well before cooking.

Slice off the two ends of a peeled cucumber. Rub the top across both sliced ends to draw out bitterness. Hold the cucumber upright in one hand with a bowl below. Carefully chop down repeatedly with a fine knife on the circular upper end while turning it round and round. When the entire surface is marked with cuts, slice ¼" off the top. Repeat, working your way down the entire cucumber. Once you get the hang of it, this only takes a few minutes.

Vatna (*grinding*): In place of the traditional pata-varvanta (grinding stone and pestle) use an Indian blender, with chutney attachments or a food processor. Add minimal water while grinding to avoid loss of flavour, thickness and texture. Use a spice mill for dry spices.

Waphawna (*steaming*): Vegetables, some sweets and savoury snacks are steamed in a modak patra. Any steamer or pressure cooker (*without* pressure) will work. Otherwise, fill a wide, shallow pan with water a little less than halfway up. Fit a colander of about the same size over it snugly so that steam cannot escape from the sides of the pan. Heat water to almost boiling. Place the food on muslin cloth or wax paper in the colander. Cook lightly covered for 15-20 minutes or till done.

Many pots and pans come with lipped lids, often used to reduce cooking time or steam-cook food. I call it *lid cooking*. Drinking water is poured on the lid to create a steam chamber in which foods cook. The water keeps the lid in place. It is removed periodically and a little of the warm water is sprinkled over the food to cook or moisten it.

Talna (*frying, deep and shallow*): Properly fried food is light and delicious with no underlying oil flavour. Over-frying results in chewy or burnt offerings, while under-fried food soaks up oil.

Deep-fried snacks like chakli are served at room temperature but many fried foods (puris, fish, fritters) are served hot and must be fried just before serving. Do the preparation ahead; just have your ingredients, wok, griddle and fat ready about 30 minutes before serving time.

Hot oil splatters when ingredients are put into it. Novices tend to nervously 'throw' ingredients into a wok. It is safer to get your hands closer and *gently slide food into the wok*, using its inside edge to help.

Tup (ghee) is the ideal frying medium because of its taste and high smoking point. It can be prohibitively expensive, especially for large amounts of frying but if possible, use it for frying sweets. For everything else, use any flavourless, healthy cooking oil.

The temperature of the oil or tup will fluctuate depending on how many items you fry at a time. Keep the temperature even for good results.

For deep-frying savoury food, the oil must be very hot. It should be slightly less hot for sweets. In a large wok, bring the fat almost to smoking over medium heat. Fine bubbles must rise to the surface. To test it for readiness, place your hand about 6" above the wok. If you can feel the heat, the fat is hot. Put in a tiny ball of dough. If it rises to the surface instantly, you can be sure.

Have two slotted spoons ready and a large platter lined with absorbent paper to place the fried food on. Gently slide in each piece to be fried, taking care not to break it or splash the oil. Fry as many pieces at a time as fit comfortably in the wok. Cook the first side till golden brown (check the underside for doneness); gently flip them over and cook the second side. Check again before removing from the wok. Individual recipes indicate specific frying times.

Often people do not drain fried foods well enough. Hold the food in the slotted spoon over the wok, allowing oil to drip off. Then cup it with one spoon against the side of the wok and drain further. Place it in a single layer on the paper-lined platter to remove more oil.

For shallow-frying, heat a griddle or skillet over medium heat for 3-4 minutes. Spread a little oil evenly over it with a spatula; heat for 30-45 seconds more before putting in the food. Thinner foods like bread need less oil and frying time than thicker fish fillets.Cook breads individually. Cook smaller items like fritters in batches, with room to run a spatula between them. Shallow-fry for 2-4 minutes per side, till golden brown. The second side usually needs less cooking than the first. Adjust the heat to keep it even. Allow excess oil to drain to the centre of the griddle, remove the food and drain on a paper-lined platter.

Baking: Though baking is not as common in Maharashtra as it is in northern India, some Marathi foods were 'baked' (wafolé, p. 162) in a bhatti (metal oven) or the embers of a coal fire. Electric and gas ovens work best for dishes like Patharé Prabhu karanjis (p. 328). Small Bundt pan ovens with a sand base heated on a range can be used for wafola. If you have a coal stove, use it for a genuine flavour.

   Pressure-cooking: Pressure-cooking generally yields lacklustre food. However, for hard-to-cook ingredients (meats, lentils) or when time is scarce, it can make sense. Follow your manufacturer's directions.

PRESENTATION

Savoury dishes are garnished with coriander and freshly grated coconut. Coriander is more extensively used, while coconut usually appears on breakfast dishes, lentils, salads and spiced rice dishes, which are also sometimes topped with tup (ghee) and, on rare occasions, nuts.

   Garnishes for sweets include nuts, chironji, raisins, sesame, saffron, cardamom and nutmeg. For extra special occasions, desserts might be topped with edible silver leaf (varkha).

   Tables and plates are beautifully decorated for special events, but Indian cooks rarely expend much thought on food presentation because it is usually not served in individual portions. Meals are generally family style, with guests served by the hosts. Serving bowls are replenished with hot food and garnished again before serving. Festive plates are laid out in a traditional manner, sometimes bordered by rangoli or flowers.

THE INGREDIENT PRIMER

Acids

Apart from lemons or limes, Marathi food gets it tartness from kokum, tamarind and mango and occasionally even from bor/ber berries. For a few special dishes like aluchi patal bhaji, the tart leaves of ambat chuka are used. East Indians use white vinegar in some dishes.

   Different acids add subtly different flavours and textures to food so they are not really interchangeable. When cooking with any acid, use non-reactive pans.

Kairi (*green mango*): Kairi is added to lentils or vegetables. Both green and ripe mangoes are used in chutneys, pickles and jams. Mango pits and amboli (thin sun-dried kairi sections re-hydrated before use) are also used. Oddly enough, amchur (dried mango powder) is not common in Maharashtra.

Wash and dry kairis thoroughly. Cut off and discard a thin disc of flesh around and including the stem to remove any resin oozing from the stem. Avoid getting it on your hands or eating it as it results in a painful rash (For ripe mangoes, see p. 35).

Amsul/kokum/sol/ratamba (*wild mangosteen*): Amsul (*Garcinia indica*) is indigenous to the Western Ghats, a treasure trove of nutrients. Scientists are discovering what cooks have known for aeons. Amsul helps reduce fat, fight cholesterol, purify blood, cool the body and alleviate nausea.[16]

The fresh, deep red fruit is about the size and taste of a half-ripe plum. It is pitted, the skin split in half and dried as amsul to use rather like tamarind. It is used in a digestive, cooling drink, solachi kadhi or amsulaché sar (p. 198). The seed, containing 23-26 per cent oil, is used to make chocolates, medicines and cosmetics. The bark can be used topically to treat paralysis.

Dried, sometimes salted, amsul skins are available widely and sometimes you find moist fresh amsul. Soak 2-4 amsul for 15 minutes in 6 tablespoons warm water. Gently rub and press the rinds into the water to release more flavour. Add the purplish water (and skins) to the dish.

Chincha (*tamarind*): Contrary to its name, *Tamarindus indica*, the tamarind tree has come to us from Africa. However, it has long been associated with India as its Arabic name tamr hindi (date of India) implies! Interestingly, tamarind is one of the essential ingredients in Worcestershire sauce, which was developed in India during the British Raj.

Lushly canopied tamarind trees provide shade from the sun. Children pick the tart, crunchy, raw, green pods to munch with salt, or nibble at the tangy new leaves and buds that are cooked as vegetable and put into chutneys. Vendors sell sun-sweetened, ripe, brown tamarind along with other fruity treats. Tamarind flavours vegetables and lentils and is made into a delicious, restorative beverage. Buy ripe tamarind in bulk and sun-dry it yearly, or get dried tamarind from the grocer.

Soak a walnut-sized ball of dried tamarind in 10 tablespoons of very warm water for about 15 minutes. Squeeze the pulp and press it through a strainer to remove fibrous strands, seeds and bits of peel. Soak tamarind in a little more hot water to express more flavour. This yields 12-14 tablespoons of pulp. Use less water for a thick paste. For tamarind water, use 16-20 tablespoons liquid. Refrigerate excess soaked tamarind for up to 2-3 days. Avoid commercial tamarind paste unless absolutely necessary. It lacks the fruit's sweetness and pulp.

Naral (Coconut)

The versatile, delicious coconut is a key ingredient in a lot of Marathi cooking. Tender green coconut water is highly nutritious. Khobra (dried coconut) is pressed for oil, largely used for cooking in Kerala. Marathi cooks use fresh and dried ripe coconut extensively.

Naral (fresh coconut) is available at vegetable markets; grocers carry khobra. Since it is high in cholesterol, avoid using it if you have health concerns, unless it is a critical ingredient. Substitute dairy/soya milk for coconut milk.

Crack and grate a coconut just before use. An un-cracked coconut lasts for about a week at room temperature. Once cracked, grate and store it immediately. Do not refrigerate it for more than 2 days. It will go rancid. Freeze in an airtight container.

Grab the coconut husk tightly in one hand and peel it off lengthwise. Use the indentation along the nut's equator as a marker to break it open. Hold it firmly and bang it on a sturdy floor or grinding stone or use a hammer or stone pestle. Have a bowl handy to collect the sweet coconut water. Drain out the water before splitting the coconut in two with your hands or use a blunt tool.

Naralacha chav (scraped fresh coconut): Chav is scraped or 'grated' out of the split shell; a vili (knife-scraper) is the most efficient tool. There are tabletop versions but I recommend the old-fashioned kind (p. 20).

Hold the coconut between your hands, over the scraper, facing downward so that the flesh faces the serrations. Using even forward, backward and circular motions and turning the coconut occasionally, scrape it till all the white flesh is removed (avoid the brown skin closest to the shell).

To use the tabletop scraper, set it on a firm surface and secure the suction stand. Crank the handle to scrape the coconut. Alternatively, bake the coconut halves at 120°C (250°F) for about 10 minutes to loosen the flesh. Cut it into sections within the shell and prise it out in chunks with a blunt knife. Grate it very fine on a grater or in your food processor.

If fresh coconuts are unavailable, use store-bought frozen, grated 'fresh' coconut. Freeze it in convenient portions for up to three months.

Suka khobra (dried coconut): Dried, husked coconut is available whole, split or grated. It lasts longer than fresh. Since it is very hard to cut, carefully slice slivers from the flesh outward to the skin, using a sturdy knife and cutting board,

You can substitute dried grated, unsweetened coconut for fresh coconut though its taste is quite different. Sweetened desiccated coconut works in coconut desserts. Reduce sugar accordingly.

Naralacha kol (coconut milk): Coconut milk is expressed from fresh coconuts. Canned coconut milk/packaged coconut cream works but can taste of preservatives.

To make fresh coconut milk, use ¾-1½ cups water for thick milk and 2-3 cups water for thin milk (make it as thick as you like or as the recipe requires). Heat water and pour half over the gratings. Blend or grind it into a fine paste. Place a fine meshed strainer or muslin cloth over a large bowl. Pour in the blended coconut and press the liquid through, squeezing the flesh well. This is *thick* coconut milk. Set it aside in a cup measure.

Scrape up the squeezed coconut and blend again with the remaining water. Squeeze this over the strainer, adding water if needed. The second strain is thinner than the first. Recipes indicate which to use and when. Note that a recipe calling for milk from a whole coconut requires both thick *and* thin milk.

Generally coconut milk is added toward the *end* of the cooking process. Do not boil the dish afterwards as it might curdle. Just warm through before serving. Adding a little rice or gram flour also prevents curdling.

Dairy Products

Dudh, chik, dahi, loni, tak, tup, chakka (milk, colostrum, yogurt, butter, buttermilk, clarified butter, yogurt cheese): Since these dairy products play a major role in fulfilling the protein and calcium needs of India's vegetarians, they are highly regarded ingredients.

Dudh (milk): Milk is pasteurized in urban India but not homogenized; since its butterfat content is not broken down it can be used to make home-made butter. First it must be boiled over low heat. Cool for 8-10 hours, skim off the thick, top layer of cream and store the milk, covered, in a cool cupboard or refrigerator till needed. If kept in a cupboard, boil again in the evening to prevent it spoiling.

Slowly evaporated milk makes rich, slightly caramelized solids (khava/mava/khoya). Khava is used to make or enrich sweets. If unavailable, try soft paneer (farmers' cheese), ricotta cheese or leftover burfi.

Chik (colostrum): Colostrum is the pre-milk fluid (first-milk/beestings) produced by cattle just after calving. It is rich in nutrients, antibodies and protein, but low in fat. Milkmen traditionally give it to favoured customers when a new calf is born.

Dahi (yogurt): Yogurt is produced when bacteria are introduced into milk, which make it gel and set. In our hot climate, it was only natural that cooks preserved milk by converting it to yogurt, which provides the same nutrients and calcium but has a longer life and is, due to its lactobacillus content, easier to digest. It is an important component of Marathi cooking, often eaten with rice and salt and used as a salad dressing and meat tenderizer. The famed Marathi dessert, shrikhand is made from thickened yogurt (p. 323). Fresh yogurt is fairly sweet and gets tarter with time. Check its tartness and thickness before use. Shrikhand, for instance, needs sweet, thick, full-fat yogurt. For pithla (p. 226) or patal bhaji (p. 192), thinner, tarter yogurt is fine.

DAHI
Yogurt
Time: 15 minutes + 6-8 hours setting

1 litre whole or low-fat milk
2 tsp yogurt, as starter

- Boil milk in a deep, heavy-bottomed pan. Pour it into a wide bowl.
- Cool to just over room temperature. Dissolve yogurt into it.
- Rest covered in a warm, stable place for 6-8 hours, till firm.
- Refrigerate to cool and prevent further souring.

LONI
Butter
Special equipment: churning stick, churn

Till recently, housewives made butter at home.

- Boil raw or non-homogenized milk over medium-low heat daily for a week.
- Cool it for 6-8 hours. Skim off the thick, top layer of cream and put it into an airtight container. Also collect the cream at the bottom of the pan, when empty. Refrigerate.
- After 2-3 days of collecting cream, mix in 1 tsp yogurt.
- After 7 days, put the sour cream in a churn or deep pan.

- Mix well with the churning stick, add a little cold water and churn with firm steady strokes *only* in one direction for 5-7 minutes, till the butter starts clumping and separating.

- Gradually add some cool water to separate the solids from the liquid.

- When butter rises to the top, stop churning *immediately* or it will dissolve.

- Strain it out with your hand, pressing tightly into a lump.

- Wash butter in cold water 2-3 times to remove tartness. Refrigerate or make it into tup (opposite).

Tak (buttermilk): The liquid left behind after making butter is buttermilk. It is naturally tart, nutritious, easy to digest and refreshing. Drink it plain, with salt or sugar (see buttermilk drinks, pp. 367-368), mix it with hot white rice or use it in tart sauces like patal bhaji (p. 192) or kadhi (p. 229).

Tup (ghee/clarified butter): Unsalted butter is heated till its water evaporates and milk solids collect at the bottom of the pan below a layer of pure clear tup. Tup has a higher smoking point than butter and in the old days, those who could afford it used it for cooking, especially deep-frying sweets.

It gives food a unique richness, and because it is considered cooling, it is often paired with jaggery, sugar or spices that can cause skin eruptions. Eaten in moderation, tup provides energy, lubricates the joints and intestines, prevents constipation, helps in maintaining a healthy weight (unlike some fats) and keeps the arteries free of blockage.

TUP

(Ghee/Clarified Butter)

Makes: 150-170 gms   Time: 30-45 minutes

500 gms home-made or store-bought butter

- Put the butter in a churn or heavy-bottomed pan that *seems* too large, to prevent the tup from boiling over.

- Heat gently, checking often to prevent burning. Do not stir the butter but swirl the pan around a little.

- Reduce the heat if the butter is warming up too quickly. It makes a rattling noise as it bubbles and boils. This reduces when it is done so keep an ear out. It can easily overheat.

- To test, put in a drop of water. If it sputters instantly, the tup is ready.

- You will be left with about one-third the weight you started with. The milk solids (beri) will be crisp and pinkish-brown.

- Take the pan off the heat and tilt it slightly to allow the liquid and solids to separate further.

- Cool tup to room temperature before straining into a glass jar. Cover tightly *only* when completely cool.

- Tup solidifies easily. If you use it frequently and the weather is cool, store it in a cool, dark spot on your kitchen counter. For occasional use, refrigerate for up to 2-3 weeks.

- The slightly caramelized beri is delicious with sugar, spread on bread or eaten with poli. Enhance vegetables or shira with its rich flavour.

CHAKKA
Yogurt Cheese
Makes: 500-750 gms   Time: 6-8 hours
Special equipment: cheesecloth, string/twine

Chakka, essentially yogurt without its liquid content, is used to make shrikhand (p. 323). Use it for dips or cheesecake too! (For a quick dip, whip chakka with minced garlic, red chilli powder, salt, cumin powder, a pinch of sugar and finely chopped coriander leaves.)

1 kg home-made or store-bought, firm, preferably full-fat yogurt

- Place cheesecloth in a colander or strainer over a bowl. Arrange the extra cloth over the sides.

- Pour in yogurt. Bring the edges of the cloth together and tie them tight, just above the yogurt, making a round, firm ball. The whey will immediately begin to drain out.

- Hang the pouch from a height (kitchen cupboard handle/sink faucet) to drain, with the bowl beneath to catch the liquid. Or leave the pouch in the colander or strainer, occasionally transferring the nutritious whey into another container. (Drink it or use for kneading puri dough or making yogurt-based gravies.)

- Drain yogurt for 6-8 hours. When it feels firm and the pouch is dry, scrape the thick, granular chakka into a container. Stretch the cloth tight to scrape off the last bits with a knife or spoon.

- Use chakka immediately or refrigerate covered for up to 2-3 days.

Fruits and Vegetables

Alu (*Colocasia esculenta*): Taro is a tropical plant grown in standing water for its starchy corms and leaves. The corms are cooked like potatoes, seasoned with cumin. The leaves, rich in vitamins and minerals, are used to make aluchi patal bhaji, served at weddings, and the famous aluchi vadi, a savoury gram flour-filled roll.

Clean them well. Alu can cause an allergic reaction so scrape off excess fibres thoroughly with the back of a knife blade. Rub or cook alu with tamarind juice to alleviate itchiness.

Amba (*ripe mango*): The mango, a fruit of the *Mangifera*, a tropical evergreen fruiting tree, is probably native to India or South East Asia. There are many Indian species. The mango holds a significant place in Indian culture: the leaves are used in Hindu rituals and as decoration; the mango shape, koiri (paisley), is a classic design element in rangoli, textiles and jewellery; the ripe fruit is eaten sliced or puréed, used in savoury dishes, desserts and candy, and preserved in pickles and jams (for green mango, see p. 27).

Avla (*Indian gooseberry, dongri avla and rai avla/amla*): Many Indians believe an avla a day keeps the doctor away! Avla are native to South and South East Asia, mentioned in ancient medical texts and an ingredient in numerous Ayurvedic tonics (triphala, hair oil, etc.). They are considered the richest natural source of vitamin C, are high in antioxidants, and have antibacterial, antiviral and laxative properties. They raise protein levels and 'activate the adrenaline response which protects against tremors and convulsions'.[17] Avla also aid digestion, cool the body and fight nausea.

Three fruits go by the name 'avla' or 'Indian gooseberry' though they bear no botanical connection, and only a superficial resemblance, to the English gooseberry. Though not frequently used as an acid, all three are used for their medicinal properties.

The large dongri avla (*Embelic myrobalan*) is often bigger

than a golf ball, very pale green, with a shiny skin and an astringent taste. It is used in moravla, a sweet preserve-tonic. The smaller dongri avla, also growing in the hills, has much less flesh. It is also used in moravla.

The rai avla (*Chebulic myrobalan*) is ½"-1" across, distinctly pale yellow-green, slightly flat at the ends, with ridges on its surface like a tiny, peeled orange. Inside is a seed with sharp flanges that match these sub-divisions. The tree, with leaves like large curry leaves, never grows higher than about twenty feet. Children like to pick and eat rai avla from the tree. They are also boiled, seeded and dried and used as a mouth freshener and digestive, made into chutneys, pickles and a beverage.

Karla (*bitter gourd*): This fruit-vegetable (*Momordica charantia*) from the gourd family (*cucurbitacae*) is popular all over Asia. In Maharashtra, it is categorized as phal-bhaji (fruit-vegetable). Helpful in controlling diabetes and digestive problems, it is also being tested for HIV treatments. It can be stuffed, sautéed, fried, or made into chutneys and pickles. The skin is usually scraped off with the back of a knife, the flesh allowed to rest before cooking to release excess bitterness.

Kelphul (*banana blossoms*): The banana is an ancient native of South East Asia. The fruit is, of course, one of the world's most complete natural nutritional offerings. India boasts many banana sub-species and plantains. They are eaten ripe and raw, cooked like a vegetable. Kelphul are cooked in various Indian regions (to peel, see p. 178). Banana leaves are used for wrapping, cooking and serving food.

Paley-bhajya (*leafy greens*): Many wild and cultivated leafy vegetables are popular: red/green-leafed math (amaranth, also called rajgira), spinach, fenugreek, ambat chuka, chakvat, tandulja, etc. Cooked fairly simply, they can be interchanged.

Greens are often flavoured with mustard seed or garlic (especially strong-smelling greens). Sometimes another vegetable (potatoes, onions) or legume (split, husked mung, peanuts) is added to make a nutritionally complete dish (use 4 parts greens to 1 part vegetable/legume).

Clean greens in several changes of water before rinsing, because they are gritty. Soak well in a bowl of water. Remove greens before emptying the bowl so grit and sediment does not fall back on to the leaves. Repeat if needed. Finally, rinse under running water. Drain and chop fine.

Phanas (*jackfruit*): Jackfruit is a large, unwieldy, prickly-skinned coastal fruit. Nestled inside are fragrant yellow sections of flesh covering meaty seeds. The raw and ripe flesh and seeds are cooked as vegetables, and fritters and wafers are made from the unripe fruit.

To cut jackfruit, oil your hands and a sturdy knife: white sticky secretions from the fruit's skin hamper cutting and cause itching. Re-oil the knife and hands as needed. On a chopping board, with a good grip on the fruit, cut into the hard skin lengthwise from top to bottom and split the fruit down the middle. Extract the sections, removing surrounding fibres. Slice the tender sections to expose the seeds. To peel their inedible, plastic-like coats, first cook the seeds till tender in the pressure cooker with ½ cup of water, for about 5 minutes after the cooker reaches full pressure (2 whistles); or on the stove top in 1 cup of water, tightly covered for 15-20 minutes.

Shevgyachya shenga (*drumsticks*): Shevgyachya shenga, the flavourful pods of the drumstick (*Moringa oleifera*) tree, which grows in semi-arid tropical and sub-tropical regions, are rich in vitamins and minerals. They are in season from March to May. Wash the pods well. Remove the tough fibres from the skins with the help of a sharp knife. Cut the pods into lengths according to the recipe.

Tondli (*ivy gourd*): Tondli (*Coccinia grandis*), a fruit-vegetable from the gourd family, *cucurbitacae*, has oblong, pale to dark green fruit (1"-2" long, at most 1" thick) with light white striations and a thin skin that crisps nicely when sautéed. Tondli have a fruity taste and texture. They are sautéed, stuffed, added to lentils or spiced rice.

Ginger and Garlic

Ala (ginger): Ginger, a rhizome of *Zingiber officinale*, may have originated in India. Marathis use fresh (ala) and dried ginger (suntha) to overcome nausea, reduce inflammation and soothe sore throats. For a quick cough syrup combine ¼ tsp grated ginger or ginger juice, 1 tsp honey and a little lime juice.

Lasun (garlic): Aromatic garlic (*Allium sativum*), a bulb of the onion family, has antibacterial, anti-fungal and antioxidant benefits. It may help treat the common cold, prevent heart disease and control late onset diabetes.

Grains, Flour and Pasta

A wide variety of grains are used in Maharashtra, whole or ground into flour. The flours are used to make breads, pancakes, steamed or fried savouries, sweets, porridges and numerous desserts, and to thicken gravies.

Gahu (wheat): Today refined and unrefined wheat flour is the most popular bread flour in Maharashtra. 'Globally, wheat nourishes more people than any other grain.'[18] A source of B vitamins, iron, magnesium and manganese, it provides the most protein.[19] Many people leave some chaff in the flour for roughage.

Rava (semolina): The hard endosperm sifted out of non-durum wheat[20] during milling is rava, farina or cream of wheat.[21] Cream of wheat and wheat are milled fine, medium or coarse. So the term rava also refers to granular flour of other grains.

Tandul (rice): Rice, the staple food for 65 per cent of India's population, is grown all over India in three different growing seasons annually.[22] It is rich in protein, thiamine, niacin, riboflavin, dietary fibre (when not overly polished) and crucial amino acids.

In coastal Maharashtra, rice is the staple but it is revered everywhere as the essence of life and served at special meals. Though India is known for its fragrant, long-grained basmati rice varieties, only affluent Indians can afford it; if the middle-class uses basmati, it is for special occasions. Short-grained rice (like the Marathi ambey-mohur, with its mango blossom fragrance; surati kolam, etc.) are used for everyday cooking.

Rice flour is used for breads, pancakes and dumpling covers, to add crunch and to thicken gravies. When washed and shade-dried before milling it yields very white, delicate 'washed-rice' flour (dhutlelya tandulacha peeth). Rice is pounded into flakes (pohé): thin (patal), for chivda; medium (madhyam), for raw or cooked pohé; and thick (jadey), for deep-fried chivda. Rice is also puffed (churmura) and children like to crunch it plain. Puffed, unhusked rice (lahya) used to be a common snack food.

Jwari and bajri (sorghum and millet): Sorghum (jwari) and pearl millet (bajri) came to India from Africa thousands of years ago and are excellent low-rainfall crops, suitable for many regions of Maharashtra. They are common sources of nutrition for some of the world's poorest labouring people. Sorghum is high in phosphorus, iron, potassium, thiamine and niacin.[23] Pearl millet is rich in calcium, iron and manganese.[24] Traditional hand-flattened bread (bhakri) is made from either flour. For most of the year, people prefer sorghum; pearl millet is popular in the winter because it produces heat in the body.

Hill millet (vari, varai) is grown like ragi (finger millet/nachni) as a food and fodder crop. Its very small, highly nutritious, light textured grain is often cooked like rice for fasts.

BHAJNI
Multigrain Flour
Makes: 6-7 cups

Several grains are roasted (bhajné means to roast) and ground together to make bhajni, a unique multigrain flour. The distinctively flavoured, highly nutritious, versatile blend traditionally consists of pearl millet, sorghum, wheat, rice and other cereals with lentils, salt, coriander seed and cumin seed. Also try our quick speed-of-light multigrain flour (p. 113) or buy it ready-made.

2 cups sorghum (jowar)
1 cup rice

Introduction   39

1½ cups split, husked Bengal gram (chana dal)
1½ cups split, husked black gram (urad dal)
1 cup wholewheat flour (atta)
1 cup coriander seeds
½ tsp fenugreek seeds (methi)

- Wash, clean and air-dry each ingredient separately.

- Roast each on a hot griddle for 7-10 minutes.

- Cool completely for 4-7 minutes before finely grinding ingredients together.

- Store in an airtight container.

Pasta: Traditionally, home-made pastas are used all over Maharashtra. The most common, shevaya (wheat vermicelli) is now usually shop-bought. In the Konkan, people eat rice flour shevaya, sometimes dunked into jaggery-sweetened coconut milk and slurped.

Gavhlé are tiny wholewheat pasta, shaped between thumb and forefinger into ½" long, ¹/₁₀" thick rolls with tapered ends. These are generally made annually and sun-dried before being stored. By twisting them slightly you get a curly variation. Since they cook quickly, gavhlé can be thrown into kheer (p. 310) at a moment's notice. Sarolya, long pasta-twists, are also used in kheer (p. 311), while shengula is a loop-shaped, savoury sorghum pasta (p. 120).

Herbs, Spices and Spice Blends

Spices and herbs have medicinal and digestive properties and infuse food with wonderful flavour. They agitate the taste buds and start off the digestive process even before food is consumed. Breathing in their aromas, as they are being toasted, ground or heated in oil, increases appetite and salivation. Some aid digestion or render ingredients digestible. Others help preserve food, a significant consideration in hot climates, and one reason why they are so widely used in tropical Asian countries.

India has long been associated with spice. Explorers discovered new continents while seeking its legendary aromatic riches. Naturally, Indian cuisine reflects this abundance. Over time, invaders from different parts of the world—Europe, China, the Middle East—colonized the subcontinent, bringing along their culture, religious beliefs, cuisines and ingredients, some of which were adopted and indigenized.

Across India, a plethora of spices and herbs are used whole or ground, fresh or dried, raw or seasoned in oil, singly or with other spices. There are many unwritten rules about their use. Traditionally, some are exclusively for savouries, others appear in sweets or beverages, while yet others cross over.

Mustard seeds, asafoetida and turmeric are a classic Marathi seasoning combo (also used individually). When coriander and cumin seed powders are used together, it is in a 2:1 ratio. Bay leaves tend to be used in rich meat, rice or lentil dishes. Curry leaves flavour salads, vegetables and legumes. Coriander leaves are a garnish.

Buy whole spices fresh as they lose their aroma and flavour in 4-6 months. To store longer, minimize degeneration by storing them whole in an airtight container, in a cool, dark place or in the freezer to prevent bug infestations. Avoid buying pre-ground spices: their quality is questionable and they lose aroma and flavour quicker than whole spices.

Cleaning: Pick over whole spices for twigs, stones and other undesirable hard bits. Debris does not get ground up and could damage your spice mill.

Toasting: Spices are toasted to release their aromas and essential oils and make them easier to powder. Toast on a hot griddle over medium-low heat. Stir often till browned and aromatic. Initially they may take a while to brown but once they heat up they will be ready quickly. (If the griddle is too hot, they will burn.) Some oil (less than 1 tsp) on a hot griddle enhances toasting.

Grinding: Grind spices fresh, using a mortar-pestle, spice grinder or coffee mill. Keep separate mortars and pestles for pungent and sweet spices.

Today, turmeric and asafoetida are rarely ground at home as both are easily available powdered. For home grinding, use a heavy-duty mortar or blender.

Seasoning: See the Phodni (Seasoning) Section (pp. 21–23).

Herbs

Bay, curry and coriander leaves are the most commonly used herbs in Marathi cooking. While bay and curry leaves are seasoned in hot oil to release their aromas, coriander leaves are usually used raw. Bay leaves are generally dried before use but curry and coriander leaves should be bought on a daily/weekly basis. Wrap them in paper or cloth towels and refrigerate in a box. Wash and dry them just before use.

Sacred or holy basil (tulsi) has great religious significance and is traditionally grown in every Hindu garden. Though used in medicinal teas, it has no other role in Marathi cooking per se.

Kadhi limba (*curry leaf*): The curry tree (*Murraya koenigii*) is said to be indigenous to India. Its leaves (kadhi patta) are used to flavour lentils, vegetables, salads and meat. Their essential oils contain carotene, riboflavin, iron, calcium and zinc. Eating them can help prevent tooth decay.

These leaves may be the root of the word 'curry', which has erroneously become a synonym for Indian cuisine. They have a pungent and unique flavour. Traditional Marathi families have a curry tree in their gardens and pluck fresh leaves as needed. They are also available at vegetable stands. Refrigerate leaves, wrapped in paper towels inside plastic bags for up to 7-10 days. Rinse leaves, pull them off the stem and pat dry before use.

Kothimbir (*coriander leaf, cilantro, Indian parsley, Chinese parsley*): The leaf of the coriander plant (*Coriandrum sativum*, parsley family) reigns supreme as the Indian garnish of choice. It is also used to make spice pastes and chutneys. The fruits, called seeds, are a spice (p. 44).

Coriander is one of my favourite herbs. I always keep a large bunch on hand. With its fresh, crisp taste, it brightens up any dish. Pick through it to remove yellowing or rotting branches and store in a glass of water or refrigerate, wrapped loosely in paper in an airtight container for 3-7 days.

Before using coriander, soak it briefly in water to remove grit. Chop it fine just before use or it will wilt. Do *not* mince it as you might basil. This only bruises and blackens the leaves, making them watery and tasteless.

Tamal patri (*Indian bay leaf*): Indian-bay leaves (*Cinnamomum tamala*) come from a tree closely related to the cinnamon. Of the laurel family, like Mediterranean bay, it is said to have originated in northern India. The leaves were used in ancient Roman cookery and perfumery and were popular with the Mughals in India. They are usually sold and used dried, staying flavourful for several months if properly stored in an airtight container in a cool, dark place. They are used whole or ground for spice blends. If Indian bay leaves are unavailable, Mediterranean bay or laurel leaves are a less flavourful substitute.

Spices

Badishep (*fennel seeds/anise seeds*): Fennel (*Foenilicum vulgare*) and anise seeds (*Pimpinella anisum*) are actually fruits. Both are referred to as badishep in Marathi. In India, fennel is more commonly used in cooking and as a digestive.

Dalchini (*cinnamon*): Cinnamon is the bark of an evergreen laurel tree (*Cinnamomum zeylanicum*) native to Sri Lanka, south-west India and parts of Burma. It has a warm, sweet taste with antioxidant and anti-microbial properties. It may help reduce blood sugar, cholesterol and triglycerides. It is also said to help stomach ailments, from indigestion to dyspepsia, and relieve coughs and colds.

Cinnamon is used not only in spice blends and to spice rice and meat dishes but also to flavour tea and desserts. Indonesian cinnamon bark (*Cinnamomum burmanii*, another laurel) is similar to Sri Lankan cinnamon, comparable in taste.

Nagkesar (*cinnamon fruit*): has several names—cinnamon buds, cassia buds, cinnamon flowers, etc. Picked while still unripe, nagkesar resembles cloves. Much less aromatic than cinnamon, it has a mild sweet taste and is used in spice blends like Kolhapuri masala (p. 49).

Dhaney (*coriander seeds*): The fruits of the *Coriandrum sativum* plant, often called seeds, add a rich, lemony-coconut flavour to Marathi foods. Dhaney taste great in meat and vegetable dishes and add wonderful texture to gravies. Toast them over low heat for 2-3 minutes just before grinding. Coriander and cumin seed powders used together are called dhaney-jirey.

Halad (*turmeric*): Indian cooking has used the rhizome (often called root) of the turmeric plant (*Curcuma longa*) for millennia. Whether it originated in South or South East Asia, today, India is its largest producer and consumer, using 80 per cent of the crop domestically.[25] Due to its yellow colour, turmeric is sometimes called 'Indian saffron'.

This member of the ginger family is aromatic when fresh but is generally used dried and powdered in seasonings, as an antiseptic and to help foods retain, even intensify, natural colours during cooking. Turmeric leaves are used to wrap foods for steaming, they infuse a subtle flavour and aroma too. Hot, sweet turmeric milk is an excellent remedy for sore throats and coughs.

Halad is important in religious ceremonies and rituals. Marathi married women's foreheads are adorned with it and with vermilion (kunku). It is also used in dyes, as a skin cleanser, complexion enhancer and an antiseptic for wounds.

Hinga (*asafoetida*): Hinga comes from *Ferula asafoetida* (the parsley family). Of Central Asian origin, it has been used in India for millennia, both medicinally and in seasonings. Juice released by the roots of this plant hardens to a resin-like substance. This is powdered and used pure or compounded (as in commercial asafoetida powder).

Asafoetida is pungent, reminiscent of garlic. A small pinch goes a long way. Marathi Brahman communities while traditionally eschewing garlic and onion, use hinga quite happily. It is commonly added (like garlic and cumin) to lentils, to break down their proteins, making them more digestible.

Jaiphal and jaipatri (nutmeg and mace): Nutmeg (*Myristica fragrans*) was thought to be of Indian origin but probably originated in the Mollucas (Indonesia). Widely grown in South India, it has long been associated with Indian cooking. It is not a nut but the aromatic kernel of an apricot-like fruit. Used to flavour desserts, it aids digestion and has sedative properties. Buy whole nutmeg to grate directly over foods.

Mace (jaipatri), the thin tissue between fruit and kernel, is powdered and used in rice and meat dishes.

Jira (cumin seeds): Cumin fruit ('seeds', *Cuminum cyminum*, parsley family) are ubiquitous in India. They are used whole or ground. With a lightly aromatic flavour, digestive properties and iron content, cumin is frequently used in fasting foods and in dishes for invalids and children. Lightly toast cumin over low heat for 2-3 minutes before use (see dhaney).

Jira, kala/shah (cumin, black/royal): Though *Bunium persicum* is different from *Cuminum cyminum*, shah jira resembles cumin and so is also called jira. These smaller, darker, thinner fruit flavour special rice dishes or feature in spice blends like goda masala (p. 48). If unavailable, cumin will do.

Kali miri (black pepper): Black pepper, cultivated for millennia, originated in the Malabar and lent its heat to Indian foods long before the arrival of New World ingredients like chillies. Pepper is thought to aid digestion, fight coughs and colds, treat stomach ailments and improve appetite. It is still used as an alternative to, or along with, chillies.

Keshar (saffron): The stigmata of the *Crocus sativus* flower are known and valued around the world as saffron. It may have originated in Crete but India, Spain and Iran are its biggest producers now. Luckily the world's most expensive spice is so flavourful, you need only a few strands to flavour a dish!

Each flower has three red stigmata, painstakingly harvested from autumn blooms, dried and sold as strands or powder. The more flavourful strands give a pleasantly delicate taste and pale yellow-orange colour to food. Soak saffron in warm water or milk before adding it (with its soaking liquid) to food.

Lavang (cloves): Cloves are the highly aromatic, hot-tasting buds of the *Syzygium aromaticum* (myrtle family). Native to the Mollucas, they appear frequently in Indian cuisines. They are used in Marathi seasonings, spice blends and paan. Cloves and clove oil relieve toothaches. People also occasionally suck or chew on them after a meal.

Methi (fenugreek): Methi leaves (*Trigonella foenum-graecum*, bean family) are cooked as a vegetable but its bitter, aromatic seeds are used in seasonings, pickles and spice blends. Said to have medicinal properties, methi seeds are given to post-partum mothers to increase lactation. They help relieve stomach ailments and may be good for skin problems.

Mirchi and mirchichi pud (chillies and red chilli powder): The chilli, though associated with Indian cuisine for several centuries, is a relatively new entrant, coming to Asia from the Americas via Europe about 500 years ago. It was quickly assimilated throughout the subcontinent.

Chillies are actually berries (of plants in the nightshade family). Their flavours range from mild and sweet to intolerably hot. Fresh green or dried red chillies are used whole, slit, chopped, ground or powdered. Of the dried varieties, Sankeshwari (from the Kolhapur region), Bedgi (from around Hubli), Rasampatti and Kashmiri Deghi chillies are commonly used.

Since the heat of chillies varies, adjust their quantity appropriately. If dried red chillies are unavailable, use good quality, unadulterated (bright red) ready-made red chilli powder, or cayenne powder. Thai bird chillies are a great alternative to fresh green chillies.

Mohri (mustard seeds): Mustard seeds (cabbage family, three varieties: black *Brassica nigra*, white-yellow *Brassica hirta* and brown *Brassica juncea*) are common in Indian cooking. Mustard seed oil is not common in Maharashtra but appears in some of our recipes.

Ground mustard (*mohrichi dal*), bright yellow and more pungent than whole seeds, is used for pickles and salads. Grind it fresh.

Ovalajwainlcarum: Ajwain fruits (*Carum copticum*, parsley family) have an oregano-like flavour. Since they are said to relieve stomach aches, they are used in hard-to-digest dishes. The leaves also make delicious fritters.

Triphala (*Goa spiceberries*): Triphala/tirphal (*Zanthoxylum rhetsa*), used on India's west coast, appears largely in Marathi fish dishes and spice blends. If unavailable, use juniper berries or omit it.

Veldoda (*green cardamom and black cardamom*): Native to South Asia and part of the ginger family, aromatic black cardamom (*Amomum subulatum*) seeds are used in savoury dishes; the better flavoured green (*Elettaria cardamomum*) work for sweet and savoury recipes. They are frequently added to Indian spiced tea (masala chai).

For sweet dishes, peel whole pods and grind the seeds in a mortar with a pinch of sugar, for really fine powder. Use black cardamom whole, sautéed in hot oil. You can remove it from the dish but the seeds are pleasant to bite into. In fact, green cardamom is used as a mouth freshener.[26]

Spice Blends

Spices are combined into various blends or masalas. Different communities have their own unique mixes, easy to use when complex flavour is needed quickly.

Today, most spice blends like goda, Kolhapuri, kanda-lasun (onion-garlic)/ghati masala and metkut (a long-lasting yellow spice powder of raw rice, lentils, fenugreek seeds, turmeric, asafoetida, etc. which is eaten mixed with hot white rice and tup or served as a sauce with yogurt) are available ready-made. When buying such blends, use a highly recommended grocer or spice merchant for quality products.

Some blends (CKP masala, Sonari masala and bottle masala) are still usually made at home. Store home-made masala in clean, dry, airtight ceramic jars in a cool place.

GODA/KALA MASALA
Classic Marathi Spice Blend
Makes: about 1½ kg   Time: 1 hour

Maharashtra's equivalent of garam masala is used for vegetables, lentils and meat. Many cooks still prepare their own blend. There is some debate whether goda and kala masala are the same. Some say they are not, others that only Marathi Brahmans traditionally used goda masala, yet others refer to goda masala *as* kala masala. Here is one recipe.

125 ml vegetable oil
15 gms (6-7) bay leaves (tej patta)
15 gms dagad phul (rock flower – optional)
250 gms dried coconut (kopra), grated (optional)
100 gms dried red chillies
50 gms cumin seeds
25 gms (2½ tbsp) royal cumin (shah jeera)
350 gms sesame seeds (til)
500 gms coriander seeds
25 gms cassia buds (nagkesar)
20 gms (4 tbsp) cloves
20 gms cinnamon
10 gms (1 tbsp) black peppercorns
25 gms (2½ tbsp) powdered asafoetida (hing)
20 gms (2 tbsp) turmeric powder
4-5 tsp coarse or kosher salt

- Gently heat ½ tbsp oil on a griddle. Toast each ingredient separately, except turmeric and salt, in the order listed above for 2-7 minutes each. Toast over medium heat, stirring frequently, till aromatic.

- Toast larger quantities in batches. Reheat griddle and oil as required.

- Put toasted ingredients in a large bowl. Powder them fine, in batches if needed. Mix in turmeric.

• Store masala in jars. To store masala long term, spread coarse salt over it before closing the lid tightly.

Note: For long-lasting masala, omit coconut. Garam masala is an adequate substitute for goda.

KOLHAPURI MASALA
Kolhapur Spice Blend
Makes: 850 gms   Time: 45-60 minutes
Contributor: Anuradha Samant

Anuradha moved to Kolhapur from Mumbai when she married Jay. She quickly learned the traditional dishes favoured by her in-laws. Kolhapuri masala is an extremely spicy blend that flavours virtually any lentil, meat or vegetable dish. It is the essence of the famed four-dish mutton fiesta, Kolhapuri Mutton (p. 243). When no side dish is available, poor folk might even just eat their bhakri with a little Kolhapuri masala mixed with oil. This blend lasts 6-8 months and is generally made twice a year.

1" piece of ginger
50 gms garlic
1 small bunch of coriander leaves, washed and dried
½ cup vegetable oil
50 gms sesame seeds (til)
25 gms (2½ tbsp) poppy seeds (khus-khus)
125 gms dried coconut chunks (kopra)
10 gms (1 tbsp) black peppercorns
60 gms (6 tbsp) coriander seeds
20 gms (2 tbsp) cumin seeds
2 x 4" sticks cinnamon
10 cloves

5 gms (5 blades) mace (javitri)
2" stick turmeric root or 1½ tsp powder
1 tsp fenugreek seeds (methi)
1 tsp mustard seeds
⅛ portion of a nutmeg (jaiphal)
4 bay leaves (tej patta)
1 tsp dagad phul (rock flower – optional)
2 cassia buds (nagkesar)
Seeds of 2 green cardamoms
Seeds of 1 black cardamom
5 gms (1½ tsp) lump asafoetida (hing)
500 gms red chilli powder
2 tsp salt

- Grind ginger, garlic and coriander leaves to a paste without water.

- Gently heat ½ tbsp oil on a griddle. Toast sesame seeds for 3-5 minutes over medium heat. Re-oil the griddle. Toast poppy seeds for 3-5 minutes. Grind them together and set aside.

- Re-oil the griddle. Toast coconut for 3-7 minutes, till golden and fragrant. Powder it fine.

- Toast the remaining ingredients separately over medium heat, in the order given, except turmeric powder (if used), chilli powder and salt. Toast each ingredient for 2-7 minutes, on a lightly oiled griddle, oiling and reheating griddle as required.

- Finely grind each ingredient separately. Place in a large bowl.

- Combine them with garlic paste, coconut, turmeric powder (if used), chilli powder and salt. Mix well, sifting the masala through your fingers to break up lumps.

- Store immediately in airtight containers.

Note: Wash your hands well after mixing the blend.

BOTTLE MASALA
Classic East Indian Spice Blend
Makes: ½ kg   Time: Several hours over several days
Special equipment: Dark glass bottles

East Indian cooks use a variety of spice blends, and bottle masala is a unique feature of their cuisine. According to Jeanne D'Penha, 'Every family makes its special blend, typically with small variations that alter pungency, flavour and even colour, and result in that unique "better-than-yours" taste. The recipe is a closely guarded family secret, passed down through generations.

'It is made after the harvest in the summer, since spices must be dried in the hot sun. They are bought from trusted grocers, cleaned and sun-dried for 2-3 days. Scores of bottles are carefully washed and sun-dried so they are absolutely clean, sanitary and dry: a drop of water could spoil a whole batch of masala.'

My friend Sameera Khan is researching the East Indian community for a book on Mumbai's Khotachiwadi (an East Indian and Marathi Hindu residential enclave). 'Bottle masala was originally hand pounded . . .' she says. 'Some families prepare the ingredients and have them ground at a mill. On average, East Indian households use 6-8 bottles of masala yearly. They also use spice mixtures like poorij, a yellow masala for fish, and fresh blends like khudi (p. 235) and fritard, which is used with fried onions and includes red chillies, ginger, garlic, pepper, saffron, cumin, cloves, cinnamon, cardamom, tamarind or kokum, and dry coriander leaves, ground into a paste.' Vegetables are more lightly cooked, usually with onions, pepper, green chillies and a little coconut milk or finely ground fresh coconut.

I adapted this recipe from several available accounts, reducing quantities to a manageable amount.

100 gms dried red Rasampatti chillies
75 gms dried red Kashmiri Deghi chillies
75 gms coriander seeds
25 gms (2½ tbsp) turmeric powder
12 gms (2½ tsp) poppy seeds (khus-khus)
12 gms (2½ tsp) sesame seeds (til)
12 gms (3½ tsp) yellow mustard seeds
12 gms (3½ tsp) cumin seeds
12 gms (3½ tsp) black peppercorns
7 gms (1¾ tsp) green cardamoms
7 gms (7 x 1" sticks) cinnamon
7 gms (1½ tbsp) cloves
7 gms wholewheat grains (gehun)
7 gms (1 tsp) split, husked Bengal gram (chana dal)
3½ gms (1 tsp) royal cumin seeds (shah jeera)
3½ gms (2 pieces) bay leaves (tej patta)
3½ gms (4¼ tsp) cassia buds (nagkesar)
3½ gms sesame flowers (optional)
3½ gms (3½ blades) mace (javitri)
3½ gms cubeb pepper (kababchini)
3½ gms (1 tsp) powdered asafoetida (hing)
1 gm (⅓ tsp) fennel seeds (badi saunf)
½ nutmeg (jaiphal)

- Clean and dry ingredients separately (except nutmeg) in the sun for 6-8 hours or roast them slowly on a hot dry griddle (traditionally an earthenware pot), till aromatic and crisp.

- Grind nutmeg fine. Place it in a large bowl. Grind chillies fine and add to the nutmeg.

- Separately grind or pound the other ingredients fine. Mix them with the powdered spices.

- Fill into dark glass bottles.

CKP MASALA

Chandraseniya Kayastha Prabhu Spice Blend
Makes: over 1¼ kg   Time: 30 minutes

This is the traditional CKP blend for lentils, vegetables and meats.

Vegetable oil for toasting
50 gms fennel seeds (saunf)
250 gms coriander seeds
1 kg dried red chillies

- Gently heat ¼ tbsp oil on a griddle. Toast each ingredient separately, in the order given, over medium heat, in batches if required, oiling and reheating griddle as needed.

- Combine spices and grind fine in batches.

- Store in airtight containers for up to 6 months.

SONARI MASALA

Daivadnya Spice Blend
Makes: 4 kg   Time: 1-1½ hours

The Daivadnya community uses Sonari masala for matkichi usal, kobichi bhaji, meat and fish. This recipe makes a large amount. Store under a layer of coarsely ground rock salt for 6-12 months or halve the quantity of ingredients.

Vegetable oil for toasting
250 gms coriander seeds
50 gms cumin seeds
25 gms (2½ tbsp) royal cumin seeds (shah jeera)
25 gms cinnamon
12-13 gms (3½-4 tsp) black peppercorns
5 gms (1 tbsp) cloves

25 gms (2½ tbsp) mustard seeds
2½ kg dried red chillies

- Gently heat ¼ tbsp oil on a griddle. Toast each ingredient separately, in the order given, over medium heat, in batches if required, oiling and reheating griddle as needed.

- Combine them and grind fine in batches.

- Store in airtight containers.

Note: Instead of Sonari masala use 1 tbsp red chilli powder, ²⁄₃ tsp coriander powder, ½ tsp powdered garam masala and ¹⁄₃ tsp cumin powder.

Legumes/Pulses

Beans, Nuts, Whole and Split Lentils: Legumes form an essential part of the largely vegetarian 'mainstream and peninsular' Indian diet. Not surprisingly, India is the world's largest producer, importer and consumer of pulses or dried legume seeds used for human consumption. However, many legumes are also important fodder crops that help improve and conserve the soil and are used by farmers to rejuvenate it between other plantings.

The legume family consists of whole and split lentils, beans, peanuts and peas. It also includes clovers, vetches, even oddly enough, tamarind! Lentils are a good source of protein, calcium, iron, phosphorous, vitamins A and B, and essential amino acids. Beans, also high in protein, are rich in soluble fibre and vitamins A and C.

Cleaning, soaking and sprouting: Clean legumes before use. Systematically shuffle them a bit on a large parat or tray to easily pick them over for stones, husks and other debris.

Many require soaking and/or sprouting before consumption. This takes 8-48 hours. One cup of dry beans yields 3-4 cups of soaked beans so measure accordingly.

Generally, legumes are soaked overnight. Soak 1 cup dry legumes in 3 cups water. In cold weather, use warm (*not* hot) water. During the process of germination legumes release unpleasant odours. Rinse them several times and refresh the water. Do not worry about the bubbly scum (excess protein, etc.) that floats to the top. Skim or drain it off.

To sprout legumes, soak and drain off the soaking water after 12-15 hours. Wrap them completely in a damp cloth and place in a bowl for 8-12 hours, till sprouts poke through the cloth. Occasionally sprinkle the package with water, particularly in dry weather. Rinse again before use.

Cooking: In the West, legumes are often eaten raw or very lightly cooked to retain their crunch. In India they are more completely cooked to ensure digestibility and to eliminate germs.

Pick over soaked/sprouted lentils or beans to remove hard, unsprouted/spoilt grains. When cooking lentils there is a tendency for the water to boil over, so keep the pan partially covered or use a deep one. Cook 1 cup of lentils in 2½ cups fresh, unsalted water.

Bengal gram and udid (urad) dal, used for flavouring foods, are sometimes toasted first or sautéed. Toss them lightly over low heat till golden or they get hard or chewy.

Harbhara (Bengal gram): Several varieties of Bengal gram (*Cicer arietinum*) are popular in India. Two (chickpeas/garbanzo beans) are not widely used in Maharashtra. But the third, Bengal gram (harbhara/chana), a type of vetch, is popular both fresh-green and dried. The fresh beans are eaten raw or cooked like green peas.

Brown/dark green dried gram is rehydrated before use for 2-6 hours in tepid water and cooks easily and quickly. It is one of the few legumes cooked in *salted* water.

Harbharyachi dal and besan (split, husked Bengal gram and gram flour): Split, husked Bengal gram is harbharyachi dal. Being rather gassy and heavy, it is rarely cooked as a lentil dish but flavours salads, vegetables, chivda, etc. It is occasionally eaten on its own in vatli dal (p. 96). Harbharyachi dal needs little soaking. To use as flavouring, soak 1 tablespoon in 3-4 tablespoons of water for 10-12 minutes. Drain and add to your dish after the seasoning.

Besan is harbharyachi dal ground into flour, a commonly used, versatile ingredient. Even the tart leaves of the harbhara bush are eaten when tender, cooked as a tasty bhaji sometimes thickened with besan!

Harbhara roasted in the shell are called phutané/chivda dal. They are salted and eaten as a snack or added to other snacks (chivda, chikki, etc). Roasting enhances their texture and flavour, making them easy to chew. Phutané are available from street vendors or packaged at grocery stores. Interestingly, they are also a popular Middle Eastern snack.

Kulith (*horse gram/vetch*): This vetch (*Glycine tomentosa*) is grown as a forage crop. Its small grain-like legumes are ground into flour (kulthacha pith).

Masur (*whole brown lentils*): Masur (*Lens culinaris*) has a meaty, peppery flavour. Split, husked masur is orange-red in colour, but in Maharashtra it is generally preferred whole. If possible, soak it for 1-2 hours before cooking. Otherwise, cook a little longer or pressure-cook.

Matar (*green peas*): Although actually a legume, green peas (*Pisum sativum*) are considered a vegetable. Growing on vines in pods, they are usually harvested in winter. An excellent source of dietary fibre, they are rich in folic acid and vitamins K, B and C. Dried whole green/yellow peas (vatana), rich in iron, calcium, protein and fibre, are a favourite too. Unlike fresh peas they need soaking overnight.

Matki (*brown mung beans/gram*): Mung beans/gram are an ancient legume, said to be native to India. There are hundreds of varieties of mung but the two most commonly used in Maharashtra are brown and green (below). Clean, wash and soak brown mung in a bowl of water overnight. After 12-24 hours, rinse and use. (To sprout, see p. 54. Test sprouts by biting into one. It should be crunchy but easy to chew.)

Mug and mugachi dal (*green mung beans/gram and mung dal*): Green mung (*Vigna radiata*) is sprouted like matki (above). It tastes great raw in salads. The beans are husked and split to make mugachi dal, which is yellow. They are nutritious, quick-cooking and easy to digest. Clean, rinse and soak mung 30 minutes before using.

Shengdane (*peanuts*): Peanuts (*Arachis hypogaea*) are a much loved snack in Maharashtra, eaten raw, roasted, fried. They are also powdered to thicken gravies and make chutneys, and cooked whole or in pieces.

Peanuts require no soaking but are often roasted before use till evenly golden, aromatic and crunchy. Unless otherwise specified, skin them before powdering or using whole in recipes. Store peanuts in a dry airtight container for up to 2-3 weeks. Kept too long they go rancid. If needed, toast them lightly before use.

Turichi dal (*pigeon peas/yellow lentils*): Pigeon peas (*Cajanus cajans/Cajanus indicus*) are probably native to India but spread to Africa long ago and made their way around the world from there. India is the largest producer of pigeon peas and many Indians eat them regularly.

Tur, grown both as a food and forage crop, is versatile and drought-resistant, tolerating almost any kind of soil. It grows on bushes/creepers in long thin pods remotely resembling green pea pods. Protein-rich tur is said to have medicinal properties. Even its leaves are used to treat sores. The fresh 'peas' are delicious raw or lightly boiled and salted. To make tur dal (split, husked yellow lentils), they are split, husked and dried, often lightly coated with castor oil. The un-oiled variety cooks easier and tastes better. Tur just requires washing before use, but if possible, soak it for 30-60 minutes to quicken cooking.

Udid (*black mung beans/gram*): Black gram (*Vigna mungo*) is infrequently used in Maharashtra. However, split, husked udid is used as flavouring and to make papad.

Val (*bitter beans*): Bitter, meaty val, a smaller variety of pavta beans (*Dolichos spicatus,* lablab, hyacinth beans), are considered a delicacy. They are used whole or split. Clean and soak overnight or till they germinate. Skin them and rinse before cooking.

Sweeteners

Gul, sakhar, pak (jaggery, sugar, syrups): Although white granulated sugar is urban India's most common sweetener, the traditional jaggery (gul) is widely used in rural parts and even urban cooks require it for certain time-honoured dishes.

The word 'jaggery' comes from the Indo-Portuguese 'jagara' and the Sanskrit 'carkara', which shares the root with the English word *sugar*! This unrefined sugar can be made from palm sap or sugarcane juice and is processed without chemicals, synthetic additives or preservatives. East and South India produce much palm jaggery; in Maharashtra, sugarcane being an important crop, jaggery usually means unrefined cane sugar.

Jaggery has sweetened Marathi food for centuries; its place in the Marathi kitchen is assured. It is used in desserts and snacks but also frequently added to lentils and vegetables to enhance natural flavours.

Sugarcane juice is thickened by boiling, set in moulds (traditionally buckets) and sold by weight in hunks/blocks (dhepa). Gul varies in colour, taste and texture. The more refined the gul, the lighter its colour (brown to golden). It can be sticky, hard or soft, sweet or slightly salty, so taste it before use.

As a good source of iron, calcium, folic acid and vitamins, gul is considered highly beneficial to health. It helps purify blood, improve liver function and breathing. Due to its high calorie content, it used as an energy booster. And since, unlike refined sugar, it contains salt, it was used for re-hydration in hot weather. Offering water and a lump of jaggery was the customary and polite way to greet a midday guest.

Sugar and gul can be used interchangeably for most recipes but for those that *require* jaggery, only dark brown sugar makes a tolerable substitute. Many sweets and desserts need syrups. Both sugar and jaggery can be cooked with water into syrups of different consistencies.

Miscellanea

Dagad phul (lichen/rock flower): This fragrant, flaky lichen is typically used in garam, goda and Kolhapuri masalas. If unavailable, omit it.

Khaskhas (poppy seeds): Tiny poppy seeds (*Papaver somniferum*) add crunch and richness to Marathi desserts and thicken gravies. Said to be cooling, they are often added to summer foods. Roast gently before grinding.

Khaycha chuna (edible/slaked lime): Edible/slaked lime is used most often in paan. It helps neutralize excess acid and 'release the alkaloid'.[27] It is also used to process avlas.

Papad: Just one generation ago, most condiments and appetizers were made at home. Today, in urban Maharashtra, they rarely are. Fortunately a huge variety is available at grocery shops.

Papads (crunchy appetizers) come in all shapes and sizes and are made from several ingredients (mugachi dal, udid dal, potatoes, sago, rice, semolina, wheat, etc.), flavoured with salt and spices, shaped and dried. To serve, they are deep or shallow-fried, toasted or roasted over an open flame. They add flavour and crunch and are often a digestive, eaten at the end of a meal.

Til (sesame seeds): Sesame seeds (*Sesamum indicum*) are rich in protein, amino acids, vitamin B, iron and calcium. Other oils are now replacing sesame oil, traditionally used in Marathi cooking. The seeds are used in spice blends (goda masala, p. 48), winter sweets and vegetable dishes. Sesame stars in the Sankranti sweets tilachi vadi/til-gul (p. 336). Sesame seeds are available un-husked and husked. For convenience use husked, white sesame seeds, lightly toasted.

Turathi (pigeon pea stalks): Turathi refers to tur stalks: tur + kaathi (stick) = turathi. In Varhad, stout, dry turathis are used to shape pasta (sarolya, p. 311).

Turti (alum powder): Turat means astringent. This astringent salt is often used as a preservative in pickling as it helps maintain crispness (moravla, p. 300). It is found at grocery or spice shops.

Varkha (edible silver leaf): Edible silver is made from thinly beaten real silver. It adds sparkle to sweets and desserts, fun to use occasionally. Since it is tasteless and the quantity of silver is minimal, eating it is decadent but not harmful.

Breakfast Dishes

A specially prepared breakfast is not traditionally Marathi. Many people may eat no breakfast at all and country folk eat the same food they would for other meals, to break their fast: millet, rice or sorghum bhakri with leftover vegetables or a condiment, or rice porridge (pej) with a vegetable, meat or fish pickle.

The urban working class may eat wheat polya, or these days, bread or a bun, perhaps dunked in hot, sweet, milky tea. For some middle-class families, a summer breakfast treat could be rice or stale bhakri and yogurt with fresh pickles. Sometimes, middle and upper-middle-class people eat sattuché pith (seven-grain flour mixed with water or milk and eaten plain or sweetened) or lately, more Western dishes (cornflakes, eggs, etc.). The dishes in this section are essentially snacks but they work well for breakfast or brunch.

GUL-POHÉ
Beaten Rice with Milk and Jaggery
Serves: 2   Time: 25 minutes

This delicious breakfast requires no cooking.

1 cup thick beaten rice (pohé)
2 cups milk
6-8 tsp grated jaggery or brown sugar
¼ cup grated fresh coconut

- Put rice in a bowl. Heat 1 cup of milk to lukewarm. Soak the rice in it for 15-20 minutes till it crushes easily between thumb and finger.

- Dissolve jaggery or sugar in the remaining milk. Combine the milk and rice, crushing any jaggery lumps without breaking the grains.

- Fold in coconut. Serve immediately.

KANDÉ-BATATÉ POHÉ

Spiced Beaten Rice with Potatoes and Onions
Serves: 6   Time: 30-40 minutes

Pohé is easy to make and delicious any time of day. Tomatoes and carrots add colour; green peas cook quickly; curry leaves and asafoetida are optional. Serve pohé unembellished or with chivda, yogurt, pickles or coriander-coconut chutney, and chai.

500 gms medium or thick beaten rice (pohé)
1 large potato or 100 gms shelled green peas or other vegetable
Up to 2½ tsp salt
A pinch of sugar
¼ tsp turmeric powder

2 medium onions, finely chopped
Juice of 1-2 limes

Seasoning:
5 tbsp vegetable oil
1½ tsp mustard seeds
½ tsp turmeric powder
A pinch of asafoetida powder (hing – optional)
3-4 green chillies, sliced
10-12 curry leaves (optional)

Garnish:
3 tbsp grated fresh coconut
3 tbsp finely chopped coriander leaves

- Briefly rinse rice in a colander under running cold water. Drain well and rest covered for 20-30 minutes. Check once or twice. Press a grain between thumb and forefinger: if crushed easily, it is soft enough to cook. If dry, sprinkle a little water over, mixing through gently with a fork.

- Wash, peel and cut potato into ½" dice. Clean and chop other vegetables into even, bite-sized chunks. Before cooking the rice, gently stir in 2 tsp salt, sugar and turmeric.

- Heat oil for seasoning in a large pan over medium heat, till almost smoking. Add mustard seeds and let them pop.

- Reduce heat to low and add turmeric and asafoetida. Stir briskly. Raise heat to medium. Stir in chillies and curry leaves (if used).

- Add onions and sauté for 3-4 minutes, till translucent. Stir in vegetables and sauté well.

- Season with a pinch of salt, reduce heat and cook covered for 5-7 minutes, till almost tender. Stir occasionally.

- Gently mix in softened rice, separating any lumps. Steam-cook covered for 5-10 minutes, stirring occasionally.

- Mix in lime juice and turn off the heat. The rice should be soft and vegetables cooked.

- Serve steaming hot, garnished with coconut and coriander leaves.

PHODNICHI POLI
Spiced Bread Sauté
Serves: 2-4   Time: 20 minutes

Many recipes, like phodnichi poli, are born of Marathi frugality. Make this dish with day-old chapattis, stale loaf bread or leftover rice (phodnicha bhat). Serve with yogurt and pickles.

6-8 one-day-old chapattis or bread slices, or 2 cups cooked rice
1 large onion, minced
¼ tsp red chilli powder
¼ tsp turmeric powder
2 medium tomatoes, diced (optional)
1-1½ tsp salt
A pinch of sugar

Seasoning:
1½ tbsp vegetable oil
½ tsp mustard seeds
¼ tsp cumin seeds (optional)
4-5 curry leaves (optional)
2-3 small green chillies, sliced

Garnish:
Juice of 1 lime (optional)
4-6 sprigs of coriander leaves, finely chopped

- Shred chapatti or bread (if used), then crush it roughly, rubbing it between fingers and palms.

- Heat oil for seasoning in a skillet. Add mustard seeds and let them pop. Add cumin and curry leaves (if used) and chillies. Stir and add onion. Sauté for 2-3 minutes over medium heat before adding chilli powder and turmeric.

- Stir in tomatoes (if used). When they release their liquid (almost immediately), add chapatti, bread or rice, mix well and sauté over medium-high heat for 3-4 minutes.

- Reduce heat to low, mix in salt and sugar. Cook for 3-5 minutes longer.

- Sprinkle in a dash of lime juice (if used) and garnish with coriander leaves.

SABUDANYACHI KHICHADI

Savoury Sago with Potatoes and Peanuts
Serves: 4   Time: 5-8 hours soaking + 30 minutes cooking
Contributor: Sheetal Joglekar

Sabudanyachi khichadi, often served for fasts, is a satisfying comfort food.

2 cups sago (sabudana)
1½ tsp salt
A pinch of sugar
¾ cup roasted, coarsely ground peanuts
3-4 tbsp tup (ghee)
2-3 green chillies
1¼ tsp cumin seeds
2 small potatoes, peeled and cut into small cubes

Garnish:
2 tbsp grated fresh coconut
2 tbsp finely chopped coriander leaves

- Rinse sago briskly and thoroughly in a small-holed colander or strainer several times under running cold water. Sago is starch, so over-rinsing or warm water will melt the pellets. Drain well, shaking out excess water.

- Place sago in a covered bowl to plump up for 5-12 hours. Occasionally check that the pellets are softening up. Press one between thumb and forefinger: if it is crushed easily, it is soft; if hard and dry, run a cold stream of water over it briefly, turning the translucent pellets over. They are ready when they expand, soften and turn milky-white.

- Before cooking the sago, gently mix in salt, sugar and peanuts.

- Heat tup in a large, deep pan, till almost smoking. Reduce heat to medium-low. Add chillies and cumin. Stir. Add potatoes, sauté briefly and cook covered for 4-5 minutes, till opaque.

- Gently mix in sago. Steam-cook covered for 10-12 minutes, stirring occasionally to prevent clumping. Each pellet should be cooked yet separate. The khichadi is done when the pellets turn translucent again.

- Serve garnished with coconut and coriander leaves, with khamang kakdi (p. 138).

Note: Use oil *only* if tup is unavailable. This dish can be served to fasters only if cooked in tup.

KOLHAPURI KHICHADI

Kolhapuri Savoury Sago with Potatoes and Peanuts
Serves: 4   Time: 5-8 hours soaking + 30 minutes cooking
Contributor: Anuradha Samant

- Use 4 tbsp coriander leaves and more coconut (4-5 tbsp for the paste, 2 tbsp for garnish). The other ingredients are as for sabudanyachi khichadi (p. 67).

- Grind peanuts, coconut, chillies and 2 tbsp coriander leaves into a fine paste. Mix with soaked sago before adding it to the seasoning. Cook as given for sabudanyachi khichadi.

SHIRA, GODE

Steamed Sweet Semolina
Serves: 4   Time: 30 minutes
Contributor: Meera Marathe

Marathi gode shira is made with very well roasted semolina. It is my brother Sameer's favourite. Shira is also a popular picnic food, eaten with poli or puri and batatyachi bhaji (p. 164). Poli and puri dough are even stuffed with leftover shira, rolled out gently and roasted or fried to make shiryachi poli (p. 349) or puri.

Until recently, shira was made only with jaggery. Before machine milling became common, semolina was thicker, being pounded roughly at home in a mortar and pestle. This thick texture held up well to the bold taste of jaggery. Today, different thicknesses of semolina *are* available. Choose appropriately for sugar or jaggery shira.

4 tbsp tup (ghee)
1½ cups semolina (sooji/rava)
1½-2 cups water or equal parts water and milk

¾ cup sugar or grated jaggery, or more to taste
3-4 green cardamoms, powdered
12-15 seedless raisins (kishmish)
4-6 almonds, slivered
A pinch of freshly grated nutmeg (optional)

- Heat tup in a heavy-bottomed wok over medium-low heat. Roast semolina, stirring frequently for 8-12 minutes, till evenly pinkish-brown and aromatic.

- Meanwhile, bring the liquid to a boil. When the semolina is roasted, gradually stir in the liquid.

- Steam-cook covered over low heat for 5-7 minutes. Stir the fluffed up semolina.

- Add sweetener. The shira will become damp and runny. Cook covered for 5-7 minutes, till it fluffs up again.

- Stir in most of the cardamom, raisins and nuts, retaining some for garnish. Turn off the heat.

- Garnish with the remaining cardamom, raisins and nuts. Grate nutmeg over the hot shira and serve.

The Essential Marathi Cookbook

SATYANARAYANACHA SHIRA
Heavenly Semolina
Serves: 4-6   Time: 20 minutes
Contributor: Sudhakar Marathe

This shira, made for Satyanarayana pujas, gets its richness from
a lot of sugar and tup. 'It is made as an offering and as prasad for
guests,' Dad says. 'The more flavoured and fragrant the banana,
the better the shira.'

125 gms tup (ghee)
125 gms semolina (sooji/rava)
1 cup milk
¼ cup water
125 gms sugar
125 gms banana slices
Dried fruit in multiples of 5
¼ tsp powdered green cardamom

- Make as for shira, gode (p. 69) with these ingredients. Serve
  in small quantities as prasad or a snack.

SHIRA, TIKHAT
Steamed Semolina with Vegetables
Serves: 4   Time: 30 minutes
Contributor: Meera Marathe

Tikhat shira with yogurt, mango pickle or coconut chutney, and
chivda is one of our family's favourite weekend breakfasts. The
semolina can be roasted ahead of time and refrigerated in an
airtight container. Bring it to room temperature before making
shira. Use any vegetables, chopping them fine for quick cooking.

1½ cups semolina (sooji/rava)
2-2½ large onions, finely chopped
2 tbsp diced tomato
2 tbsp diced carrot
2 tbsp shelled green peas
1 tsp salt
1½ tbsp tup (ghee)
Lime juice to taste

Seasoning:
3 tbsp vegetable oil
¾ tsp mustard or cumin seeds
1 tsp split, husked black gram (urad dal)
6-8 curry leaves
2 green chillies, sliced

Garnish:
2 tbsp grated fresh coconut
3-4 sprigs of coriander leaves, finely chopped
4-5 fried cashew nuts (optional)

- Roast the semolina (p. 70) without tup in a large skillet. Transfer to a bowl.

- Bring 1½ cups of water to a boil. Wipe out your skillet, add oil for seasoning and heat till almost smoking. Reduce heat, add mustard or cumin seeds and let them pop. Add dal, curry leaves and chillies. Stir well. Add onions and sauté for 2-3 minutes.

- Mix in vegetables, 1½ cups of boiling water and salt. Bring to a rolling boil and gradually pour in semolina, stirring continuously to prevent lumps. Stir in the tup.

- Steam-cook covered for 8-10 minutes, stirring occasionally to prevent sticking. The shira is ready when the semolina fluffs up. If it appears slightly dry or raw, sprinkle with a little water, stir and steam again, covered, for 2-3 minutes.

- Mix in lime juice. Serve piping hot, garnished with coconut, coriander leaves and fried cashew nuts.

TANDULACHI UKAD

Steamed Rice Flour with Mustard Seeds and Buttermilk
Serves: 2-3   Time: 15 minutes

This Konkanastha breakfast dish is made with rice flour. It requires constant stirring and tastes best hot, so make it just before serving. Easy on the stomach, it makes a great supper dish too.

3 cups buttermilk
1½ cups rice flour
¾-1 tsp salt

Seasoning:
3-4 tbsp vegetable oil
¾ tsp mustard seeds
4-6 curry leaves
A pinch of asafoetida powder (hing)
¼ tsp turmeric powder
1-2 long green chillies, sliced

Garnish:
4-6 sprigs of coriander leaves, finely chopped

- Pour buttermilk into a medium bowl. Add rice flour, 1 tbsp at a time, whisking to make a smooth paste. Stir in salt.

- Heat oil for seasoning in a pan over medium-high heat. When it is almost smoking, reduce heat to medium. Add mustard seeds and let them pop.

- Add curry leaves, asafoetida, turmeric and chillies. Stir briskly and turn down the heat.

- Gradually pour the rice paste over the seasoning. Raise the heat to medium-low. Cook for 8-12 minutes, stirring continuously. The ukad is ready when the liquid has evaporated, leaving behind a firm, fluffy mass.

- Serve piping hot, garnished with coriander leaves.

Breakfast Dishes   73

TANDLELACHI UKAD

1¾ cups rice flour
½-1 tsp salt

Seasoning:
3-4 tbsp vegetable oil
½ tsp mustard seeds

Snacks & Teatime Treats

Snacks

Snacks are an important part of Indian social life. In fact, I dare say there is no other nation with such fondness for the social ritual of snacking and such a plethora of sweet and savoury snacks.

In Maharashtra, a multitude of fresh snacks ranges from the simple (bhel, harbharyachi usal, etc.) to those requiring more preparation (bataté vadé, pangya, etc.). There are also longer lasting snacks, prepared in advance, eaten at room temperature when desired and made in bulk for festive platters on occasions like Diwali or weddings: chakli, kadboli, karanji, chivda, shev, Shankarpali, ladu, etc.

So it is unfortunate that, as a society, we are increasingly buying such treats ready-made. Often people believe they are too difficult to make at home or that they lack the time or the experience to make them. Actually many are simple, needing only a little planning. Try them out when you feel up to it. You might build a repertoire of treats that work for you. Certainly you will notice a difference in their quality.

Note: Though shev is an important snack mentioned here as a topping for various dishes, I do not include the recipe which requires too much oil and fuss for most contemporary kitchens. Bhel is also missing since most people now go out to eat it!

BHADANG
Puffed Rice Snack Mix
Serves: 10-12   Time: 20 minutes

Gather your ingredients and you are done in under 30 minutes!

250 gms puffed rice (murmura)
1½-2 tsp salt
¾ cup peanut or vegetable oil
10-15 curry leaves
120 gms dried coconut (kopra), finely slivered
150 gms peanuts

Spice powder:
2 cloves
1" stick cinnamon
2 tsp metkut (optional)
¾ tsp ground black pepper
½ tsp red chilli powder
½ tsp coriander seeds
½ tsp cumin seeds
1 tsp sugar

- Crisp the puffed rice in an oven preheated to 120°C (250°F) for 5-7 minutes, if needed, turning occasionally. Transfer it to a large bowl.

- Grind spice powder ingredients fine. Add salt and toss with the puffed rice.

- Heat oil in a small skillet till almost smoking. Reduce heat to low and sauté the curry leaves, coconut and peanuts, browning them ever so slightly for 3-4 minutes.

- Briskly stir the curry leaf mixture into the rice to distribute the flavourings. They settle at the bottom so toss it before serving.

- Store, once cool, in airtight containers.

CHAKLI
Crunchy Multigrain Spirals
Makes: 20-30 chaklis   Time: 1-1½ hours
Special equipment: chakli press/pastry bag with a large, star-shaped nozzle, banana leaves/plastic sheets/wax paper, paper-lined platter
Contributor: Surekha Sirsikar

A chakli that is crunchy but not hard, soft but not mushy, with just the right amounts of salt, spice and shortening that make it what we call, 'khuskhusheet' is a rare treat. The best I have ever eaten are my grandmother's. She learnt the recipe from her mother-in-law, Laxmibai Sirsikar, who made them with rice flour and lots of butter. My health-conscious grandmother preferred bhajni (recipe below).

Chakli-making is time-consuming—an all-day affair at Aji's because she made so many at a time—and it will probably take you a few tries before you get it right. But a khuskhusheet chakli is worth it.

Ready-made bhajni is now available at Marathi grocery stores (around October-November) but your best bet is to have the flour ground from ingredients you prepare yourself.

Bhajni flour:
1 kg short-grained rice
500 gms split, husked Bengal gram (chana dal)
250 gms split, husked black gram (urad dal)

Chakli:
680 gms bhajni
⅓ cup vegetable oil or melted shortening
1½ tsp salt
1½ tsp red chilli powder
½ tsp asafoetida powder (hing)
2 tsp sesame seeds (til)
1 litre vegetable oil

Bhajni flour:

- Rinse and drain the rice well. Dry it thoroughly, spread out on a large clean cloth in a shaded spot outdoors for 3-6 hours.

- Roast dried rice and lentils separately for 15-20 minutes each, in a large, dry wok, till fragrant and toasted, stirring frequently.

- Cool, combine and grind the ingredients into flour.

- Store in an airtight container.

Chakli dough:

- Measure bhajni into a bowl. Rub in oil or shortening with your hands. Mix in salt, spice powders and sesame seeds.

- Pouring in a little cool water at a time, knead to make a firm, squeezable dough, a little looser than chapatti dough. Set aside for 15-20 minutes.

Forming the chaklis:

- The chakli press (sorya) has different stencils. Use the star-shaped one for chaklis. A pastry bag with a large, star-shaped nozzle works too.

- On a clean surface, lay out clean banana leaves, plastic sheets or wax paper on which to form the chaklis.

- Fill the press three-quarters full with dough and place the top portion gently over it. Position the press 6" above the non-stick surface and push its top steadily into the dough. Simultaneously, turn it clockwise in a spiral motion so it falls on to the surface, forming a 3" spiral. Lift the press upward with a flicking motion and stop pushing, to break the ribbon of dough. Press the end of the spiral against the chakli so it stays together during frying. Shape the remaining chaklis 1" apart.

- If using a pastry bag, fill it with dough as for icing. Shape spirals as above.

Frying:

- Heat oil in a wok till almost smoking,

- Gently peel off each chakli and slide it into the wok. Fry 4-6 at a time, for 45-90 seconds on the first side. Turn them carefully when golden and fry for less than 1 minute on the other side, till golden brown. Drain well before removing them from the wok.

- Arrange chaklis on the paper-lined platter.

- The chaklis will be firm when fried correctly, but break very easily while hot, so cool completely before serving or storing. Store flat in an airtight container for up to 2-3 weeks.

KHARVAS

First-Milk Custard
Serves: 4-6   Time: 30 minutes
Special equipment: steamer

Fresh colostrum (p. 30) is used to make kharvas; a sweet, saffron-yellow, cardamom-speckled custard with a silky, squeaky texture. Very thick, first-day colostrum is best for kharvas. If using second- or third-day colostrum, reduce milk by $1/3$ cup.

250 ml colostrum
250 ml milk
3-4 tbsp sugar or jaggery, or to taste
5-6 green cardamoms, powdered

- Stir colostrum, milk, sweetener and powdered cardamoms together till the sweetener dissolves.

- Steam custard in a shallow pan for 15-20 minutes, till set.

- Cool before cutting into squares.

- Serve at room temperature or chilled.

PARATLELA CHIVDA
Beaten Rice Snack Mix
Serves: 10   Time: 30 minutes
Contributor: Meera Marathe

Chivda is extremely popular in Maharashtra, essential on a Diwali platter, and served on significant social occasions such as engagements and weddings. It is so often paired with ladu that the two are referred to as one, 'ladu-chivda'. Paratlela literally means stir-fried.

50 gms un-skinned peanuts
70 gms desiccated coconut (kopra), slivered
50 gms roasted Bengal gram (phutané)
500 gms thin beaten rice (pohé)
1½-2 tsp salt
1½ tsp mango powder (amchur)
1 tsp sugar
2 tbsp seedless raisins (kishmish – optional)

Seasoning:
4 tbsp peanut oil
1½ tsp mustard seeds
1 sprig curry leaves
1½ tsp cumin powder
¾-1 tsp turmeric powder
4-5 dried red chillies or 1 tsp red chilli powder

- Heat oil for seasoning in a wok over medium heat for 3-5 minutes, till hot and bubbling. Add mustard seeds and let them pop. Add curry leaves, cumin, turmeric and chillies or chilli powder and sauté briefly.

- Mix in peanuts and coconut and stir-fry for 3-4 minutes, till golden. Stir in roasted gram. Add beaten rice and stir-fry for 10-12 minutes, till crisp but not brown. Mix in salt, mango powder, sugar and raisins.

- When cool, store in an airtight container. Serve hot or at room temperature.

Note: Beaten rice, peanuts and coconut burn easily, so stir them often, lifting and flipping ingredients briskly. Avoid over-handling beaten rice as they disintegrate. They also get damp and chewy. If needed, sun-dry the rice for a few hours or toast for 5-7 minutes, in an oven preheated to 120°C (250°F) for 5-7 minutes, turning occasionally.

SPEED-OF-LIGHT CHIVDA

Quick Snack Mix
Serves: 5-6   Time: 15 minutes
Special equipment: paper-lined platter

500 ml vegetable oil
250 gms thick beaten rice (pohé)
2 tsp coriander seed powder
1 tsp fennel powder (badi saunf)
½ tsp cumin powder
½ tsp red chilli powder
½ tsp ground black pepper
⅛ tsp asafoetida powder (hing)
¼ tsp sugar
A handful of roasted peanuts or cashew nuts (optional)
Salt to taste

- Heat oil in a wok. Deep-fry beaten rice for 4-7 minutes over medium-low heat, till crisp and golden, turning occasionally. Drain thoroughly and place on the paper-lined platter.

- After 5-7 minutes, toss beaten rice in a large bowl with the spices, sugar, nuts (if used) and salt.

SHANKARPALI

Savoury Flaky Pastry Squares
Makes: about 200 Shankarpali   Time: 1-1½ hours
Special equipment: karanji/pastry crimper, paper-lined platter
Contributor: Meera Marathe

Make these crunchy flaky savoury or sweet squares (opposite page).
The trick is getting the flakiness just right. Like chaklis, well-
made Shankarpalis are 'khuskhusheet'.

> 400 gms sifted refined flour (maida)
> 2-3 tbsp tup (ghee)
> 2-2½ tsp salt
> ½-2 tsp red chilli powder
> 1½ tsp cumin seeds
> ¾ tsp ajwain/carum
> ½-1 litre vegetable oil for frying

- Place flour in a bowl. Make a well in the middle and pour in
  tup and salt. Rub the tup thoroughly into the flour. Mix in
  spices.

- Gradually add up to ½ cup water to bring the ingredients
  together. Use water sparingly, stopping as soon as the dough
  comes together. Knead it for 5-7 minutes, till soft and smooth.
  Rest covered for at least 30 minutes.

- Divide the dough into smooth lumps the size of tennis balls.
  Roll each ball evenly into a 12" wide, ¼" thick circle.

- Using a pastry crimper or knife, cut equidistant parallel lines
  across each circle to make even strips; turn the board
  90 degrees to cut equidistant parallel lines, perpendicular to
  the first. This makes small squares of dough. For diamonds,
  cut the circle similarly, but at an angle.

- When 1-2 circles are cut, heat oil in a large wok over medium
  heat. Fry 20-30 squares for 1-2 minutes, till evenly golden

and crisp, turning them if needed. Some will flip over themselves; some will puff up.

- Drain a few at a time and place on the paper-lined platter.

- While one batch is being fried, roll and cut the next ball of dough. (Or prepare all the squares first, covering them with a damp cloth to prevent drying.)

- Store cooled Shankarpalis in an airtight container for up to 2 weeks.

GODE SHANKARPALI
Sweet Flaky Pastry Squares
Makes: about 200 Shankarpali   Time: 1–1½ hours
Special equipment: karanji/pastry crimper, paper-lined platter
Contributor: Meera Marathe

400 gms sifted refined flour (maida)
2-3 tbsp tup (ghee)
A pinch of salt
100-150 gms powdered sugar
1 tsp powdered green cardamom
Up to 1 cup water
½-1 litre vegetable oil for frying

- Follow the method given in the previous recipe, using these ingredients.

Teatime Treats

BATATYACHA KEES
Grated Potato Sauté with Cumin
Serves: 4   Time: 15 minutes
Contributor: Sudhakar Marathe

2 large potatoes or sweet potatoes, grated
½-¾ tsp salt
½ tsp turmeric powder
1-1½ tsp red chilli powder
A pinch of sugar
3-4 tsp ground peanuts

Seasoning:
1½ tbsp tup (ghee)
½ tsp cumin seeds

Garnish:
3-4 sprigs of coriander leaves, finely chopped
½ medium lime

- Squeeze extra starch from the grated potatoes. Mix in salt.

- Heat tup for seasoning in a skillet. Add cumin seeds and let them pop.

- Add turmeric and potatoes and sauté for 2-3 minutes over medium heat. Stir in chilli powder and sugar. Reduce the heat and steam-cook covered for 5 minutes.

- Mix in ground peanuts. Cook covered for 3-4 minutes more, stirring occasionally.

- Garnish with coriander leaves and lime wedges or lime juice.

Variations: You can deep-fry the potatoes till crisp and golden; sprinkle with cumin powder, mango powder, chilli powder and salt. Or add salt, chilli powder, fried peanuts, cashew nuts and raisins to make potato chivda.

BATATA VADA

Spicy Potato Croquettes
Serves: 4-6   Time: 45-60 minutes
Special equipment: paper-lined platter
Contributor: Anuradha Samant

Bataté vadé might be Maharashtra's best-known snack. In Mumbai the spiced potato, crisp-battered fritters are served as 'vada-pav', one or two smashed in a soft bun, smothered with spicy garlic chutney. They are also great plain or with chutney or ketchup.

Filling:
4 medium potatoes
2 green chillies
1 tbsp coriander leaves
1 medium onion, minced
1 tsp lime juice
1 tbsp ginger-garlic paste
1-1½ tsp salt

Seasoning:
1 tbsp vegetable oil
¼ tsp mustard seeds
¼ tsp cumin seeds
¼ tsp asafoetida powder (hing)
A pinch of turmeric powder
5-6 curry leaves

Batter:
1 cup gram flour (besan)
2 tbsp rice flour

1 tsp red chilli powder
1 tsp coriander seed powder
1 tsp cumin powder
½-¾ tsp salt
1 tbsp hot vegetable oil

2 cups vegetable oil for frying

Filling:

- Boil potatoes for 15-20 minutes, till tender. Cool, peel and mash them smooth, not pasty. Grind chillies and coriander leaves into a paste.

- Heat oil for seasoning in a skillet. Add mustard seeds and let them pop. Stir in cumin, asafoetida and turmeric. Add curry leaves and onion and sauté for 2-3 minutes.

- Add 1 tsp water, lime juice, ginger-garlic paste and salt. Mix in the potatoes. Cook covered for 2-3 minutes.

- Cool to room temperature and stir in the chilli-coriander paste. Shape the filling into 2"-3" balls.

Batter:

- Combine all batter ingredients in a bowl. Slowly stirring in up to 1 cup of water, make a batter thick and heavy enough to coat the potato balls without too much dripping off.

Frying:

- Heat 2 cups oil in a medium wok till almost smoking. Dip vadé in the batter, drain off excess and slide them gently into the wok. Fry 4-5 vadé at a time over medium heat for 2 minutes per side, turning over when golden brown. Keep the heat even. Drain well and place on the paper-lined platter.

Note: For **Vada-Pav**, toast white rolls or pav lightly. Stuff vadé into them and top with a spicy garlic chutney (p. 273).

DADPÉ POHÉ

Crunchy Beaten Rice with Onions and Lime
Serves: 6-8   Time: 25 minutes

This crunchy treat uses raw pohé. Prep ingredients (do not cut onions too far in advance as they get smelly) and combine them briskly but lightly just before serving!

Pohé:
2 medium onions, minced
2 small tomatoes, minced (optional)
1 tsp grated ginger (optional)
3-4 green chillies, sliced
1 large fresh coconut, grated
A pinch of sugar
1-1½ tsp salt
Juice of 3 medium limes
500 gms thin beaten rice (pohé)
3 tbsp peanuts (optional)

Seasoning:
2 tbsp vegetable oil
½ tsp mustard seeds
A pinch of asafoetida powder (hing)
½ tsp turmeric powder
5-6 curry leaves
2-3 dried red chillies

Garnish:
5-6 sprigs of coriander leaves, coarsely chopped

- Put onions, tomatoes and ginger (if used), chillies, coconut (reserve 1½ tbsp for garnish), sugar, salt and lime juice in a large bowl.

- Stir in unwashed beaten rice and allow it to soak up the juices. Soak for 3-5 minutes for crunchy pohé, longer for softer pohé.

- Heat oil for seasoning in a small wok. Add mustard seeds and let them pop. Stir in asafoetida, turmeric, curry leaves and red chillies. Pour the seasoning over the beaten rice.

- Mix well, add peanuts (if used), and serve immediately, garnished with reserved coconut and coriander leaves.

SODYACHÉ KANDA POHÉ
CKP Beaten Rice with Dried Shrimp
Serves: 2-4   Time: 30 minutes
Contributor: Sheela Pradhan

Shrimp:
100 gms dried shrimp, cut into 2-3 pieces each
1 tsp salt
1 tbsp vegetable oil

Spice paste:
1-2 green chillies or to taste
3-4 cloves garlic
1" piece of ginger
¼ tsp turmeric powder
1 tsp red chilli powder

Pohé:
2 tbsp vegetable oil
7-9 curry leaves
250 gms thick beaten rice (pohé)
3 medium onions, minced
2 medium potatoes, cubed
½ tsp salt

Garnish:
2 tbsp grated fresh coconut
5 sprigs of coriander leaves, finely chopped

- Soak shrimp in water for 10-20 minutes.

- Grind chillies, garlic and ginger to a fine consistenty. Stir in turmeric and chilli powder.

- Drain shrimp, rinse well and marinate with the spice paste and salt.

- Heat 1 tbsp oil in a large pan. Sauté shrimp for 2-3 minutes over medium heat, till tender. Transfer to a small bowl.

- Add 2 tbsp oil to the same pan. Sauté curry leaves briefly over medium heat. Make pohé as given in kandé-bataté pohé (p. 64) using these ingredients.

- When ready, add cooked shrimp.

- Garnish with coconut and coriander leaves.

- Serve piping hot.

MATARCHI KARANJI
Savoury Green Pea-Filled Crescents
Makes: 6-12 Time: 1 hour
Special equipment: pastry crimper, paper-lined platter

Fresh green pea or harbhara-filled crescents are fabulous. Prepare the filling the day before or while the dough rests. Bring refrigerated filling to room temperature before using.

Pastry:
100 gms sifted refined flour (maida)
1½-2 tbsp vegetable oil or tup (ghee)
A pinch of salt

Seasoning:
1 tbsp vegetable oil or tup (ghee)
1 tsp cumin seeds

¼ tsp turmeric powder
1-2 green chillies, sliced (optional)
½" piece of ginger, grated

Filling:
50 gms (1 small) onion, minced (optional)
250 gms tender fresh green peas or fresh green gram (harbhara)
1 tsp salt
Juice of ½ a lime
1 tsp goda masala (p. 48) or garam masala powder
A pinch of sugar (optional, for mature peas)

Karanjis:
Milk for sealing karanjis
½-1 litre vegetable oil for frying

Pastry:

- Place flour in a large bowl. Make a well in the middle. Add oil or tup and salt, rubbing them into the flour. Gradually adding up to 1 cup of water, make a firm, flexible dough.

- Knead for 5-7 minutes. Rest covered, for about 30 minutes.

Filling:

- Heat oil for seasoning in a small skillet over medium heat. When the oil is almost smoking, add cumin seeds and let them pop. Lower heat and stir in turmeric, chillies and ginger.

- Add onion and sauté for 4-5 minutes, till golden and softened.

- Raise the heat to medium-high, add green peas or gram and sauté briefly. Reduce the heat to low and cook covered for 7-15 minutes, till tender. Stir occasionally.

- Test a green pea or gram for doneness; add salt, lime juice, goda or garam masala and sugar (if needed). Steam through.

- Cool the filling completely before making karanjis.

Karanjis:

- Have ready a pastry crimper, paper-lined platter, damp dishcloth and some milk by the rolling board. Knead the dough briefly. Divide it into 1½" balls, flatten lightly into discs and cover with the damp dishcloth.

- Roll a ball into a 4"-6" disc. Put 1-1½ tbsp of filling on the half closer to you, leaving a clear ¼" edge.

- Dot the edges of the circle with milk; it helps seal the pastry shut. Fold and press the upper half over the filling on to the lower half, forming a semicircle.

- Cut around the edge with the crimper to create a scallop-edged crescent (or pinch the dough at ¼" intervals for a fluted edge).

- Use scraps to make more karanjis. Store crescents close to each other on a platter, covered with the dishcloth.

- When you are nearly done forming the karanjis, heat oil in a wok. Fry 2-3 karanjis at a time over medium heat for 1-2 minutes. Turn them when golden brown. Some will flip over themselves and some will puff up. They are ready when evenly golden, crisp and firm. Keep the heat even.

- Drain each well and place on the paper-lined platter.

- Serve karanjis hot or at room temperature with coriander chutney (p. 277) or ketchup.

PANGYA

Padmakar Kaka's Rice Flour Treat
Serves: 4-6   Time: 40 minutes
Contributor: Usha Marathe

My father's older brother Padmakar had a sweet smile and a gentle spirit. He died quite young. His wife Usha and sons, Pramodan, Niranjan and Sudarshan shared some of Kaka's favourite recipes. Usha Kaku recalls, 'Kaka was a thorough gentleman and had a very healthy lifestyle. If he was recovering from a fever, he would ask me to prepare pangya because they are light on the stomach and easy to digest.'

Ai Aji (who made them for Kaka when he was a child) gave her the recipe.

1 cup grated jaggery
2 cups rice flour
1 tbsp + 2-4 tbsp unsalted butter
A pinch of salt
½ cup milk
4-6 tbsp vegetable oil
2-3 small banana leaves, washed, dried and cut into foot long sections

- Combine jaggery with rice flour, 1 tbsp melted butter and salt. Add enough milk to make a very thick batter, dissolving the jaggery completely.

- Butter both sides of a banana leaf. Spread batter on half of it. Fold and press the top over and on to the batter. Repeat with the remaining leaves.

- Heat 1-2 tbsp oil in a large skillet over medium heat. Shallow-fry packets for 3-4 minutes, till the underside turns brown and the batter begins to firm up. Gently flip packets over and cook till brown.

- Rest briefly on a cutting board.

- Carefully unfold packets, remove pangya and slice into small slabs.

- Serve with sweet lemon pickle.

SABUDANYACHÉ VADÉ
Tasty Sago-Potato Cakes
Serves: 4   Time: 6-8 hours soaking + 40 minutes cooking
Special equipment: paper-lined platter
Contributor: Medha Marathe

3 large potatoes, boiled
1 cup sago (sabudana), soaked for 6-8 hours (p. 67)
2-3 green chillies, sliced or 1½ tsp red chilli powder
3-4 tsp ground peanuts
½ tsp cumin seeds
1 tsp salt
A pinch of sugar
1 tbsp finely chopped coriander leaves
2 cups vegetable oil

- Peel potatoes and mash well. Coarsely mash in the soaked sago, chillies, peanuts, cumin, salt, sugar and coriander leaves.

- Heat oil in a wok till almost smoking. Meanwhile, make 1"-1½" balls of the sago mixture and flatten slightly.

- Deep-fry 4-5 vadé at a time for 1-2 minutes per side, till light golden, turning them over when the first side is done. Drain well and place on the paper-lined platter.

- Serve hot with chutney or ketchup.

VATLI DAL

Tangy Bengal Gram Hash

Serves: 2   Time: 8-12 hours soaking + 20 minutes cooking
Contributor: Mira Gokhale

Vatli dal is often served on Anant Chaturdashi, the last day of the Ganpati festival. Kairichi dal (opposite) is a raw version.

1 cup split, husked Bengal gram (chana dal), cleaned and rinsed
1 tsp lime juice
2 tbsp grated green mango (optional)
½-1 tsp salt
½ tsp sugar

Seasoning:
3 tbsp vegetable oil
½ tsp mustard seeds
½ tsp turmeric powder
1 green chilli, sliced
1 tsp grated ginger (optional)

Garnish:
2 tbsp grated fresh coconut
⅛ cup finely chopped coriander leaves (optional)

- Soak gram in 2 cups water, covered, in a warm place for 8-10 hours. When it is so soft that it breaks apart when lightly pressed, drain it. Clean it once more. Grind to a grainy consistency, adding 1-2 tbsp water at a time (up to 7 tbsp). It should be moist, not runny.

- Heat oil for seasoning in a skillet over medium-high heat for 2-3 minutes. Add mustard seeds and let them pop. Stir in turmeric, chilli and ginger (if used).

- Reduce heat to medium and mix in gram, lime juice, mango, salt and sugar. Steam-cook covered for 10-15 minutes. Stir occasionally, adding water, if needed.

- Serve garnished with coconut and coriander leaves (if used).

KAIRICHI DAL
Raw Bengal Gram Hash with Mangoes
Serves: 2-4   Time: 8-12 hours soaking + 20 minutes cooking

A popular dal in the mango season, kairichi dal is often served at Marathi baby showers (dohalé jevan).

1 cup split, husked Bengal gram (chana dal)
¼ cup grated green mango
1½ tbsp grated fresh coconut
¾-1 tsp salt
A pinch of sugar
2 sprigs of coriander leaves + extra for garnish, finely chopped

Seasoning:
1 tbsp vegetable oil
½ tsp mustard seeds
A pinch of asafoetida powder (hing)
A pinch of turmeric powder
A pinch of red chilli powder (optional)
1 green chilli, sliced

- Clean, soak and grind the gram as described opposite for vatli dal.

- Mix the gram with grated mango, coconut, salt, sugar and 2 sprigs of finely chopped coriander leaves.

- Heat oil in a wok over medium heat. Add mustard seeds and let them pop. Add spice powders and chilli.

- Stir well and mix the seasoning into the gram.

- Garnish with coriander leaves.

Grains

Craina

Bread

Maharashtra boasts such a vast variety of (mostly unleavened) breads that I include only the basics. Hand-flattened bhakris made of millet or sorghum are one of three common staples, particularly for working-class folk. The others are wheat breads (polya) and rice breads. On the coast, rice is also used for pancakes. And various grains are combined with spices to make bhajni, used for spiced pan breads (thalipeeth).

Bhakris made of dough mixed with milk or sugarcane juice are called dashmi, eaten in the evening; gakar is a wheat bread, thick as a bhakri and roasted like one, but about the size of a puri. There are special, sweet stuffed breads (puran poli, shiryachi poli), pancakes like dhirda, with or without vegetables; thin pancakes called ghavan served with a thin jaggery and coconut milk sauce.

Breads are eaten morning, noon and night. Some, like thalipeeth, are generally eaten fresh; others like bhakri are also relished stale. Leftover bread is never thrown out. It might be crumbled and eaten with milk, dipped in tea or made into various sweet and savoury snacks.

Here are some bread-making tips (also see individual recipes):

- For bhakris, mix the dough at cooking time. Do not knead it.

- For wheat breads (poli, puri, etc.), the dough *must* rest after kneading for the gluten to relax and the breads to be soft and pliable. Prepare dough 30 minutes prior to cooking.

- Use water sparingly, when making dough. Add a little at a time as needed.

- Add a pinch of salt to *all* sweet bread doughs and more than a pinch to basic bread doughs to improve flavour and digestibility.

- Spread tup on freshly made polya and phulkas to maintain softness.

- Serve unsalted butter with hot pan breads like thalipeeth or dhirda. Place it away from the bread to prevent melting.

- With all savoury pan breads and pancakes, yogurt, butter, chutneys, pickles and salads are great accompaniments.

BHAKRI
Hand-Flattened Millet or Sorghum Bread
Serves: 6   Time: 30 minutes

Unrefined millet or sorghum bhakri flour is more affordable, filling and nutritious than wheat flour. Rural folk still subsist on bhakri and though many urban folk have transitioned to wheat bread, they occasionally hanker for earthy, dense bhakri too. Bhakris take skill to make, being flattened and roasted over an open fire (preferably wood or coal) by hand. The best bhakris have two separate layers, a thin top one and a thicker bottom layer.

For the quintessential Marathi experience, break an onion with your fist, peel and eat it with salt and a bhakri. If you like, spread butter or tup (ghee) between the bhakri layers.

Mix only enough flour for 2 bhakris at a time. Once roasted, mix flour for the next two. Use 1 cup flour per large bhakri (usually enough for one person).

6 cups sifted pearl millet (bajra) or sorghum (jowar) flour + 1 cup for rolling
Up to ½ cup water + 2-3 tbsp slightly warm water per cup of millet flour (for sorghum, use cold water)

- Heat a griddle well over low heat.

- In a parat or mixing platter, mix flour with a little water at a time to make an elastic dough.

- Make a ball of dough that sits comfortably within your palm. Start flattening it on a floured board with one hand, alternately tapping and rotating *in one direction*. The tapping flattens the dough; the rotating keeps the shape increasing evenly in a circle. If necessary, sprinkle on more flour. Shape the bhakri till it is thin but still thick enough to lift and flip on to the griddle at one go.

- Put the bhakri, bottom side up, on the griddle. Wet your hand and rub water evenly and smoothly over the bhakri. In 1-2 minutes, it will begin to lift a little in places. Rotate it a few times to roast it evenly on the underside. Then push it to the side of the griddle and flip it over. After about 1 minute, rotate it a few times as before.

- Move the griddle off the heat and place the bhakri gently over direct heat to puff up. Turn it a few times with tongs so it roasts nicely all over without charring. Or simply roast longer on the griddle, cooking each side only once.

- Usually cooks stand the roasted bhakri against the stove or a wall to cool. You could fold it in half and put it in a container without closing the lid. Hold the hot bhakri on one palm and chop down on it with the edge of the other hand firmly, folding the bhakri in one smooth motion.

GHADICHI POLI
Layered Wholewheat Bread
Serves: 1   Time: 35 minutes

A poli is the middle-class urban equivalent of bhakri. Make the dough pliant enough to roll comfortably, but not so soft that it sticks to the rolling board, pin or griddle.

Dough:
100 gms sifted wholewheat flour (atta)
A pinch of salt
¾ tbsp vegetable oil

For rolling:
2-3 tbsp refined flour (maida), in a bowl
2 tbsp vegetable oil, in a bowl
Tup (ghee) for spreading

- Place flour in a parat or mixing platter. Make a well in the middle. Add salt and oil and rub them into the flour with your fingers.

- Adding up to ½ cup lukewarm water very slowly, bring the flour together.

- Knead dough very thoroughly for 5-7 minutes, rolling the ball over and over, pressing down and forward to fold and refold it, making it firm, smooth and pliant. Rest covered for 20-30 minutes.

- Place a round box, the rolling flour, rolling oil and tup close at hand.

- Divide the dough into 2-3 flattened balls that fit comfortably in the centre of your palm. Cover with a clean dishcloth.

- Press one ball very lightly in the rolling flour. Roll it out on the board with a slightly circular motion *in one direction*, turning the flattened dough occasionally. Apply gentle pressure on the edges.

- When it is about 4" wide, spread some oil lightly on half the upper side. Fold the dough into a semicircle. Spread oil lightly on the upper part; then fold it into a triangle.

- Dip this lightly in flour, dust evenly and roll out with a circular motion, pressing gently on the edges. The dough should turn around on the board with the pressure of the rolling pin. Or lift and turn it occasionally, shaping it into a 9"-10" round poli.

- Heat a griddle well over medium heat for 2-3 minutes.

- Lift the poli between your hands and spread it carefully on the griddle. Start rolling your next poli but keep an eye on the roasting bread.

- When it begins to show small bubbles on its surface and to get pink-brown, after about 1 minute, press all its edges gently with the end of the rolling pin or a folded cloth. With the same cloth, move the poli around on the griddle to cook evenly. Check by lifting the edge whether the bubbles are evenly spread out. Gently press down on uncooked spots.

- Turn the poli over in one smooth motion. If rolled well, it should almost immediately puff up. Rotate it a little to make sure it is cooked on the second side, for about 1 minute.

- Take it off the griddle, carefully crushing it to release the steam. Spread tup on both sides before placing it in a container.

- Do *not* cover polya till they are completely cool or they get soggy. Reheat the griddle before cooking the next poli.

- Serve polya with a meal or jam. They make great wraps for dry vegetable, lentil or meat fillings.

Note: Refrigerate dough for up to 2 days. Bring it to room temperature and knead before making polya.

Variation: **Sakhar Poli (Simply Sweet Bread)**: Kids love sugar polya. Prepare ghadichi poli dough as described above. Flatten and roll each ball out about 4" wide. Spoon 1½ tsp sugar in the centre. Wrap the dough round it and seal shut. Dip it into the rolling flour. Roll gently and evenly into a 6" poli. Heat a skillet and grease it with oil or tup. Roast the poli gently for 1-3 minutes per side. Overcooking will make these polya chewy.

PHULKA
Puffed Wholewheat Bread
Makes: 3-4 phulkas   Time: 30 minutes

The ingredients and process for phulkas, *unfolded* polya, are the same as for ghadichi poli (p. 103). Phulkas are smaller, not layered and taste best hot off the griddle.

- Roll phulkas 6" wide. Roast lightly only once on each side.

- Move the griddle off the burner, turn the heat low and roast the phulka over the open flame, a few seconds per side, till it puffs up. Use tongs to move and roast it evenly.

- Remove from the heat, crush lightly to release the steam and spread with tup before serving or storing.

POLICHA LADU
Chapatti-Jaggery Balls
Makes: 4-6 ladus   Time: 15 minutes

4-6 one-day-old chapattis
2 tbsp tup (ghee)
½ cup grated jaggery, softened
4-6 peanuts, ground
½ tsp sesame seeds (til – optional)

- Shred chapattis, tearing them into progressively smaller bits. Crush them into a coarse powder, with some texture. For more texture, tear but do not crush them.

- Rub in tup. Crush in softened jaggery. Add peanuts and sesame.

- Add more jaggery or tup if needed, making sure it is not too sweet or greasy.

- Press a handful of mixture in one palm and shape it with the other into a 1½" ball.

- Refrigerate for up to 2 days.

TANDULACHYA PITHACHI BHAKRI
Hand-Flattened Rice Flour Bread
Serves: 3-4   Time: 30 minutes
Contributor: Mohsina Mukkadam

My friend Mohsina recently received her doctorate, with her dissertation on medieval Marathi food. She is a Malvani Muslim from Revdanda (near Alibag and Murud Janjira) where, she says, men were traditionally served scrambled eggs or fried bananas with chapatti for breakfast. Women ate leftover rice bhakri with atwal (the previous night's fish).

Though this dough is made from cooked flour, you can also use raw rice flour, kneaded like wheat flour for polya.

A pinch of salt
1 cup rice flour

- Bring 1 cup of water to a boil, add salt, reduce heat and slowly stir or whisk in rice flour, till smooth. Cook for 4-7 minutes, stirring continuously. When the mixture is glassy and shiny, turn off the heat.

- When cool enough to handle, knead for 4-5 minutes, to make a pliable soft dough. (Do not wait too long or the mixture will seize up and not be malleable.)

- Divide it into lime-sized balls. Set aside covered.

- Rice bhakris are rolled or hand flattened and roasted like polya (p. 103).

Special Breads

PURI
Airy Fried Bread
Serves: 2   Time: 30 minutes
Special equipment: paper-lined platter

Usually 4-5 of these delicious, special-occasion breads are enough to satisfy a person, especially if there is rice to follow. Knead enough dough just in case!

If made right, purya are light and airy. They pair well with desserts (shrikhand, amras, shevayachi kheer), rassas and potato bhaji.

200 gms sifted wholewheat flour (atta)
A pinch of sugar
A pinch of salt
2 tbsp + ½ tbsp + 2 cups vegetable oil

Dough:

- Make ghadichi poli dough (p. 103) using the flour, sugar and salt, but use 2 tbsp oil. The dough should be slightly firmer in consistency.

- When well kneaded, pour ½ tbsp oil on your palms and knead again. This extra oil smoothens and gives it a better consistency. Rest covered for 30 minutes.

- Divide the dough in half. Roll each half into a long sausage shape, about 1" thick. Cut this into small, even discs. Set aside covered with a dishcloth.

- Roll out each disc, as you would polya, but do *not* use flour.

Instead, dab oil on the board before rolling.

- Purya must be rolled flatter at the edges than in the centre. Start at the centre of the dough and move your rolling pin outward, gently but evenly, turning the puri occasionally as it increases in size. Press the edges gently with the rolling pin and flatten dough into a 3"-3½" wide puri.

- Roll out at least 10 purya before you start frying. Keep them covered to prevent drying.

Frying:

- Meanwhile, heat 2 cups oil in a wok over medium-high heat till nearly smoking. Reduce heat slightly.

- Fry 1-4 purya at a time, sliding each one in along the side of the wok. It will first sink to the bottom of the wok but rise immediately. Touch it gently with a slotted spoon to help it rise. Press down in the centre and the edges so it puffs up like a ball. Turn it over.

- The second side needs less time to cook. When golden brown, quickly remove the puri and drain it over the wok. Hold the slotted spoon against the side of the wok to drain further.

- Place it on the paper-lined platter as you continue frying the other purya. Do not pile too many purya on each other. They should retain their airy shape.

FUGIA

East Indian Fried Bread

Makes: about 100 fugia Time: 8 hours rising + 1 hour making
and frying
Contributor: Jeanne D'Penha

Fugia (balloon in Marathi) *will* puff up like balloons. They must be
light and hollow inside to be tasty. They are made for East Indian
feasts, usually eaten with sarpatel (p. 253) and taste best hot.

1 kg sifted refined flour (maida)
A pinch of sugar
¼ tsp salt
1 cup thick coconut milk or dairy milk
2 eggs, beaten
12 gms yeast
1 tsp baking powder
Up to 1 litre vegetable oil

- Place flour in a large bowl. Make a well in the middle. Add
  sugar and salt. Stir in coconut milk and bring the ingredients
  together to make a thick dough. Knead well.

- Add the eggs. Mix in yeast and baking powder. The dough
  should be thick but light enough to form balls.

- Rest tightly covered in a warm place overnight.

- Mix dough once more before forming fugias. If too soft, stir
  in a little flour; if too dry, mix in 1-2 tbsp water.

- Heat 2 cups oil in a wok till bubbles form at the bottom.
  Keep some water handy to moisten your hands so the dough
  does not stick to them.

- Form a fugia by grasping the dough with the left hand and
  squeezing it through the space between thumb and forefinger.
  A golf-size ball of dough will form at the top of your fist.

- Lift this fugia gently off with your right hand and put it into the oil carefully. Cook 2-3 fugia at a time over medium heat for 1-2 minutes. Remove when brown on *one* side, holding it gently against the side of the wok to drain further.

TIKHATAMITHACHI PURI

Spicy Fried Bread
Serves: 2   Time: 30-40 minutes
Special equipment: paper-lined platter

Spiced purya are an excellent snack and travelling food. They last longer than regular purya, taste great with chutneys, pickles and thick yogurt or onion salad. They make you rather thirsty, so have plenty of tea or water on hand!

200 gms sifted wholewheat flour (atta)
A handful of fenugreek (methi) or spinach leaves, finely chopped (optional)
2 tbsp gram flour (besan – optional)
½ tsp red chilli powder
½ tsp cumin seeds or coarse cumin powder
½ tsp nigella seeds (kalaunji) or sesame seeds (til) – optional
½ tsp turmeric powder
1 tsp salt
2 tbsp vegetable oil + 2 cups for frying

- Make puri dough (p. 108) but add the above spices when blending in salt and oil.

- Roll and fry like purya.

- Tikhatamithachya purya are more likely to become oily so drain very well after frying. Serve hot or at room temperature.

- Store when cool, in an airtight container.

Assorted Grain Pan Breads
& Pancakes

THALIPEETH
Spiced Multigrain Pan Bread
Serves: 4   Time: 30 minutes
Special equipment: banana leaves/wax paper/plastic sheet

Thalipeeth is bread made from bhajni (p. 39), which has a dense, spicy taste. If you cannot make bhajni but still want to make thalipeeth, try the speed-of-light bhajni opposite. Finely chopped vegetables vary the taste of thalipeeth. Thalipeeth dough is mixed just before cooking; kneading makes it chewy. Cook the first side of the thalipeeth covered and the second uncovered.

2 cups speed-of-light multigrain flour (opposite) or bhajni (p. 39)
¾ tsp salt
¼ tsp red chilli powder
5-6 tbsp vegetable oil + extra for cooking

- Place flour in a bowl, make a well in the middle and add salt, chilli powder and 5-6 tbsp oil. Mix with one hand while slowly pouring in up to ½ cup water with the other, to make a firm, pliable dough.

- Keep a bowl of water handy. Make 2" balls of dough that fit into the palm of your hand.

- Place a banana leaf, wax paper or plastic sheet on the countertop. Put the dough on it and flatten gently into a circle, using the fingers and palm of your hand. If necessary, dip your fingers in water to prevent sticking and to help loosen too-firm dough. The thalipeeth should be 6" wide.

- Make a hole in the centre to help it cook quicker. Sometimes cooks make more holes across the entire surface!

- When 3-4 thalipeeths are ready, heat and lightly oil a griddle till smoking hot.

- Gently peel the thalipeeth off the non-stick surface and place it on the griddle. Cook covered for 1-1½ minutes, till brown, occasionally drizzling a little oil around its edges and in the centre to crisp it. When done, the steam from the lid will splutter on the griddle.

- Flip the thalipeeth over. Cook uncovered for 1-2 minutes, till brown and crisp, drizzling oil around it (less than ¼ tsp).

- Serve hot off the griddle.

SPEED-OF-LIGHT MULTIGRAIN FLOUR
Makes: 2 cups

1 cup sorghum flour (jowar)
½ cup sifted wholewheat flour (atta)
2 tbsp rice flour
2 tbsp gram flour (besan)
1 tsp split, husked black gram (urad dal), powdered (optional)
1 tsp fenugreek seeds (methi), powdered (optional)
A pinch of salt

- Combine all ingredients and store in an airtight container.

VARHADI RURAL THALIPEETH
Varhadi Pan Bread

My father's friend Uma Dadegaonkar from Varhad, the north-east region of Maharashtra, says, 'Once the crops of various pulse grains such as udid, mug, harbhara, tur and so on are ready, then they are split to make various dals. During this process, some of the new shoots (plumules) and some broken grain are left and spill out of the sieves used. This is known as kalna in Varhad, the poor man's grain for thalipeeth.

'These are mixed with sorghum and ground into slightly coarse flour. Make this into dough with salt, chilli powder and finely chopped leafy vegetables. Cook and serve in the same way as the other thalipeeths.'

THAPOLE
Multigrain Vegetable Pancakes
Serves: 6   Time: 40 minutes
Contributor: Medha Marathe

Thapole batter is patted by hand (hence the name, 'something that is patted') on to a hot griddle.

1 cup sifted wholewheat flour (atta)
1 cup sorghum (jowar) or pearl millet (bajra) flour
1 cup gram flour (besan)
1 cup wheat bran (optional)
1 tsp red chilli powder
¼ tsp turmeric powder
¼ tsp asafoetida powder (hing)
1½-2 tsp salt
1 cup shredded vegetables (cabbage, fenugreek leaves, carrot, pumpkin or onion)
1 tbsp + 1 cup vegetable oil for cooking
½-¾ cup sour yogurt or buttermilk

- Combine dry ingredients, vegetables and 1 tbsp oil in a bowl. Pour in yogurt or buttermilk and beat the batter to a thick, creamy consistency.

- Heat and generously oil a griddle over medium heat. Pour on a ladleful of batter, carefully spreading it with your fingers into a 4" wide, less than ¼" thick disc. Cover with a lid.

- Cook the first side for 1-2 minutes till brown. Flip it over and cook covered for a further 2 minutes, till done.

- Serve hot.

DHIRDA

Spicy Pancakes
Serves: 4   Time: 30-40 minutes

Dhirdi, rich-tasting, egg-less pancakes, can be made with virtually any grain and lentil flour combo (wheat, rice, sorghum, gram, mung). Experiment! Use fine flour for thin dhirdi, a coarser grind for thicker ones. Very finely chopped onion, coriander leaves, tomato, cabbage or leafy greens in the batter are delicious!

120 gms gram flour (besan)
120 gms rice flour
1¼ tsp salt
¾ tsp red chilli powder or 1 green chilli, minced
1 small onion, minced
4-5 sprigs of coriander leaves, finely chopped
Up to 1 cup vegetable oil

- Combine flours with salt and chilli powder or chilli. Whisk together with a little water, adding up to 1 cup as needed to make a thin batter of pouring consistency (like that of a dosa or European pancake batter).

- Stir in onion and coriander leaves.

- Place a griddle over medium heat till almost smoking. Smear with oil.

- Pour on a ladleful of batter, immediately spreading it with the back of the ladle in a circular fashion till evenly thick and 6"-8" wide. It begins to cook right away, its edges becoming lacy like those of a crêpe or dosa.

- Cook for 2-3 minutes, making sure it does not burn. Drizzle oil around it (less than ¼ tsp) so it crisps.

- When it is easy to lift off, gently flip it over. Cook for 1-2 minutes, spooning oil around its edges. Press lightly to brown it, for 1-2 minutes longer.

- Serve hot.

AMBOLI
Fermented Rice Flour Pancakes
Serves: 2   Time: 8-12 hours fermenting + 45 minutes cooking

Konkani amboli resemble South Indian dosas. Traditionally, a hot coal is dunked into the batter for a unique, smoky aroma and flavour. Serve amboli with chutney or a meat or fish dish.

200 gms rice-lentil flour (opposite)
1½ tsp salt
1 hot coal (optional)
1 cup vegetable oil

- The night before you want to make ambolya, combine flour and salt in a bowl. Stir or whisk in up to 2 cups warm water to make a thin batter of pouring consistency (like that of a dosa or crêpe batter).

- Heat a coal till red-hot. Using tongs, plunge it into the batter. Cover immediately. Remove and discard the coal after 5 minutes.

- Rest batter covered in a warm place overnight. The fenugreek in the rice-lentil flour helps it rise. The next day it will have increased in volume and be fluffy, slightly fermented and sour. Stir briskly.

- Heat a griddle for 3-4 minutes, till very hot. Oil it lightly. Pour on a ladleful of batter, immediately spreading it with the back of the ladle in a circular fashion till evenly thick and 6"-8" wide. For softer amboli, it should be a little thicker than a dosa.

- Cook covered over medium heat for 2-3 minutes. When bubbles form on the surface and the underside is golden, gently flip the amboli over. Cook uncovered for about 2 minutes, till golden.

- Serve hot.

RICE-LENTIL FLOUR
Makes: 625 gms

500 gms rice
125 gms split, husked black gram (urad dal)
½ tbsp fenugreek seeds (methi)

- Wash rice. Drain and dry completely in a warm, shaded spot for 4-8 hours.

- Grind it into flour with the gram and fenugreek seeds.

- Store in an airtight container.

Assorted Grain Dishes

BAJRICHA KHICHDA
Millet-Lentil 'Rice'
Serves: 4   Time: 40 minutes
Special equipment: winnowing fan
Contributor: Prabhavati Gopalrao Deshpande

Millet is one of the staples in Beed. This one-pot, spiced rice-like dish—'khichada'—is made with millet, split, husked mung and Bengal gram. Serve it with yogurt and pickle.

500 gms pearl millet grains (bajra), washed
200 gms split, husked green mung (mung dal), cleaned and washed
1 heaped tbsp split, husked Bengal gram (chana dal)
1 heaped tbsp peanuts
1½-2 tsp salt

Seasoning:
1 tbsp + 1 tbsp vegetable oil
½ tsp + ½ tsp mustard seeds
¼ tsp + ¼ tsp cumin seeds
¼ tsp + ¼ tsp turmeric powder
¼ tsp asafoetida powder (hing)
½ tsp + ½ tsp red chilli powder
Pounded garlic to taste

• Drain millet and pound it lightly till the husk separates (or pulse gently in a food processor). Remove the husk outdoors by winnowing the grain in a winnowing fan (sup) or a large, flat plate, gently flipping it up and down and blowing away the husks.

- In a large pan, heat 1 tbsp oil for seasoning till almost smoking. Add ½ tsp mustard seeds. When they pop, add ¼ tsp each of cumin and turmeric powder and a pinch of asafoetida. Stir and add ½ tsp chilli powder and some garlic.

- Pour in double the quantity of water as millet (add more later if needed) and bring to a boil. Stir in millet, mung and Bengal gram. Cook covered for 15-20 minutes, till tender. Mix in peanuts and salt.

- Heat the remaining oil for the seasoning in a small wok over medium heat. Add ½ tsp mustard seeds and let them pop. Stir in remaining seasoning ingredients with a little more garlic.

- Pour the seasoning over the dish and serve hot.

BAJRICHÉ UNDÉ
Millet Dumplings
Serves: 4-6   Time: 30 minutes soaking + 20 minutes cooking
Special equipment: steamer
Contributor: Aruna Karande

Millet dumplings are especially prepared in the Kolhapur-Sangli region for Gatari Amavasya, the moonless day in Ashadh (June-July) and served with a roasted aubergine salad (p. 149).

500 gms pearl millet grains (bajra), washed and drained
A pinch of salt
Tup (ghee), grated jaggery and milk to serve

- Rest millet for 30 minutes and grind into a thick paste.

- Add salt and shape into 2" wide undé or dumplings.

- Steam them for 15-20 minutes.

- When cool enough to handle, crush each one on a plate and pour melted tup into the centre.

- Add jaggery and milk. Eat steaming hot.

UKAD SHENGULÉ

Sorghum Pasta
Serves: 2-3   Time: 45-60 minutes
Contributor: Prabhavati Gopalrao Deshpande

An interesting one-pot 'pasta' meal! 'Crush the shengulé in the gravy as you eat. Some people like to pour hot kardai (safflower) oil over them too.'

200 gms sorghum flour (jowar)
100 gms gram flour (besan)
75 gms sifted wholewheat flour (atta)
1-2 tsp garlic paste
A pinch of turmeric powder
¼ tsp cumin seeds
1 tsp ajwain/carum
Up to 2 tsp salt
1½-2 tsp red chilli powder
1-2 tbsp yogurt
1 tsp hot safflower oil per serving

Seasoning:
1 tbsp safflower oil
¼ tsp cumin seeds
¼ tsp asafoetida powder (hing)
½ tsp turmeric powder

- Combine flours in a bowl.

- Lightly grind garlic, turmeric, cumin seeds and ajwain and add to the flours with a pinch of salt and half the chilli powder.

- Mix into a firm, pliable dough with yogurt and a little water. It should taste slightly tart.

- Shape a bit of dough into a 3" long, ¼" thick rod. Bend it into a circle and pinch the two ends together. This is a shengula.

- Shape the remaining dough into similar shengulé, placing them in a tray covered with a damp cloth.

- Heat oil for seasoning in a large pan till almost smoking. Add cumin seeds and let them pop. Add asafoetida and turmeric and as much of the remaining chilli powder as desired.

- Pour in 1 litre water, bring to a boil and salt it well. This will make the pasta sauce.

- Quickly add the shengulé. Cook over low heat for about 10 minutes. To test, press a shengula between two fingers. It should be firm but crumble slightly.

- If the sauce is too thin, take out a few shengulé, crush them in 1 tbsp water and mix it back into the sauce. Heat through.

- Serve the sauce with the pasta floating in it, topped with 1 tsp hot safflower oil for each serving.

Note: Any light oil will work for the seasoning but use only safflower oil over the cooked shengulé.

VARYACHA BHAT

Steamed Hill Millet
Serves: 4 Time: 10-15 minutes

Vari (hill millet) has a lighter texture and taste than pearl millet, cooks quickly and digests easily. It is often served as a fasting day dish with shengadanyachi amti (p. 223).

1 cup hill millet grains (vari ragi)

• Wash and drain the millet well.

• Combine it with 1¼ cups water in a heavy-bottomed pan.

• Cook covered over medium-low heat for 8-10 minutes, till light and fluffy. The water must be absorbed.

• Serve hot.

Variation: Flavour the millet with boiled potato, ground peanuts, chillies and cumin for a fasting day khichadi. Wash and drain 1 cup hill millet well. Heat 1 heaped tbsp tup in a medium pan. When almost smoking, add ½ tsp cumin seeds and let them pop. Add 1-2 green chillies and potato chunks and sauté for 1-2 minutes. Stir in millet. Add water, 1½ tbsp peanuts, 1 tsp salt and ½ tsp sugar. Cook covered over very low heat, as above.

Rice Dishes

Rice is a wonderful and versatile grain; easy to cook and digest, it is a great source of vitamins, other nutrients and roughage. For people under the weather, it is beneficial with yogurt or buttermilk. Serve it with warm milk and salt to children. Rich preparations are obviously special festival foods. But other ways of eating rice, for instance with metkut or lime pickle, are mouth-watering despite their simplicity. Rice goes well with any lentil preparation and with vegetable dishes and salads.

Although the pressure cooker is now ubiquitous in urban Maharashtra, stove-top cooking is still best for rice. Use a deep pan from which cooking water cannot spill over. Generally you need 2 cups water per cup of rice. Adjust the quantity depending on your rice stock. (New rice needs less than 2 cups water per cup of grain or it becomes mushy. Experienced cooks only buy or stock old rice.)

All the following hot rice dishes become even more delicious when topped with a dollop (or drizzle) of tup!

BHAT
Hot White Rice
Serves: 2   Time: 20-30 minutes

Bhat is hot, boiled white rice. Varan-bhat (yellow lentils over plain rice) is one of the most basic and satisfying Marathi meals.

1 cup short or long-grained rice

- Pick the rice grains over for debris if necessary. Rinse well to remove excess starch and dirt.

- Drain the rice and put into a deep pan. Add 2 cups water. Cook half-covered over medium-low heat, till the water comes to a boil and reduces to about the level of the rice.

- Reduce the heat to low and cook covered for 10-15 minutes, till the water is nearly absorbed.

- Check if the rice has cooked and turned from translucent to opaque. Add more water if needed, and depending on whether you like your rice grains distinct and separate or soft and mushy. Pinch a grain of rice between thumb and forefinger to test. It should be firm but mash easily.

- You can drain out excess water to make a lightly spiced soup, pej (below).

- Keep rice covered till serving time.

DAHI BHAT
Seasoned Yogurt Rice

Mix thick, slightly tart yogurt with day-old or freshly made rice for a simple, fabulous meal. Stir in some milk if needed. Make a finishing seasoning with mustard seeds, curry leaves and chillies (p. 21), if you like. Add chopped coriander leaves.

Eat with lime pickle or papad.

PEJ
Rice Gruel
Serves: 2   Time: 20-30 minutes

Pej is the extra water drained from boiled rice. It was drunk because it contained all the nutrients of the grain and husk but was easy on the stomach. It is helpful in cases of an upset stomach, diarrhoea or dysentery. Pej with some salt and tup is delicious.

This recipe is for specially prepared rice water or gruel that can be served to invalids or for breakfast. A kind of rice gruel, with the grain left in, is served both in Maharashtra and Goa. It resembles Chinese congee. In fact, pej is called kanji in North India and parts of Maharashtra.

¼ cup ambey mohor or other short-grained rice
4 black peppercorns (optional)
½" piece of ginger, grated (optional)
A pinch of salt
1 tsp tup (ghee – optional)

- Rinse rice well several times in a heavy-bottomed pan. Soak it in 6 cups water for 30 minutes.

- Add peppercorns and ginger (if used). Cook over medium-low heat for 20-25 minutes, till the rice is tender, almost falling apart.

- As a drink, serve the strained liquid with salt. As a gruel or soup, serve it with some of the cooked rice, salt and tup.

MATKI BHAT
Brown Mung-Coconut Rice
Serves: 2   Time: 30-40 minutes
Contributor: Jyoti Joshi

Legumes are highly nutritious, affordable and very popular in Maharashtra. Cooked with rice they make complete and delicious one-pot meals like matki bhat, mugachi khichadi, etc. The brown mung used for matki bhat is rich and meaty, but easy on the stomach. Soak it two days before cooking. Then matki bhat can be ready in about 30 minutes. Serve with yogurt and papad.

2 cups sprouted brown mung (matki) made from ½ cup dried
beans (p. 54)
1 cup short-grained rice
1½ tsp salt
1½ tsp sugar

Spice paste:
2 tbsp grated fresh coconut
2 small onions
3 heaped tbsp coarsely chopped coriander leaves
1½ tsp cumin seeds
8 small cloves garlic
2 green chillies

Seasoning:
2 tbsp vegetable oil
1 tsp mustard seeds
10 curry leaves
A pinch of asafoetida powder (hing)
½ tsp turmeric powder

Garnish:
1 tbsp grated fresh coconut
4-5 sprigs of coriander leaves, finely chopped

- Rinse the sprouted mung gently so the sprouts stay intact.
  Drain and check them for unsprouted/hard beans. Wash and
  drain the rice separately.

- Grind spice paste ingredients to a fine consistenty.

- Heat oil for seasoning in a deep pan till almost smoking. Add
  mustard seeds and let them pop. Stir in curry leaves, asafoetida
  and turmeric.

- Add sprouts and sauté for 1 minute over high heat. Reduce
  heat to medium-high, add ½ cup water and cook mung covered
  for 5-7 minutes.

- Meanwhile bring 2½ cups water to a boil separately.

- Add the spice paste and rice to the mung. Sauté briefly so the paste remains green.

- Stir in hot water, salt and sugar. Reduce heat to medium-low and cook covered for 15-20 minutes, till the rice is done.

- Serve garnished with coconut and coriander leaves.

MUGACHI KHICHADI
Split Mung Bean Rice
Serves: 2-4   Time: 25 minutes

This perennial Marathi favourite is easy and quick to make. Drizzle mugachi khichadi with tup or mix hot or cold milk, buttermilk, even yogurt into it for a soothing dinner. With papad and pickle you'll need nothing else. My snack-loving father says khichadi makes a great snack with chopped onions and coriander leaves!

1 cup short-grained rice
½ cup split, husked green mung (mung dal)
1 small onion, minced (optional)
1 medium potato, cut into ½" cubes (optional)
1 tsp goda masala (p. 48 – optional)
1 tsp salt

Seasoning:
1½-2 tbsp vegetable oil or tup (ghee)
¾ tsp cumin seeds
¼ tsp turmeric powder
1-2 green chillies, sliced (optional)

Garnish:
4-5 sprigs of coriander leaves, finely chopped

- Rinse the rice and dal separately, to clean and remove excess starch and protein. Drain in a colander.

- Heat oil for seasoning in a deep pan over medium heat. Add cumin seeds and let them pop. Stir, reduce the heat to low and add turmeric and chillies.

- Add onion (if used) and sauté for about 2 minutes, till golden but not crisp.

- Raise heat to medium, add potato (if used) and sauté for 2-3 minutes.

- Stir in rice and dal. Mix in 3½ cups water, goda masala (if used) and salt.

- Bring the water to a boil. Reduce the heat to low. Cook covered for 12-15 minutes, till the rice is soft but not mushy and the potato is tender. If needed, add up to ¼ cup more water and cook covered for 5-7 minutes.

- Garnish with coriander leaves and serve hot.

MASALÉ BHAT
'Wedding Special' Rice
Serves: 2   Time: 40 minutes

White rice is cooked with fragrant spices to make masalé bhat, the special rice served at many Marathi weddings. When vegetables are added, the dish takes on the vegetable's name: tondli bhat (ivy gourd rice), vangi bhat (aubergine rice), etc. Masalé bhat is also made in January at Bhogi (the day before Sankranti) with seasonal produce: green peas, beans and carrots.

This recipe serves 2 but can be increased easily. Use 1 cup rice for 4 people but increase spices only by half. Do not use more than 3-4 chillies. Other spices add heat.

½ cup rice, preferably long-grained
¼ cup vegetables (sliced ivy gourd/carrots, small, thin wedges of
aubergine – optional)
2 green chillies, sliced
1 tsp salt
½ tsp red chilli powder
2 tbsp yogurt

Spice powder:
3" stick cinnamon
4-5 cloves
1 tsp coriander seeds
1 tsp cumin seeds
½ tsp royal cumin seeds (shah jeera)

Seasoning:
2 tbsp vegetable oil
½ tsp mustard seeds
¼ tsp asafoetida powder (hing)
½ tsp turmeric powder

Garnish:
2-3 tbsp grated fresh coconut
5-6 sprigs of coriander leaves, finely chopped
10-12 cashew nuts, roasted
Tup (ghee) as required

- Clean, wash and drain the rice in a colander.

- Grind spice powder ingredients to a fine consistency.

- Bring 1 cup of water to a boil.

- Heat oil for seasoning in a deep pan. Add mustard seeds and let them pop. Add asafoetida and turmeric.

- Mix in vegetables (if used) and sauté for 2-3 minutes over medium heat.

- Add chillies and rice. Sauté well. Stir in salt, chilli powder, spice powder and yogurt.

- Pour in 1 cup boiling water. Cook over medium heat till the water begins to boil again.

- Reduce heat and cook, partly covered, for 10-15 minutes, till tender. Stir gently once or twice with a fork.

- Serve masalé bhat steaming hot, topped with coconut, coriander leaves, nuts and tup. Serve other wedding delicacies (aluchi patal bhaji, khamang kakdi, batatyachi bhaji, etc.) alongside.

VADA BHAT
'After-Wedding' Special
Serves: 4-6   Time: 5-6 hours soaking + 1 hour cooking
Special equipment: paper-lined platter
Contributor: Uma Dadegaonkar

'In other parts of India, pulao, makki di roti and sarson da sag may be considered delicious but the folk of Vidarbha, fond of eating hot, really mouth-watering dishes, especially plan to serve this vada bhat to special guests after some ceremonies like a wedding.' This dish tastes best with a thecha (pounded relish) of soaked red chillies.

200 gms split, husked Bengal gram (chana dal), soaked for 1 hour
Up to 1 litre vegetable oil
1½-2 tsp salt
½ tsp cumin powder
1 tsp coriander seed powder
100 gms split, husked green mung, soaked for 5-6 hours and drained
½-1 tsp red chilli powder or to taste
4-5 sprigs of coriander leaves, finely chopped
1 cup long-grained rice like basmati
A pinch of asafoetida

Seasoning:
1 tbsp vegetable oil
5-6 dried red chillies
5-6 curry leaves or to taste
A pinch of asafoetida powder (hing)
¼ tsp turmeric powder

- Drain Bengal gram and grind it coarsely.

- In a large wok, heat 1 tbsp oil. Sauté the ground gram for 4-5 minutes and spoon it into a bowl.

- In the same wok, heat oil for seasoning till almost smoking. Add red chillies, curry leaves, asafoetida and turmeric in quick succession. Stir briskly.

- Pour in ½ cup water. Bring to a boil. Mix in sautéed gram, 1 tsp salt and cumin and coriander seed powders. Cover pan and turn off the heat.

- After 15-20 minutes, mix in the mung, remaining salt, chilli powder and coriander leaves.

- Shape dough into 2" flat dumplings. With a spoon handle, make a hole in the centre of each vada.

- Heat 500 ml oil in a wok over medium heat. Reduce heat to medium-low. Fry 2-3 vadé at a time for about 2 minutes on each side, till golden brown. Drain and place on the paper-lined platter. Add more oil as needed.

- Meanwhile, rinse rice and cook it for 15-20 minutes, till fluffy. Set aside covered.

- To serve, mix asafoetida with 4-5 tbsp water. Mound a large spoonful of rice on each plate, make a hollow in the middle and pour in a little asafoetida water. Crumble 4-5 vadé into each hollow. Pour a spoonful of frying oil over them and mix well.

Salads

Traditionally, these 'salads' are eaten at lunch or dinner, in slightly larger servings than a condiment. They are easy to prepare and round out a meal nicely. Vegetables, uncooked or very lightly cooked (for the most part), are dressed with yogurt, spice-infused tup, and/or simply flavoured with salt, sugar and cumin. Seasoning offers virtually limitless flavour options. Peanuts and coconut, both popular in Maharashtra, are frequent additions.

Seasoned raw vegetables with or without yogurt are generally called koshimbir. Raita and dahyatli koshimbir describe un-mashed vegetables in a yogurt dressing. A cooked vegetable salad (usually in yogurt) is bharit, for which vegetables are mashed, chopped or grated.

Here is a basic salad recipe for 2-4 servings, which takes 15-20 minutes to put together; choose your vegetable and one of four great seasoning variations:

- Chop, grate or dice 250 gms vegetable of choice. Depending on the vegetable, use it raw, blanched, steamed or sautéed in 1 tsp tup (ghee).

- Lightly whisk 200 gms thick yogurt. Stir in 1 tsp salt and a pinch of sugar. For tart or thick yogurt, whisk in some milk. (You can also make the salad without yogurt.)

- Fold in the vegetable, green chillies or a dash of red chilli powder, for green vegetables. Add finely chopped onion, if appropriate. Garnish with freshly chopped coriander leaves.

Now take your pick of a seasoning!
Frothy mustard: Beat 1 tsp crushed yellow mustard in ½ tsp water with a fork till frothy. Mix it into the salad.

Whole mustard: Heat 1 tbsp tup (ghee) or vegetable oil in a seasoning wok. Add ½ tsp mustard seeds and let them pop. Stir in a chopped green chilli, if you like. Mix into the salad.

Whole cumin: Heat 1 tbsp tup in a seasoning wok. Add ½ tsp cumin seeds and let them pop. Stir in a chopped green chilli, if desired. Pour over the salad and mix well.

Cumin powder: Stir 1 tsp cumin powder into the yogurt.

Salads With Seasoning

AI AJICHA LETTUCE SALAD
Ai Aji's Lettuce Slaw
Serves: 4   Time: 20 minutes

This is lettuce salad Marathi style. Lettuce wilts quickly so prep
your ingredients but do not season or toss the salad till ready
to serve.

1 large head romaine or other lettuce, washed and dried
½ tsp salt
A pinch of sugar (optional)
Juice of 1 lime
¼-½ cup peanuts, ground

Seasoning:
1 tbsp tup (ghee)
½ tsp mustard seeds
¼ tsp red chilli powder or to taste

* Shred lettuce into a bowl. Toss with salt, sugar (if used) and
  lime juice. Add peanuts and toss again.

* Heat tup in a wok over low heat. Add mustard seeds and let
  them pop. Swirl the wok gently.

* Add chilli powder. Turn off the heat.

* Pour the seasoning over the lettuce, toss well and serve
  immediately.

KHAMANG KAKDI

Zesty Cucumber Salad
Serves: 4   Time: 15 minutes

Khamang means zesty. Here the zest comes from the seasoning on finely chopped cucumber.

1 medium cucumber, finely chopped (p. 23)
2-3 tbsp peanuts, coarsely ground
½ tsp salt
A pinch of sugar
1 tsp lime juice or tamarind paste (p. 27)
2 tbsp grated fresh coconut
1-2 tbsp coriander leaves, finely chopped

Seasoning:
1 tbsp tup (ghee)
¼ tsp mustard seeds
2-3 green chillies, sliced
½ tsp cumin seeds
A pinch of asafoetida powder (hing)

- Just before serving, toss cucumber with peanuts, salt, sugar, lime juice or tamarind and most of the coconut and coriander leaves (reserve some for garnish).

- Heat tup in a wok till almost smoking. Reduce heat, add mustard seeds and let them pop. Add chillies. Turn off the heat and add cumin and asafoetida. Mix into the salad.

- Garnish with reserved coconut and coriander leaves and serve with a meal or sabudanyachi khichadi (p. 67).

Note: Cucumbers release liquid when chopped so if you cut them much before serving, refrigerate them.

Variations:

- Try this salad with finely chopped cabbage, radish or beetroot.

- Add minced onion.

KAKDICHI DAHYATLI KOSHIMBIR
Cucumber-Yogurt Salad
Serves: 4   Time: 15 minutes

¾ cup yogurt
A pinch of sugar (if required)
4-6 tbsp milk (if required)
¾ tsp salt
½ tsp cumin powder
½ tsp red chilli powder
1 medium cucumber, finely chopped (p. 23)

- Whisk yogurt. Taste and if too tart, add sugar; if too thick, stir in milk. Add salt, cumin powder and chilli powder.

- Fold in cucumber just before serving.

KOBICHI KOSHIMBIR
Cabbage Salad
Serves: 2-4   Time: 20 minutes
Contributor: Anuradha Samant

100 gms green cabbage, grated or finely chopped
1-2 green chillies, sliced (optional)
1 tsp lime juice
1 tbsp coriander leaves, finely chopped
½ tsp salt
A pinch of sugar
3 tbsp roasted peanuts, coarsely ground (optional)

Seasoning (optional):
1 tbsp vegetable oil
1 tsp cumin or mustard seeds
¼ tsp turmeric powder
6 curry leaves

Garnish:
2 tbsp grated fresh coconut (optional)
1 tbsp coriander leaves, finely chopped

- Combine cabbage with chillies (if used), lime juice, coriander leaves, salt and sugar.

- Toss well with peanuts just before serving.

- To add the seasoning, heat oil in a wok to almost smoking. Add cumin or mustard seeds and let them pop. Add turmeric and curry leaves. Turn off the heat. Mix the seasoning into the salad.

- Garnish with coconut (if used) and coriander leaves.

Variation: My mother Meera varies this salad by adding 2 grated carrots, 1 small, very finely chopped onion, 2 tbsp grated fresh coconut or any combination of these ingredients.

GAJRACHI KOSHIMBIR

Carrot-Peanut Salad
Serves: 4   Time: 15 minutes
Contributor: Meera Marathe

3 large carrots, grated
½-¾ tsp salt
A pinch of sugar
1½ tbsp grated fresh coconut (optional)
2 green chillies, sliced
1 tsp lime juice or to taste
3 tbsp peanuts, coarsely ground

Seasoning:
1½ tsp tup (ghee)
1 tsp mustard seeds or cumin seeds
A pinch of turmeric powder

Garnish:
A few sprigs of coriander leaves, finely chopped

- Put carrots in a bowl. Add salt, sugar, coconut (if used) and chillies (or reserve them for the seasoning).

- Heat tup in a wok. Add mustard or cumin seeds and let them pop. Add turmeric and chillies (if reserved).

- Mix the seasoning into the carrots, sprinkle with lime juice and add peanuts.

- Stir well and garnish with coriander leaves.

SURNACHI KOSHIMBIR

Elephant-Foot Yam Salad
Serves: 4-6   Time: 30 minutes
Special equipment: paper-lined platter
Contributor: Maya Kale-Laud

Elephant-foot yam is very different in taste from other yams and sweet potatoes. Here it makes a crunchy, tasty salad.

1 cup vegetable oil
500 gms elephant-foot yam (suran), washed, peeled and cut into
¼" cubes
²/₃ cup grated fresh coconut
1 tbsp coriander leaves, finely chopped
1 large onion, minced
Juice of 1 large lime
2 green chillies, sliced (optional)
¾ tsp salt
A pinch of sugar

Seasoning:
2 tbsp vegetable oil
1 tsp mustard seeds
A pinch of asafoetida powder (hing)

Garnish:
1 tbsp grated fresh coconut
1 tbsp coriander leaves, finely chopped

- Heat 1 cup oil in a medium wok till almost smoking. Deep-fry the yam for 3-4 minutes over medium heat, till evenly golden. Drain well and place on the paper-lined platter.

- Combine coconut, coriander leaves, onion, lime juice, chillies (if used), salt and sugar in a bowl.

- Heat oil for seasoning in a small wok. Add mustard seeds and let them pop. Add asafoetida. Mix into the coconut-onion blend.

- Fold in yam just before serving. Garnish with coconut and coriander leaves.

TAMATYA-KANDYACHI KOSHIMBIR

Tomato-Onion Salad
Serves: 4   Time: 10 minutes

Eat this popular accompaniment (like Mexican salsa cruda) with rice and bread dishes or lentils and vegetables. If you are not fond of onion, leave it out and use ¼ cup of crushed peanuts instead.

4 large ripe, firm tomatoes, cut into ¼" dice
1 green chilli, sliced
A pinch of sugar
½ tsp salt
1 large onion, minced
¼ tsp cumin powder or hand-crushed cumin seeds

Garnish (optional):
2 tbsp grated fresh coconut
A few sprigs of coriander leaves, finely chopped

- Place tomatoes, chilli, sugar and salt in a bowl. Toss in onion and cumin just before serving.

- Garnish with coconut and coriander leaves if you like.

Variations:

- For a finishing seasoning, omit cumin. Heat 2 tbsp peanut oil in a wok. Add ½ tsp mustard seeds and let them pop. Add a pinch of asafoetida and chilli powder. Mix into the salad. Serve at room temperature, with garnish.

- **Tamatya-Kandyachi Dahyatli Koshimbir (Tomato-Onion Salad in Yogurt):** Whisk ¾ cup yogurt till smooth. If too tart, add a pinch of sugar, if too thick, stir in 4-6 tbsp milk. Add ¾ tsp salt, ½ tsp cumin powder and ½ tsp chilli powder. Fold in tomatoes and onions just before serving.

Salads With Yogurt

ALYACHA RAITA
Ginger-Yogurt Relish
Serves: 4   Time: 10 minutes
Contributor: Anuradha Samant

'In the Konkan, this raita is a must for naivedya (ritual food offerings to gods) and shraadha (obsequies).' Eat it in small quantities like a chutney.

2" piece of ginger, roughly chopped
2 black peppercorns
1 tbsp jaggery, grated
¼ tsp salt
½ cup yogurt

- Grind ginger to make a fine paste with peppercorns, jaggery and salt.

- Whip yogurt with a fork and stir in the paste.

- Serve at room temperature.

BATATYACHA BHARIT
Marathi Potato Salad
Serves: 4   Time: 25 minutes

This is a healthy alternative to mayonnaise-based potato salads.

2 large potatoes, boiled, peeled and cut into ½" cubes
¾ cup yogurt, whisked
A pinch of sugar (if required)
4-6 tbsp milk (if required)
¾-1 tsp salt
1-2 green chillies, sliced

Seasoning:
1½ tsp tup (ghee)
½ tsp mustard seeds
1 sprig curry leaves (optional)
¼ tsp turmeric powder
A pinch of asafoetida powder (hing – optional)

Garnish:
A few sprigs of coriander leaves, finely chopped

- Put potatoes in a bowl.

- Taste yogurt: if too tart, stir in a pinch of sugar; if too thick, stir in some milk. Mix in salt and chillies.

- Fold yogurt into the potatoes.

- Heat tup in a wok till almost smoking. Add mustard seeds and let them pop. Add curry leaves (if used), turmeric and asafoetida (if used). Immediately mix the seasoning into the potatoes.

- Serve garnished with coriander leaves, or refrigerate briefly.

BEETROOTCHI DAHYATLI KOSHIMBIR

Beetroot in Yogurt

Serves: 4-6   Time: 30 minutes

2 medium beetroots
1 onion, minced (optional)
¾ cup yogurt, whisked
A pinch of sugar (if required)
4-6 tbsp milk (if required)
¾-1 tsp salt

Seasoning:
1½ tsp tup (ghee)
½ tsp cumin seeds
1-2 green chillies, sliced

Garnish:
A few sprigs of coriander leaves, finely chopped

- Boil the beetroot for about 20 minutes, till soft. Peel, and grate or chop it into ¼" cubes. Combine beetroot and onion (if used).

- Taste yogurt: if too tart, stir in a pinch of sugar; if too thick, stir in some milk. Add salt.

- Fold yogurt into the beetroot.

- Heat tup in a wok. Add cumin seeds and let them pop. Add chillies. Mix the seasoning into the beetroot.

- Garnish with coriander leaves. Serve cool.

Note: When I do not have time to season the salad with tup, I just blend cumin powder, chilli powder, salt and sugar into the yogurt.

Variations:
- You can serve this salad without yogurt.

- Also try raw beets, green papaya, raw or steamed grated carrots or other tasty, crunchy vegetables.

- Toss raw or boiled, grated beetroot with any/all of the following: finely chopped onions, salt, coarsely crushed cumin seeds or powder, green chillies, lime juice, sugar.

- Instead of onions, add coarsely ground peanuts.

BHOPLYACHA BHARIT
Pumpkin-Yogurt Salad
Serves: 4-6   Time: 15 minutes

250 gms red pumpkin (kaddu), peeled and grated
1 tsp tup (ghee)
¾ cup yogurt, whisked
A pinch of sugar (if required)
4-6 tbsp milk (if required)
¾-1 tsp salt

Seasoning:
1 tbsp tup (ghee)
½ tsp mustard seeds
1-2 green chillies, sliced (optional)
5 curry leaves (optional)
A pinch of turmeric powder

Garnish:
3-4 sprigs of coriander leaves, finely chopped

- Sauté the pumpkin in 1 tsp tup. Cover and steam-cook briefly in 2-3 tsp water for about 5 minutes, till tender. (Or steam-cook/microwave the whole chunk and mash the flesh.)

- Taste yogurt: if too tart, add a pinch of sugar; if too thick, stir in some milk. Add salt. Fold yogurt into the pumpkin.

- Heat 1 tbsp tup in a wok. Add mustard seeds and let them pop. Add chillies and curry leaves (if used). Turn off the heat and add turmeric. Stir once and mix into the salad.

- Garnish with coriander leaves. Serve cool or at room temperature.

DAHI-KANDA

Onions and Green Chillies in Creamy Yogurt
Serves: 4   Time: 15 minutes
Contributor: Anuradha Samant

Traditionally, this salad is served with Kolhapuri mutton (p. 243).

3 tbsp thick fresh yogurt
3 tbsp thick fresh cream
2 medium onions, cut in ½" long slices
2 medium tomatoes, cut in ½" long slices
A few sprigs of coriander leaves, finely chopped
1 green chilli, sliced
1 tsp salt

- Combine yogurt and cream 2 hours before serving.

- Combine onions, tomatoes, coriander leaves and chillies.

- Five minutes before serving, fold in the yogurt-cream and salt. Serve cool.

VANGYACHA BHARIT
Roasted Aubergine-Yogurt Salad
Serves: 4   Time: 30 minutes

Vangyacha bharit is smoky and tangy-sweet! It can be eaten with rice, poli and other breads and gravied lentils. Keep the aubergine skin and stem intact. The skin chars while roasting, protecting the flesh and giving the dish its smokiness. Use the stem to turn the aubergine.

1 large aubergine (baingan), washed and dried
1 tsp salt
1 tbsp tamarind pulp (p. 27)
A pinch of sugar

Seasoning:
1½ tsp tup (ghee)
½ tsp mustard seeds
1-2 green chillies, sliced
¼ tsp turmeric powder
1 medium onion, minced (optional)

Garnish:
A few sprigs of coriander leaves, finely chopped

- Place the aubergine directly over an open flame or barbecue grill. Rotate periodically as it blackens, to ensure even cooking, for 7-10 minutes.

- When the skin is evenly charred and puckered, cool the aubergine in a paper bag. Remove and discard the skin.

- Mash the flesh. Stir in salt, tamarind and sugar.

- Heat tup in a skillet. Add mustard seeds and let them pop. Add chillies and turmeric and give it a stir. Add onion (if used) and sauté for 2-3 minutes.

- Combine seasoning and aubergine.
- Serve garnished with coriander leaves.

Note: Add some yogurt or very tender fresh green peas to the bharit, or flavour the seasoning oil with garlic slivers.

PACHADI
Maya Maushi's Fruit and Yogurt Salad
Serves: 8-10 as a salad; 6-8 as a dessert   Time: 20 minutes
Contributor: Maya Kale-Laud

Maya Maushi learnt this recipe from her mother-in-law, Sudhatai Kale. Pachadi can be eaten as a side dish with meat or as dessert.

4 bananas
3 oranges
2 tomatoes
2 sapota (chikoo)
3 slices fresh or canned pineapple, drained (optional)
2 guavas, seeded (optional)
500 gms yogurt
6 tbsp sugar or more, depending on tartness of yogurt
A pinch of salt
A dash of freshly ground black pepper

- Cut fruit into ½" dice. Set aside.
- Put the yogurt in a small pan and stir in sugar and salt. Place over low heat whisking and stirring for 4-5 minutes, till smooth.
- Cool the yogurt briefly. Fold in chopped fruit. Cool on the counter or refrigerate for 15-30 minutes. Grind fresh black pepper over it and serve.

Vegetables

Bhaji generally refers to unprocessed, uncooked vegetables *and* to cooked vegetable dishes. Vegetables are divided into many categories: paley-bhajya (green leafy vegetables), phal-bhajya (fruit-vegetables), kandmul (roots and tubers), etc.

This chapter consists of vegetable appetizers and main course dishes (sautéed and gravied preparations and vegetable/fruit soups). One dish of each type is served at a traditional meal.

There are many kinds of cooked bhajis. Dry sautés might be named after the vegetable (batatyachi bhaji—cooked potatoes), the occasion (upasachi bhaji—fast-day vegetable) or the flavourings (chincha-gulachi bhaji—vegetable with tamarind and jaggery). Stuffed vegetables are preceded by the prefix bharli (stuffed); vegetables in gravies are rassa, while some are occasionally referred to as amti, a term otherwise used for sour lentil soups.

Thin vegetable/fruit soups without solids are termed sar. Some greens are cooked in a batter—a thick sauce—or thin gravy with a base of yogurt, gram flour, ground peanut, coconut paste, or even water. These are patal bhajis (vegetables in a thin gravy). Others, distinctly thicker and cooked with much more gram flour, were traditionally served with a pali (iron ladle or scoop), so they are termed palivadhi bhaji (vegetables served with a pali).

Appetizers

ALUCHI VADI
Sanjiv's Favourite Leaf Roll
Serves: 2-4   Time: 45 minutes
Special equipment: steamer, cotton string, paper-lined platter
Contributor: Meera Marathe

My husband loves Mom's aluchi vadi, a spicy colocasia leaf roll.

6 colocasia (alu/arbi) leaves, washed, dried and scraped
Up to 500 ml vegetable oil

Filling:
50 gms tamarind
1-2 medium onions, minced
100 gms gram flour (besan)
1 tsp ajwain/carum
1 tbsp goda masala (p. 48) or garam masala powder
1 tsp coriander seed powder
1 tsp cumin powder
Red chilli powder to taste
1-2 tsp salt
A pinch of sugar
1 tsp ginger paste
½ tsp garlic paste (optional)

Garnish:
2 tbsp grated fresh coconut
4-5 sprigs of coriander leaves, finely chopped
1 tbsp toasted sesame seeds (til – optional)

- Sort the colocasia leaves by size (large, medium, small). Make 2 sets of the 3 different-sized leaves.

Filling:
- Make a thick tamarind paste with 10 tbsp of warm water. Use the residue to make ¾ cup thin tamarind water (p. 27).

- Combine onions with gram flour, ajwain, spice powders, salt and sugar in a bowl.

- Bind ingredients into a thick paste with the thin tamarind water. Blend in ginger and garlic (if used).

- Taste and add more salt, spices or sugar if needed.

Assembling the rolls:
- Spread out the 2 largest leaves, veined side up on the work surface. Apply a layer of thick tamarind paste and a layer of filling over each. Cover with the medium leaves (veined side up). Repeat the process of layering with the remaining leaves, ending with a layer of filling.

- Now you have 2 stacks of 3 leaves each. Roll each stack gently but tightly into a cylinder, starting at the stem end. Tie string at both ends and in the middle to hold the roll together. Some filling may squeeze out. If the rolls are longer than 6"-8", cut them in half before steaming.

To steam:
- Steam the rolls for about 15 minutes. Cool completely before frying or storing. Each roll will make 10-12 slices.

- Refrigerate whole in an airtight container for up to 3-4 days or freeze for up to a month.

- To serve, remove string, slice into thin vadya with a serrated knife, and serve plain or fried.

To shallow-fry:
- Heat 1 tbsp oil on a griddle. Over low heat, fry 8-12 vadya for 2-3 minutes. Drizzle oil around and between them as needed.

- Flip vadya when crisp and golden. Fry for 1-2 minutes.

- Oil the griddle before cooking another batch.

To deep-fry:
- Heat 1 cup oil in a medium wok till almost smoking. Fry 4-5 vadya at a time over medium heat for 1 minute, till golden brown on one side.

- Flip over and cook for 30-45 seconds. Drain well and place on the paper-lined platter.

To serve:
- Serve sprinkled with coconut, coriander leaves and toasted sesame seeds (if used).

Note: Use leftover filling to flavour another vegetable dish.

Variation: **The Low-Fat Version**: Slice the steamed roll. Arrange vadya on a serving dish. Heat 1½ tbsp oil in a seasoning wok. Add ½ tsp mustard seeds, let them pop and add ¼ tsp chilli powder. Pour seasoning over the vadya, garnish with coconut and coriander leaves and serve.

HARBHARYACHYA DALICHI VADI

Shubhangi Vaze's Bengal Gram-Coriander Bites
Serves: 2-4   Time: 5-6 hours soaking + 45 minutes cooking
Special equipment: steamer, paper-lined platter

100 gms split, husked Bengal gram (chana dal), soaked for 5-6 hours
½ tsp garam masala powder
A pinch of asafoetida powder (hing)
A pinch of turmeric powder
A pinch of red chilli powder
1 tsp sugar
1 tsp salt
100 ml vegetable oil

Spice paste:
2 packed cups coriander leaves
2 -3 green chillies
1" piece of ginger

- Drain the gram and grind it the night before you make vadya. Rest covered in a cool place.

- Grind spice paste ingredients fine.

- Mix gram, spice powders, sugar, salt and spice paste in a bowl.

- Shape into 4"-6" long rolls as thick as your thumb.

- Steam the rolls for about 15 minutes. Cool completely before cutting each into ½" thick vadya.

- On a hot, oiled griddle, shallow-fry 8-10 vadya at a time till golden. Replenish oil during the frying and before cooking more vadya.

Notes:
- Try very finely shredded cabbage leaves and lime juice in these vadya.

- Refrigerate vadya for up to 2 days. Fry just before serving.

KAP

Vegetable Fritters
Serves: 6-8 as a snack/appetizer   Time: 30 minutes

There are two kinds of vegetable fritters: kap (sliced, shallow-fried vegetables) and bhuji/vada (cooked or raw batter-dipped, deep-fried vegetables). For kap, use meaty vegetables: aubergine, potato, plantain, raw bananas, yams. Peel all these vegetables, except aubergine.

2 long or round medium aubergines (baingan) or 2 medium potatoes
½ cup rice flour
¼ tsp red chilli powder
A pinch of turmeric powder
¾-1 tsp salt
1 cup vegetable oil

- Peel potatoes if used. Slice the vegetable into ¼"-½" thick rounds.

- In a shallow dish, combine rice flour, spice powders and salt.

- Heat a griddle and smear with 1 tbsp oil. Press each vegetable slice into the rice flour to coat both sides.

- Cook 4-6 kap at a time over medium-low heat for about 2 minutes, till golden brown. Drizzle oil around them as they cook. Flip them over and cook for 1½-2 minutes, till golden.

- Serve hot.

PHANASACHI BHUJI
Jackfruit Fritters
Makes: 8-10 fritters   Time: 1 hour
Special equipment: paper-lined platter

Fritters (bhuji) are made from many vegetables, most often potato and onion. Here is an unusual jackfruit bhuji (use the same batter for other vegetables too).

Jackfruit is a little taste of heaven. Cleaning and preparing it is another matter, because of its tough, prickly skin (p. 37). Peeled jackfruit sections at the fruit seller's are a convenient option!

> 500 gms cleaned jackfruit, chopped fine
> 1 medium onion, minced (optional)
> 1 tsp + ½ tsp salt
> ½ cup gram flour (besan)
> 2-3 green chillies, sliced
> 1 tbsp mango powder (amchur)
> 1 tbsp garam masala powder
> 1 tsp ajwain/carum
> ½-1 litre vegetable oil

- Combine jackfruit, onion and 1 tsp salt. Pressure-cook for 5 minutes after the cooker reaches full pressure (2 whistles) or steam-cook them for 15-17 minutes, till tender.

- When cool enough to handle, mash the fruit slightly. Shape into 2"-3" patties.

- Mix gram flour with up to 1½ cups water to make a thick pancake-like batter. Add ½ tsp salt, chillies and spices.

- Heat oil in a medium wok. Dip patties into the batter, coating completely. Drain well to remove excess batter and slip them into the hot oil.

- Reduce heat to medium-low. Deep-fry fritters for 2-4 minutes, till brown and crisp. Flip them over if needed.

- Drain well and place on a paper-lined platter.

- Serve hot with ketchup or chutney.

SAMBAR VADI
Varhadi Coriander Rolls
Serves: 4-6   Time: 1 hour
Special equipment: paper-lined platter
Contributor: Uma Dadegaonkar

The 'sambar' in this recipe has nothing in common with the South Indian lentil sambar. In Vidarbha, coriander is called sambar because the plant resembles a bush with multiple branches, like the multi-pronged antlers of the sambar stag. Coriander is plentiful in the winter (November-December). 'Then, at least once, in every (middle class) home sambar or pudachya vadya are bound to be prepared.'

150 gms coriander leaves, cleaned before weighing
1 tbsp roasted poppy seeds (khus-khus)
1 tsp charolya (chironji)
Red chilli powder to taste (optional)
1-2 tsp salt
½ tsp kala or goda masala (p. 48)
1 litre vegetable oil

Spice paste:
4 green chillies
1 tsp cumin seeds

Seasoning:
1 tbsp vegetable oil
¾ tsp mustard seeds
A pinch of asafoetida powder (hing)
A pinch of turmeric powder

Dough:
100 gms sifted wholewheat flour (atta)
50 gms gram flour (besan)
A pinch of turmeric powder
A pinch of salt

- Chop the coriander leaves.

- Grind spice paste ingredients fine.

- Heat oil for seasoning in a wok. Add mustard seeds and let them pop. Add asafoetida and turmeric.

- Stir in the spice paste. Add coriander leaves, poppy seeds, charolya, chilli powder and salt. Sauté for 1 minute and remove from heat. Cool completely.

- Mix kala or goda masala with 1-2 tsp water and ½ tsp oil.

- In a bowl combine wheat flour, gram flour, turmeric, a pinch of salt and 1 tbsp oil. Make a puri-like dough (p. 108) using up to 1½ cups of water. Shape it into large marble-sized balls and roll them into little puris.

- Lightly apply a little kala or goda masala mixture to each puri. Place 2 tsp of the sambar mixture in the centre. Roll the outer clear part of the puri over the filling, with your fingers toward the centre from the left, then from the right so the two sides meet in the middle creating two mini-rolls. Press the open ends of the rolls shut. Prepare all the vadya in this way, keeping them covered when formed.

- Heat ¾-1 litre oil in a wok over high heat. Reduce heat to medium-high. Fry 4-5 vadya at a time for 1-3 minutes, till golden brown. Drain well and place on the paper-lined platter.

- Serve hot.

- Sambar vadya stay fresh and tasty for a week.

WAFOLA
Baba's Savoury Cabbage Cake
Serves: 4   Time: 45 minutes
Special equipment: two 9" baking tins
Contributor: Padmavati Marathe

Wafola means a steamed dish but this one is 'baked'. When Keya was younger, my father (Baba) would tease her, asking if her Mama was going to bake cabbage cake for her birthday. Now when I make it, she says we're having 'Baba's cake'.

During the years of food rationing around the Second World War, when semolina and refined wheat flour were hard to come by, gram flour-based snacks were a great alternative. Traditionally, wafola was cooked over an open coal fire but a conventional oven works!

2½ packed cups finely chopped or grated green cabbage
¾ tbsp ginger paste
1½ tsp salt
½ tsp turmeric powder
2 green chillies, sliced
1 tsp ajwain/carum
A pinch of sugar
2 tbsp + 1 tbsp + 1 tbsp vegetable oil
¼ tsp asafoetida powder (hing)
2 cups gram flour (besan)
½ tsp sodium bicarbonate (optional)
¾ cup thin, tart buttermilk or ¼ cup yogurt + ½ cup warm water

Garnish:
1 tbsp tup (ghee)
½ tsp mustard seeds
½ tsp turmeric powder
¼ tsp red chilli powder
1 tbsp grated fresh coconut
4-5 sprigs of coriander leaves, finely chopped
Juice of ½ lime

- Combine cabbage, ginger, salt, turmeric, chillies, ajwain and sugar in a bowl.

- Heat 2 tbsp oil and warm the asafoetida in it. Mix it into the cabbage. Fold in gram flour.

- Stir sodium bicarbonate (if used) into the buttermilk or liquefied yogurt. Slowly pour this into the cabbage, stirring continuously. If needed, add up to 1 cup of water to make a thin, cake-like batter.

- Grease two 9" baking tins well with 1 tbsp oil. Divide the batter between the tins.

- If possible, bake the wafolé on a coal stove, in a wide pan covered with a thick griddle. After 10-12 minutes, place some burning coals on the griddle and continue to cook for another 12-15 minutes, till the cake is done.

- Or preheat the oven to 180°C (350°F). Bake wafolé for 20 minutes. Smear a little oil over them. Bake for 10 minutes more, till the tops are golden brown and firm. Cool cakes on racks for 10 minutes, before cutting into squares.

- Heat tup for garnish in a wok. Add mustard seeds and let them pop. Add turmeric and chilli powder. Stir well and pour over the squares. Sprinkle with coconut, coriander leaves and lime juice.

- Serve hot with coriander chutney (p. 277).

Side Dishes

BATATYACHI BHAJI
Sautéed Potatoes with Mustard Seeds
Serves: 2-4   Time: 45 minutes

In Maharashtra we make dozens of dishes with potatoes. This bhaji alone has many incarnations. It is delicious with white rice, yogurt-rice, buttermilk, breads. Traditionally it accompanies jilebis, to relieve their sweetness. Batatyachi bhaji takes less than an hour to make, including boiling, peeling, chopping and seasoning the potato.

2 large potatoes
2 small onions, finely chopped (optional)
1 tsp salt
A pinch of sugar (optional)
Lime juice to taste

Seasoning:
2 tbsp vegetable oil
½ tsp mustard seeds
½ tsp cumin seeds
2 green chillies, sliced
6-8 curry leaves
A pinch of asafoetida powder (hing)
¼ tsp turmeric powder

Garnish:
3-4 sprigs of coriander leaves, chopped

- Boil potatoes till well done but firm, about 20 minutes. Peel and cut them into ½" cubes.

- Heat oil for seasoning in a heavy-bottomed skillet. Add mustard seeds and let them pop. Add cumin, chillies and curry leaves. Stir in asafoetida and turmeric. Reduce heat.

- When the chillies turn pale, add the onions (if used) and stir-fry for 3-5 minutes, till light brown.

- Add potatoes and warm through for 3-5 minutes. Sprinkle with salt, sugar and lime juice. Mix well and garnish with coriander leaves.

Note: Plan ahead. Boil some potatoes and refrigerate (for up to 3 days) till you want to make this bhaji. Bring potatoes to room temperature and cook as above.

Variations:

- Omit mustard seeds or cumin seeds.

- Stir in a little yogurt while cooking.

- Add 1 tbsp finely powdered peanuts with ¼ cup water or buttermilk to the bhaji. Stir it in to make a thickish gravy

- Add diced aubergine, capsicum or bite-sized cauliflower florets. Cabbage, spinach and other greens also taste great.

- For a fasting-day dish (batatyachi upasachi bhaji), omit onion, mustard, turmeric, asafoetida and curry leaves. Use tup for the cumin seed-chilli seasoning. Flavour with salt, sugar and lime juice.

BATATYACHYA KACHRYANCHI BHAJI
Crispy Potato Stir-Fry
Serves: 4   Time: 30 minutes
Contributor: Sudhakar Marathe

Who says only the Chinese know 'stir-fry'! This dish is a great example of *slow*, stir-fried vegetables. Dad says no one made it better than his aunt, Susheela Kaku. 'The trick is slicing the potato really thin, and stir-frying it patiently till well cooked. The slower it cooks and the more frequently it is stirred, the better it turns out.'

Do not peel potatoes if their skins are unblemished and tender. Dad's secret addition: 1 tbsp mango pickle oil!

3 medium potatoes, washed
1 tsp salt
¾ tbsp lime juice (optional)

Seasoning:
2½-3 tbsp vegetable oil
1½ tsp mustard seeds
¼ tsp fenugreek seeds (methi)
1 tsp red chilli powder (optional)
½ tsp turmeric powder
3-4 curry leaves (optional)

- Quarter potatoes lengthwise. Slice them paper-thin. The thinner the slices the quicker they cook. Soak them in water to prevent oxidation.

- Heat oil for seasoning in a heavy-bottomed skillet till almost smoking. Add mustard seeds and let them pop. Stir in fenugreek seeds, chilli powder (if used) and turmeric. Reduce heat slightly. Add curry leaves (if used).

- Drain the sliced potatoes well. Add to pan and stir-fry for 10-12 minutes, till slices are as crisp and brown as you like.

- Once the potatoes have cooked, stop stirring or the slices will break. Add salt and lime juice.

- Serve hot or cold with rice or breads.

Variation: Green plantains and yam are also delicious this way.

BHARLI BHENDI
Okra Stuffed with Coconut
Serves: 4   Time: 35 minutes
Contributor: Meera Marathe

If you eat bhendi in my neck of the woods, you will fall in love with it.

500 gms even-sized, tender okra (bhindi), washed
1-2 medium onions, minced
4 tbsp vegetable oil
¼ tsp turmeric powder
¾ tsp red chilli powder

Spice paste:
½ fresh coconut, grated
10-15 sprigs of coriander leaves, finely chopped
1 tbsp goda masala (p. 48) or garam masala powder
A pinch of sugar
1 tsp salt
Juice of 1 lime

- Dry okra thoroughly to prevent them from getting sticky. With a sharp knife, slit each about halfway up to the stem. Leave stems intact.

- Grind spice paste ingredients coarsely. Mix in onions. Stuff okras with this filling, keeping the vegetables intact. Place them on a plate till they are all filled.

- Heat oil in a large skillet. Add turmeric and chilli powder. Stir briefly.

- Carefully arrange okra in one layer in the skillet. Cook over medium heat for about 5 minutes. Add any leftover filling, reduce heat and cook covered for 5-7 minutes. Occasionally shake the pan to prevent the okra sticking.

- Uncover the pan and turn the okra carefully. Cook uncovered for 5-7 minutes, stirring if needed. Serve hot.

BHARLI VANGI

Aubergine Stuffed with Coconut and Tamarind
Serves: 4   Time: 30 minutes
Contributor: Madhavi Sirsikar

Madhavi Mami's mother, the late Vimaltai Laud, taught her this recipe. Aubergines are an acquired taste but these make it easy to get hooked.

500 gms small, round, even-sized aubergines (baingan)
3 tbsp vegetable oil
½ tsp turmeric powder

Filling:
1 tsp + ½ tsp vegetable oil
5 black peppercorns
½" stick cinnamon
3 cloves
2 tsp coriander seeds
1 tsp fennel seeds (badi saunf)
4-5 small cloves garlic
1 onion, finely sliced + 1-2 onions, minced
1 cup grated dried coconut (kopra)
1 tsp red chilli powder
1½ tsp salt

1 tsp grated jaggery or brown sugar
½ cup tamarind pulp (p. 27)
2 tsp roasted peanuts, finely ground

Garnish:
5-7 sprigs of coriander leaves, finely chopped

- With a sharp knife, slit the bottom of each aubergine halfway up to the stem. Cut crosswise and halfway up the aubergine to make a deep cross. Retain their stems. Soak them in a bowl of salted water for 10 minutes before draining.

- To prepare the filling, heat a griddle and oil it lightly. Toast peppercorns, cinnamon, cloves, coriander seeds and fennel seeds over medium heat, tossing frequently for 2-3 minutes, till aromatic. Grind spices with garlic in 1 tsp oil.

- Heat ½ tsp oil in a pan and sauté sliced onion for 4-5 minutes. Add coconut and sauté for 2-3 minutes, till golden brown. Grind this mixture into a fine paste.

- Combine the ground spices, onion-coconut paste, minced onions, chilli powder, salt, jaggery, tamarind and peanuts.

- Drain aubergines and pat them dry. Stuff them generously with the filling, keeping them intact. Set aside on a platter till they are all ready.

- Heat 3 tbsp oil in a large skillet. Stir in turmeric. Arrange aubergines in one layer. Top them with any leftover filling.

- Cook over medium heat, tightly covered with a lipped lid or metal plate. Carefully pour ¼ cup water on to the lid. When the water begins to boil, after 5-7 minutes, gently uncover the pan and pour it over the aubergines. Stir carefully. Cook covered for 5-7 minutes, till tender.

- Serve hot, garnished with coriander leaves.

BHARLI VANGI, SODE GHALUN
Aubergine and Potato Stuffed with Dried Shrimp
Serves: 4   Time: 30 minutes
Contributor: Sheela Pradhan

⅓ cup dried shrimp, coarsely chopped
250 gms (8-10 small) aubergines, washed and dried
100 gms small, even-sized, baby potatoes, washed and dried
⅓ cup vegetable oil
1 tbsp CKP masala (p. 53)
1 tsp + ½ tsp salt
½ tsp mustard seeds
A pinch of asafoetida powder (hing)

Spice paste:
5-6 small cloves garlic
½" piece of ginger
2-3 green chillies
1 tsp red chilli powder
½ tsp turmeric powder
½ tsp salt

Onion-coconut paste:
1 tbsp vegetable oil
2 medium onions, minced
½ cup grated dried coconut (kopra)
½ tbsp poppy seeds (khus-khus)
2-3 cloves
2" stick cinnamon

- Soak shrimp in water for 10-20 minutes.

- Grind spice paste ingredients fine with a little water.

- Drain shrimp well and marinate them in the spice paste for 10 minutes.

- Prepare aubergines as for bharli vangi (p. 168). Cut a deep cross at one end of each potato. Soak vegetables in salted water.

- Heat oil for onion-coconut paste in a skillet. Add onions and sauté till golden brown. Add and brown the coconut. Stir in poppy seeds, cloves and cinnamon. Grind the mixture into a fine paste.

- Clean out the skillet and heat 1 tbsp oil. Add shrimp and sauté over low heat for 5-7 minutes. Mix in onion-coconut paste, CKP masala and 1 tsp salt. Cook for 1-2 minutes till moist, not runny.

- Drain aubergines and potatoes well. Lightly salt the insides with the remaining salt.

- Stuff them with the shrimp.

- Heat the remaining oil in a large skillet till almost smoking. Add mustard seeds and let them pop. Stir in asafoetida.

- Arrange vegetables in one layer in the skillet. Cover with any leftover filling, reduce heat and cook covered for 10-20 minutes, till tender. Stir occasionally, adding water as needed to prevent vegetables from sticking.

- Serve hot.

BHENDICHI CHINCHA-GULACHI BHAJI
Tamarind-Jaggery Okra
Serves: 2-4   Time: 30 minutes
Contributor: Jyoti Joshi

All Marathi okra recipes counter its stickiness by cooking it with an acid like tamarind.

250 gms okra (bhindi), washed and well-dried
1 tbsp vegetable oil
½ tsp mustard seeds
A pinch of asafoetida powder (hing)
A pinch of turmeric powder

Vegetables   171

2 tbsp tamarind pulp (p. 27)
2" piece of jaggery, grated
¾-1 tsp salt

- Top and tail okra and slice into ¾" pieces.

- Heat oil in a medium wok. Add mustard seeds and let them pop. Stir in asafoetida and turmeric. Add okra and sauté over medium-high heat for 2-3 minutes.

- Stir in tamarind, jaggery and 2-3 tbsp water. Reduce heat. Cook covered, stirring occasionally for 12-15 minutes.

- Add salt and cook uncovered for 2-3 minutes to evaporate most of the water.

- Serve hot with ghadichya polya (p. 103).

CHANYACHI DAL GHALUN BHAJYA
Vegetables with Bengal Gram
Serves: 4   Time: 30 minutes

This lightly spiced, gently cooked bhaji is easy on the stomach and palate. Try it with different vegetables: cabbage, cauliflower, bottle gourd (lauki/ghia), snake gourd (chirchinda).

1 tbsp split, husked Bengal gram (chana dal)
500 gms any one vegetable of choice, washed and dried
1-2 green chillies, cut into 4-6 pieces (optional)
¾ tsp salt
¼ tsp sugar (optional)

Seasoning:
1 tbsp vegetable oil
¾ tsp mustard seeds
A pinch of asafoetida powder (hing)
A pinch of turmeric powder

Garnish:
1½ tbsp grated fresh coconut
4-5 sprigs of coriander leaves, finely chopped

- Soak gram in ¼ cup water for 10-20 minutes before cooking. Shred cabbage (if used) fine. Cut other vegetables into ½" pieces.

- Heat oil for seasoning in a medium wok or skillet till almost smoking. Add mustard seeds and let them pop. Stir in asafoetida and turmeric.

- Add chillies (if used) and raise the heat to high. Drain gram and add it with the vegetable. Sauté briefly.

- Reduce heat to medium-low, cover pan with a lipped lid or metal plate, and pour ¼ cup water on to the lid. Cook for 4-5 minutes. Stir and add some warm water from the lid into the pan if needed or to make a gravy.

- Cook covered for 7-10 minutes, till the vegetable is tender but slightly crunchy; cook cauliflower slightly longer than gourd and cabbage.

- Stir in salt and sugar. Heat through.

- Garnish with coconut and coriander leaves.

Variations:

- For gourd, add 1 tsp coriander seed powder and ½ tsp cumin powder when almost cooked.

- When adding coriander and cumin, add ¾-1 tsp goda masala (p. 48), particularly for snake gourd.

GAVARI/PAPDICHI BHAJI
Green Beans with Marathi Spice
Serves: 2-4   Time: 25 minutes

One of the first vegetables I can remember eating are my mother's crunchy green beans, finely sliced, lightly sautéed and topped with fresh scraped coconut! Cook French beans, cluster beans (gwar ki phalli), or pretty much any 'green' bean, this way.

250 gms French beans or other green beans, washed and trimmed
1 medium onion, minced (optional)
1-1½ tsp salt
1 tsp grated jaggery or sugar
1 tsp goda masala (p. 48)
1 tbsp grated fresh coconut
2 tsp lime juice (optional)

Seasoning:
2 tbsp vegetable oil
1 tsp mustard seeds
¼ tsp turmeric powder

Garnish:
1 tbsp grated fresh coconut
4-5 sprigs of coriander leaves, finely chopped

- Top and tail the beans. Line up 4-6 beans at a time and chop them fine (break sheet and cluster beans into 3-4 pieces).

- Heat oil for seasoning in a medium skillet. Add mustard seeds and let them pop. Add turmeric.

- Add onion (if used) and sauté for 2-3 minutes over high heat.

- Add beans and stir-fry for 2-3 minutes. Stir in up to ¼ cup water, reduce heat to medium and simmer covered for 10-12 minutes.

- Uncover pan, stir and reduce the heat to low. The beans should be bright green and most of the water should have evaporated.

- Add salt, sweetener and goda masala. Cook uncovered for about 5 minutes, stirring occasionally. Add more water if needed.

- Mix in coconut and steam-cook the beans for 1-2 minutes.

- Sprinkle with lime juice and serve hot, garnished with coconut and coriander leaves.

KANDMUL
Quick-Cooked Monsoon Veggies
Serves: 4   Time: 45 minutes
Contributor: Medha Marathe

This traditional dish is usually cooked in the monsoon, especially in the month of Shravan. In the old days, vegetables were steamed in their own juices in a brass or earthenware pot with a tight lid. Kandmul is served with jwari bhakri (p. 102) and yogurt or with white rice. Chavli, rajgira, batua, tandulja, amaranth (lal math/cholai bhaji), spinach or any leafy greens can be used.

4-5 colocasia (alu/arbi) leaves
1 large bunch of any leafy greens
3 x 3" pieces of red pumpkin (kaddu)
2 corncobs
1 ridged gourd (toori)
2 small aubergines (baingan)
1 large potato
1 sweet potato
6" piece of snake gourd (chirchinda)
3" piece of bottle gourd (lauki/ghia)

Spice paste:
3-4 green chillies

Vegetables   175

½ fresh coconut, grated
1-2 tsp tamarind pulp (p. 27) or lime juice
A pinch of sugar
1 tsp salt

- Wash all vegetables well. Peel fibres off the colocasia leaves. Stem the other greens. If using tender spinach, keep the stems but remove excess fibres. Chop greens fine.

- Grind spice paste ingredients fine.

- Combine greens and pumpkin with ½ cup hot water in a large pan. Cook tightly covered over low heat for 15-20 minutes.

- Slice the corncobs into thin discs. Chop the remaining vegetables into 1½" cubes.

- Add vegetables to the pan with ½ cup hot water (use more as needed). Cook covered for about 15 minutes, till tender.

- Stir in spice paste. Raise the heat.

- Bring to a boil, simmer for 2-3 minutes, and serve.

KANDYACHI BESAN LAVUN BHAJI
Rustic Onion-Gram Flour Sauté
Serves: 4   Time: 30 minutes

Sautéed onions are coated with gram flour; ajwain and ginger make the dish more digestible.

3 tbsp vegetable oil
¼ tsp cumin seeds
1 tsp ajwain/carum
½ cup sifted gram flour (besan)
1 tsp grated ginger
¼ tsp red chilli powder or to taste

¼ tsp turmeric powder
1½ tsp salt
3 large onions, finely sliced lengthwise
1 tsp mango powder (amchur) or juice of 1 lime (optional)

Garnish:
4-5 sprigs of coriander leaves, finely chopped

- Heat oil in a large skillet. Add cumin seeds and ajwain and let them pop. Gradually add gram flour, stirring continuously. Sauté over medium-high heat for 5-6 minutes, till well browned. Mix in ginger, chilli powder, turmeric and salt.

- Add onions and sauté briefly. Sprinkle up to ½ cup of water over the onions and stir so they don't clump together. Cook covered for 5-10 minutes, stirring occasionally, till translucent. Mix in mango powder or lime juice (if used).

- Garnish generously with coriander leaves.

- Serve hot or cold with bhakris (p. 102), polya (p. 103) or yogurt-rice (p. 124).

Variation: **Oli Kandyachi Besan Lavun Bhaji (Rustic Moist Onion-Gram Flour Sauté):** For a moister dish, whisk 1 cup yogurt with the gram flour. Make the seasoning and sauté onions well. Slowly stir in gram flour-yogurt paste. Cook as above for 10-12 minutes, stirring frequently, till thickened.

KELPHULACHI BHAJI
Banana Blossom Stir-Fry
Serves: 4-6   Time: 1 hour cleaning + 30 minutes cooking
Contributor: Meera Marathe

1 medium banana blossom pod
½ cup split, husked mung (mung dal), yellow lentils (arhar/toover) or
black gram (urad dal)
½ cup grated fresh coconut
1 tsp garam masala powder
½ tsp coriander seed powder
½ tsp red chilli powder
1 tsp grated jaggery or to taste
½ tsp salt or to taste
2 tsp tamarind pulp (p. 27)

Seasoning:
2 tbsp vegetable oil
¼ tsp mustard seeds
⅛ tsp asafoetida powder (hing)
½ tsp turmeric powder
1 tsp cumin powder

Garnish:
1 tbsp grated fresh coconut
6-10 sprigs of coriander leaves, finely chopped

Cleaning the blossoms:
*   Before cleaning the blossoms, oil your hands or they will turn purple. Remove and discard the thick red outer layers of the banana pod. The edible flowers/baby bananas under each layer are encased in inedible plastic-like sheaths. Gently peel and discard these. At the heart of the flower is a solid spear-shaped part that tastes like cabbage. Chop it and the blossoms fine.

Bhaji:

- Wash the dal and soak it in ½ cup water for 30 minutes.

- Cook blossoms and dal with the water for 15-17 minutes, till well done. Drain well.

- Heat oil for seasoning in a large skillet to almost smoking. Add mustard seeds and let them pop. Stir in asafoetida, turmeric and cumin powder.

- Add the blossoms and dal and sauté.

- Mix in coconut, garam masala, coriander seed powder and chilli powder. Cook covered for 10 minutes, stirring occasionally.

- Stir in jaggery, salt and tamarind and cook for 2-3 minutes longer.

- Serve hot, topped with coconut and coriander leaves.

LAL BHOPLYACHI BHAJI

Fenugreek-Scented Pumpkin
Serves: 4-6   Time: 20 minutes
Contributor: Jyoti Joshi

1 kg red pumpkin (kaddu)
1 tsp grated jaggery or to taste
¼ cup peanuts, ground (optional)
1-2 tsp salt
1 tbsp grated fresh coconut

Seasoning:
1 tbsp vegetable oil
¼ tsp mustard seeds
¼ tsp fenugreek seeds (methi)
2 dried red chillies
½ tsp turmeric powder

A pinch of asafoetida powder (hing)
6-8 curry leaves (optional)

- Carefully peel off the pumpkin's thick, hard rind. Cut the flesh into 1½"-2" cubes (they shrink when cooked).

- Heat oil for seasoning in a pan, Add mustard seeds and let them pop. Add fenugreek seeds, chillies, turmeric, asafoetida and curry leaves.

- Add the pumpkin and sauté.

- Cover the pan with a lipped lid or metal plate. Pour some water on it. Add some as needed to the bhaji. Cook for 3-5 minutes. Halfway through, stir in jaggery, peanuts and salt.

- Stir in coconut just before serving. Serve hot.

MATHACHI BHAJI
Red Leafy 'Greens'
Serves: 4   Time: 35 minutes

Pair any of Maharashtra's favourite greens with legumes, onions or potatoes for a traditional paley-bhaji or 'dish of leafy greens'.

200 gms amaranth (cholai bhaji) or other leafy greens
50 gms sprouted green/brown mung, split, husked mung (mung dal),
peanuts, onions or potatoes
½ tsp salt
A pinch of sugar (optional)

Seasoning:
2 tbsp vegetable oil
1 tsp mustard seeds
¼ tsp asafoetida powder (hing)
¼ tsp turmeric powder

4-5 green chillies or 1 tbsp red chilli powder
1 tbsp ginger and/or garlic paste

Garnish:
2 tsp grated fresh coconut (optional)
4-5 sprigs of coriander leaves, finely chopped

- Clean and wash the greens. Drain, but do not dry them. Finely chop the leaves. Wash, peel and dice potatoes (if used) into ½" cubes. Chop onions (if used) fine.

- Heat oil for seasoning in a large skillet, till almost smoking. Add mustard seeds and let them pop. Stir in asafoetida, turmeric and chillies or chilli powder. Add ginger and/or garlic and sauté.

- Stir in legumes or vegetable and cook for 2 minutes. Sprinkle with several tablespoons of water. Cook covered over low heat for 12-15 minutes, till legumes or vegetables are tender. Stir occasionally.

- Mix in the greens. Cook covered for 7-10 minutes.

- Stir in salt and sugar.

- Serve garnished with coconut (if used) and coriander leaves.

METHICHI BHAJI

Garlicky Fenugreek Greens
Serves: 2   Time: 20 minutes

Once when I was eight, my mother served fenugreek for lunch.
Try as I might, I could not swallow it. It was too bitter but I 'had
to finish what was on my plate'. I finally downed it rather
unhappily. Now I love methichi bhaji and when I told Keya (then
age three) this story, she immediately asked me to make methi for
her. Imagine my surprise when she eagerly devoured it!

1 large bunch of fenugreek leaves (methi) or other leafy greens
1 medium onion, minced (optional)
A pinch of sugar
¼ tsp red chilli powder (optional)
¾-1 tsp salt

Seasoning:
1½ tbsp vegetable oil
¾ tsp mustard or cumin seeds
A pinch of asafoetida powder (hing)
¼ tsp turmeric powder
3-8 small cloves garlic, minced

- Wash greens well and chop them.

- Heat oil for seasoning in a medium wok or skillet, till almost
  smoking. Add mustard or cumin seeds and let them pop. Stir
  in asafoetida and turmeric.

- Add garlic and sauté for 1-2 minutes, till aromatic and golden
  brown. Add onion and sauté for 3-5 minutes, till brown.

- Raise the heat, add greens and sauté for 3-4 minutes, till wilted.
  Cook covered over low heat for 7-10 minutes. Sprinkle in
  sugar and chilli powder.

- For slightly tough leaves, add up to ¼ cup water and simmer
  for 2-3 minutes. Add salt once the bhaji is cooked.

- Serve hot.

PHANASACHI BHAJI

Jackfruit Sauté

Serves: 4   Time: 45-60 minutes cleaning + 20 minutes cooking
Contributor: Meera Marathe

Though ripe jackfruit flesh is delicious, raw jackfruit also makes
a wonderfully meaty side dish.

1 kg flesh of a small unripe jackfruit (seeds optional)
A pinch of turmeric powder
1-1½ tsp salt
1 tsp ginger paste
1 small clove garlic, crushed (optional)
3-4 green chillies, sliced
1 tsp garam masala powder

Seasoning:
4 tbsp vegetable oil
½ tsp cumin seeds

Garnish:
2 tbsp grated fresh coconut
4-5 sprigs of coriander leaves, finely chopped

- Clean the jackfruit (p. 37). Boil and peel the seeds. Cut seeds
  and fruit into bite-sized pieces.

- Pressure-cook the fruit with 2 tbsp water and a pinch each of
  turmeric and salt for 5 minutes after the cooker reaches full
  pressure (2 whistles) or cook covered in a pan, with ¼ cup
  water for 10 minutes. Drain.

- Heat oil for seasoning to almost smoking in a medium skillet.
  Add cumin seeds and let them pop.

- Add jackfruit and sauté for 2-3 minutes. Add the seeds.

- Stir in ginger, garlic (if used), chillies, garam masala, remaining

salt and up to ¼ cup water, if needed. Simmer covered for
5-10 minutes.

- Serve hot garnished with coconut and coriander leaves.

PHANASACHYA BIYANCHI BHAJI
Spicy Jackfruit Seed Sauté
Serves: 2   Time: 20 minutes

30 peeled and boiled jackfruit seeds (p. 37)
2-3 green chillies, sliced
½ tsp turmeric powder
1 tsp salt
1 tsp garam masala powder

Seasoning:
1 tbsp vegetable oil
½ tsp cumin seeds

Garnish:
2 tbsp grated fresh coconut
4-5 sprigs of coriander leaves, finely chopped

- Slice jackfruit seeds fine.

- Heat oil for seasoning in a skillet till almost smoking. Add
  cumin seeds and let them pop.

- Reduce heat, add chillies, turmeric and jackfruit seeds. Sauté
  for 2-3 minutes, then cook covered for 4-5 minutes.

- Add salt and garam masala. Cook for 5-7 minutes more.

- Serve garnished with coconut and coriander leaves.

TONDLICHI BHAJI
Ivy Gourd Sauté
Serves: 2-4   Time: 30 minutes

Dry-sauté tondli or add a little water for a thin gravy to sop up with polya. Thinner slices make a crisper bhaji while thicker chunks and wedges give a soft, meaty taste.

500 gms ivy gourd (tendli), washed
¼ tsp red chilli powder
1 tsp goda masala (p. 48 – optional)
¾-1 tsp salt
A pinch of sugar

Seasoning:
2 tbsp vegetable oil
¾ tsp mustard seeds
A pinch of asafoetida powder (hing)
¼ tsp turmeric powder

Garnish:
2 tbsp grated fresh coconut
4-5 sprigs of coriander leaves, finely chopped

- Cut the ends off the gourd. Slice them into ¼"-½" discs or lengthwise in quarters.

- Heat oil for seasoning in a medium wok or skillet till almost smoking. Add mustard seeds and let them pop. Add asafoetida and turmeric.

- Add gourd and sauté over high heat for 3-4 minutes.

- Stir in chilli powder. Reduce the heat to medium-low. Cover the pan with a lipped lid or metal plate. Pour ¼ cup water into it. Cook gourd for 4-5 minutes. Stir, adding warm water from the lid if needed.

- Add goda masala and cook gourd covered for 5-7 minutes, till tender but slightly crunchy.
- Stir in salt and sugar. Heat through for 1 minute.
- Garnish with coconut and coriander leaves.

Gravied Accompaniments

BATATYACHA RASSA
'Saucy' Potatoes
Serves: 4-6   Time: 35-45 minutes

A rassa (literally juice) is a vegetable in a thickish gravy. My favourite is Mom's potatoes in a tangy tomato sauce! Mix things up to suit your taste: substitute almost any other fruit, vegetable or tuber for the potato; add cauliflower, fresh green peas or baby onions; or use buttermilk for the sauce. My sister-in-law Dhanashree's family likes spicy rassa so they add 2 teaspoons garlicky ghati masala to the seasoning.

4 medium potatoes, washed and peeled
100-200 gms cauliflower, green peas or other vegetable
2 large onions, minced or blended with 4 tbsp water
4-6 medium tomatoes, cut into ½" dice
2 tsp goda masala (p. 48) or garam masala powder
1½ tsp cumin powder (optional)
1-2 tsp salt
A pinch of sugar
A pinch of red chilli powder or ground black pepper (optional)

Seasoning:
2-3 tbsp vegetable oil
¾ tsp mustard seeds
½ tsp cumin seeds
1½-2 tbsp ginger-garlic paste
2-3 green chillies, sliced
1 tsp turmeric powder

Garnish:
A few sprigs of coriander leaves, finely chopped

- Cut potatoes into 1" cubes, placing them in water to prevent discolouration. Cut other vegetables into bite-sized chunks.

- Heat oil for seasoning in a deep pan till almost smoking. Add mustard seeds and let them pop. Add cumin and ginger-garlic paste. Sauté for 4-5 minutes, till golden and aromatic.

- Add chillies, turmeric and onion. Sauté for 3-5 minutes, till golden.

- Stir in tomatoes and cook on high heat for 2-3 minutes, till they soften and release their juice.

- Add drained potatoes and sauté for 2-3 minutes. Reduce heat, add water to just cover potatoes and cook covered for 5-7 minutes. Stir occasionally. If potatoes are undercooked, add more water and cook for 3-5 minutes more.

- Add other vegetables. Cook for 7-10 minutes.

- Stir in goda or garam masala, cumin powder, salt and sugar.

- For really spicy rassa, add chilli powder or ground black pepper. Mix well.

- Cook for 5 minutes more, till potatoes are tender.

- Serve garnished with coriander leaves.

- This rassa is wonderful with rice, polis, varan and kandya-tamatyachi koshimbir.

DUDHI-KAJUCHI SONARI AMTI

Goldsmith's Bottle Gourd and Cashew Sauce
Serves: 2   Time: 30 minutes
Contributor: Meeheika Karekar

My husband's friend, Meeheika (Mikki) lives in England but visits Mumbai twice a year to see her father. 'This dish is a complete winner in our family during Ganpati, when we don't eat meat. The amti is meaty and rich.' Her aunt, 'Tiger' taught Mikki how to cook her community's traditional food. 'Tiger surpasses her culinary skills with this dish. She says this amti is the marriage of the humble marrow to the wealthy cashew nut.'

1 tbsp vegetable oil
250 gms bottle gourd (lauki/ghia), peeled and cut into 1" chunks
2 small onions, finely chopped
15-20 cashew nuts (a little less than the quantity of gourd)
1 tbsp Sonari masala (p. 53)
1" stick cinnamon
1 tsp sugar
A pinch of turmeric powder
A pinch of asafoetida powder (hing)
1-2 tsp salt
1 tsp gram flour (besan)
Coconut milk made from 1 coconut (p. 29)

Garnish:
4-5 sprigs of coriander leaves, finely chopped

- Heat oil in a medium pan. Add all ingredients except the gram flour, coconut milk and coriander leaves. Mix well. Cook covered for about 10 minutes.

- Make a thin paste with the gram flour and a few drops of water. Stir it into the vegetable with the coconut milk.

- Cook for 5-10 minutes more till the raw smell of gram flour disappears. Add a little more coconut milk if the sauce looks too thick. It should have a pourable, but not watery, consistency.

- Garnish with coriander leaves and serve over hot white rice.

KAKDICHI AMTI
Gravied Cucumber
Serves: 4   Time: 30 minutes

Serve this unusual gravy over hot white rice for a light supper when you wish to avoid onion and garlic!

2 tsp tup (ghee)
2-3 green chillies, sliced
250 gms cucumber, peeled and cut into 1" chunks
½ cup tamarind pulp (p. 27)
¾-1 tsp salt
A pinch of sugar

Spice paste:
½ fresh coconut, grated
1 tsp coriander seeds
½ tsp mustard seeds
1 tsp rice grains
½ tsp turmeric powder

- Grind spice paste ingredients fine.

- Heat tup in a pan. Stir in chillies. Add cucumber and a little less than ¼ cup water. Simmer covered for 4-5 minutes, till tender.

- Add tamarind and boil for 2-3 minutes.

- Add the spice paste and mix well. Bring to a boil once more.

- Stir in salt and sugar. Do not boil the amti after adding salt.

KHATTA

Clatter-Pot Vegetables
Serves: 4   Time: 1 hour
Contributor: Medha Marathe

Mangal Kaku's maternal grandmother gave her the recipe for a year-round, mixed vegetable dish. 'Khatta gets its name from the fact that it sat bubbling (khadkhadné) on the stove for hours. Today it can be made in a pressure cooker to save time.'

1 cup yellow lentils (arhar/toover), cleaned and washed
3 x 3" pieces of red pumpkin (kaddu), cut into 1" chunks
2 medium aubergines (baingan), cut into 1" chunks
2 corncobs, cut into 1" discs
1 large potato, cut into 1" chunks
2 drumsticks, strung and cut into 1" strips
1 ridged gourd (toori), cut into 1" chunks
6" piece of snake gourd (chirchinda), cut into 1" chunks
½ cup elephant foot yam (suran), cut into 1" chunks
½ cup unripe jackfruit flesh, cut into 1" chunks
½-1 tsp salt
¼ cup tamarind pulp (p. 27)
¼ tsp turmeric powder
A pinch of asafoetida powder (hing)
2-3 Goa spiceberries (triphala – optional)

Spice paste:
½ fresh coconut, grated
1 medium onion
2-3 dried red chillies
1 tsp salt

- Grind spice paste ingredients fine.

- Bring 2½ cups of water to a boil. Cook dal in it over medium-low heat, stirring occasionally.

- Add the pumpkin. Continue to cook for about 15 minutes, till the dal is very soft and the pumpkin is falling apart.

- Stir in remaining vegetables and 1 cup of water. Cook covered for 15-20 minutes, till the vegetables are tender. Stir occasionally and add more water if needed.

- When the water has reduced to a thick gravy, mix in salt, spice paste, tamarind, turmeric, asafoetida and spiceberries (if used). Simmer for 3-5 minutes.

- Serve with hot white rice and papad.

PALAKCHI PATAL BHAJI
Spinach in Buttermilk
Serves: 4 Time: 25-30 minutes
Contributor: Surekha Sirsikar

My grandfather Anna loved Vahini Aji's patal bhaji. You will too.

1 tbsp split, husked Bengal gram (chana dal)
2 tbsp peanuts
250 gms (2 bunches) spinach
1 tbsp gram flour (besan)
1 cup yogurt or 2 cups thin buttermilk
1½ tbsp vegetable oil or tup (ghee)
1½ medium onions, minced
1 tbsp slivered dried coconut (kopra – optional)
1-1½ tsp salt

Seasoning:
1-1½ tbsp vegetable oil or tup (ghee)
¾ tsp mustard seeds
½ tsp turmeric powder
1 tsp grated ginger (optional)
2-3 green chillies, sliced
4 small cloves garlic (optional)

- Soak gram and peanuts in 6 tbsp water for 30 minutes before cooking. Cook gram and peanuts in their soaking water for 3-5 minutes. Drain and set aside.

- Clean spinach, wash and chop fine. Blanch in 500 ml boiling water for 2-3 minutes. Drain well and set aside.

- Mix gram flour and yogurt or buttermilk in a bowl till smooth.

- Heat 1½ tbsp of the fat in a pan. Sauté onions for 4-5 minutes, till translucent.

- Add spinach, gram and peanuts. Sauté over low heat for 4-5 minutes.

- Stir in the gram flour-yogurt mixture, raise heat to medium, bring to a boil and cook for 3-4 minutes. Add coconut. Reduce heat and simmer for 3-5 minutes. Mix in salt.

- Heat the fat for seasoning in a wok. Add mustard seeds and let them pop. Stir in turmeric, ginger, chillies and garlic. Cook for 15-20 seconds, till aromatic and golden.

- Pour the seasoning over the spinach, stir once, cover pan and set aside for 2-3 minutes.

- Serve hot with hot white rice or chapatti.

SHENG SOLA
Winter Solstice Stew
Serves: 4-6   Time: 45-60 minutes
Contributor: Aruna Karande

Many ingredients for this 'patal' bhaji are available only around the winter solstice so people look forward to eating it then at Bhogi. It is eaten with bhakri—sesame (in the stew) and millet (in the bread) provide essential heat and calories for the body.

2 spring onions, chopped
1-1½ tsp salt
½-1 tsp red chilli powder
50 gms shelled green 'pavta' beans (p. 57)
50 gms shelled green gram (hara chana)
50 gms carrot, peeled and cubed
50 gms shelled green peas
1 medium aubergine (baingan), cubed
1 medium potato, peeled and cubed
A few fresh French beans, chopped
A few green bor/ber berries
A small piece of jaggery, grated

Spice paste:
50 gms sesame seeds (til)
1" piece of ginger
7-8 cloves garlic
2 tbsp peanuts
5 sprigs of coriander leaves, finely chopped

Seasoning:
100 ml vegetable oil
¾ tsp mustard seeds
½ tsp cumin seeds
A pinch of asafoetida powder (hing)
½ tsp turmeric powder

Garnish:
1 tbsp grated dried coconut (kopra)
5 sprigs of coriander leaves, finely chopped

- Heat a griddle well. Toast sesame for 4-6 minutes, till golden and aromatic. Grind fine with the remaining spice paste ingredients.

- Heat oil for seasoning in a deep pan. Add mustard seeds and let them pop. Stir in cumin, asafoetida and turmeric.

- Add spring onions and sauté for 2-3 minutes. Mix in spice

paste, salt and chilli powder. Stir for 5-7 minutes, till the oil begins to rise to the top.

- Add remaining vegetables and berries. Steam-cook for about 5 minutes, while bringing 2-4 cups water to a boil in a separate pan.

- Mix hot water and jaggery into the stew. Cook vegetables for 7-12 minutes, till tender. Garnish with coconut and coriander leaves.

SHEVGYACHYA SHENGANCHA RASSA
Divine Drumsticks
Serves: 4   Time: 30 minutes

Drumsticks are a summer delicacy. Though their skin is not edible, drumsticks are cooked with it intact because their flavourful, astringent flesh is minimal. Drumsticks absorb the flavour of ingredients they are cooked with, which makes them fun to suck and chew on. Grip the pods between the teeth and pull the flesh and edible seeds out.

5 tender drumsticks, strung and cut into 2" lengths
½ cup tamarind pulp (p. 27)
1-1½ tsp salt
½ tsp sugar

Spice paste:
½ cup grated fresh coconut
1 tsp rice grains
1 tsp coriander seeds
½-1 tsp red chilli powder
½ tsp turmeric powder

Seasoning:
1 tsp vegetable oil

½ tsp mustard seeds
A pinch of asafoetida powder (hing)
¼ tsp turmeric powder

- Soak drumsticks in water for 15 minutes.

- Grind spice paste ingredients fine with 1-2 tbsp water.

- Heat oil for seasoning in a pan. Add mustard seeds and let them pop. Stir in asafoetida and turmeric.

- Add the drained drumsticks and sauté briefly. Cook covered in ½ cup water for 10-15 minutes. They will change colour and soften.

- Stir in tamarind. Bring to a boil and cook for 2-3 minutes. Lower heat to a simmer, add spice paste and cook for another 3-5 minutes.

- Stir in salt and sugar.

- Serve hot with rice or polya.

Soups

KAIRICHI AMTI
Gravied Green Mango
Serves: 4   Time: 30 minutes

My great grandmother Laxmibai came from Sawai verim (now in Goa). Her husband Manjunath Sirsikar was from Sirsi (North Karnataka), near the Maharashtra border. They had 14 children and 47 grandchildren.

As a doctor in the (erstwhile) Central Provinces and Berar State Medical Department my great grandfather had lived in the Central Provinces (Nagpur, Berar-Dhule, etc.) so when he retired, the family settled in Nagpur.

Laxmibai loved to cook and to eat. She taught this and other recipes to her daughter-in-law, Vahini Aji. The Marathes make a similar soup, adding curry leaves and mango-pickle spice.

1 large green mango, washed dried and peeled
1 fresh coconut, grated
¾ tsp coriander seeds
¾ tsp red chilli powder
½ tsp turmeric powder
2" piece of jaggery, grated
1 tsp rice flour (optional)
¾-1 tsp salt

Seasoning:
1½-2 tbsp vegetable oil
½ tsp mustard seeds
A pinch of asafoetida powder (hing)
1 tsp fenugreek seeds (methi)

- Remove the mango pit (reserve it for another purpose). Quarter the fruit and chop it into ½" pieces. Grind ⅓ of the coconut with coriander seeds, chilli powder and turmeric. Marinate the mango in this paste for at least 30 minutes.

- Extract milk from the remaining coconut (p. 29).

- Heat oil for seasoning in a pan till almost smoking. Add mustard seeds and let them pop. Add the asafoetida and fenugreek seeds.

- Stir in the mango with its marinade. Cook over low heat for 5-7 minutes, till tender.

- Add coconut milk and jaggery. For a thicker or smooth sauce, whisk in rice flour. Bring to a boil and turn off the heat.

- Serve with hot rice, tup and papad.

SOLACHI KADHI
Kokum-Coconut Soup
Serves: 2-4 Time: 1-4 hours soaking + 30 minutes preparation

Solachi kadhi (amsulaché sar) is drunk as a digestive with seafood or following a meal, since kokum aids digestion and alleviates nausea. Lately, it has become popular in Mumbai, being served at Gomantak and Malvani restaurants.

10-12 kokum (amsul) skins
1 fresh coconut, grated
1 tsp salt
A pinch of sugar (optional)

Seasoning:
1 tbsp tup (ghee)
1 tsp cumin seeds
A pinch of asafoetida powder (hing)

1 green chilli, sliced
1 dried red chilli, broken into pieces
2-5 curry leaves (optional)

- Soak kokum in 1½-2 cups boiling hot water for 1-4 hours. Squeeze them to express more flavour. Discard the skins (or munch on them).

- Extract coconut milk (p. 29). Add it to the kokum water with salt and sugar.

- Heat tup in a wok till almost smoking. Add cumin seeds and let them pop. Stir in asafoetida, chillies and curry leaves (if used).

- Mix the seasoning into the kadhi. Cover for 2-3 minutes.

- Serve at room temperature. Do *not* reheat the kadhi.

MOLLY
Patharé Prabhu Coconut Soup
Serves: 2-4   Time: 40 minutes
Contributors: Deepak & Ujwal Mankar

Molly sounds as if it might be from Kerala but it is a tangy-spicy Patharé Prabhu soup. Serve it with hot white rice or as an after-dinner beverage.

1" piece of ginger, peeled and sliced into thin rounds
1 green chilli
½ cup thick + 1 cup thin coconut milk, made from 1 coconut (p. 29)
1 tsp rice flour
1-1½ tsp salt
Juice of one lime

Garnish:
4-5 sprigs of coriander leaves, finely chopped

- Boil the ginger and chilli in ¼ cup water for 3-5 minutes.

- Whisk rice flour into the thin coconut milk till smooth. Heat it in a medium pan over low heat for 1-2 minutes. Add the ginger-chilli water, whisking or stirring continuously. Cook, stirring for 5-7 minutes, till slightly thickened.

- Add thick coconut milk and warm through for about 3 minutes. Turn off the heat when it comes to a boil.

- Stir in salt and lime juice.

- Serve the molly, garnished with coriander leaves.

SANTOSH
Tomato-Coconut 'Contentment'
Serves: 6   Time: 1 hour

The day her grandchildren arrived at her home in Dehnu Road for summer vacation, Vahini Aji would make their special farmaish (request). I always wanted santosh with rice and tup. If you *must* have accompaniments, serve bharli bhend (p. 167) and masurichi usal (p. 216).

750 gms tomatoes
2 tbsp tup (ghee) or vegetable oil
2 small red onions, minced
1 tsp grated ginger
1¼ tsp cumin seeds
¾-1 tsp red chilli powder
1½-2 tsp salt
Thin and thick coconut milk made from 1 coconut (p. 29)
1-2 tbsp rice flour or gram flour (besan – if required)
A pinch of sugar (if required)

Garnish:
5-6 sprigs of coriander leaves, finely chopped

Tomato Purée:

- Blanch tomatoes in 1 litre boiling water for 3-5 minutes, till they soften and the skin begins to split.

- Cool tomatoes slightly and skin them. Squeeze skins to extract juice and discard skins.

- Mash or purée tomato flesh and juice into a thickish pulp. Strain purée and discard seeds.

Santosh:

- Heat tup or oil in a deep pan over low heat. Sauté onions for 4-7 minutes, till they turn pink. Do not brown them.

- Add ginger and cumin seeds and sauté briefly.

- Stir in tomato purée, chilli powder and salt. Simmer for 5-8 minutes.

- Gently mix in the thick coconut milk. The soup will be a delicate salmon colour.

- Taste it. If the flavour of tomatoes and coconut is balanced (neither too sweet nor too tart), raise the heat slightly. If it needs more coconut, add the thin milk. If the soup seems too thin, slowly stir in the rice flour or gram flour. If it is too tart, add a pinch of sugar.

- Bring the soup just up to a boil but do not let it boil.

- Garnish with coriander leaves.

- Serve with hot white rice and tup.

Variation: **Speed-of-Light Version:** When you lack time but want contentment, try this: Purée and strain 750-800 gms canned whole tomatoes in juice (add up to 4 cups water to blend and liquefy). Then follow the above method using the listed ingredients. Replace the fresh coconut with 375-450 ml canned coconut milk. Add 50 ml of coconut milk to the santosh at a time as needed. Do not dilute the tomato flavour.

Legumes

Legumes

The word dal, which means cooked lentils in some other parts of India, refers to raw split, husked lentils in Maharashtra and to dishes made from them like kairichi dal (p. 97).

Rice and lentils, frequently paired as a meal across India, together provide the maximum source of protein for most Indians. Both contain important amino acids and when combined, complete the body's required amino acid profile. Lentils are also served with breads like poli and bhakri, delicious when dipped or soaked in the lentil gravy.

Marathi people have a great fondness for whole legumes or kad dhanya (grains which can be sprouted). Soaked or sprouted whole legumes are cooked as usal, seasoned and served in a thick sauce. Boiled, split lentils are varan. The preparation is almost always thick. Sadha varan or goda varan refers to basic, cooked yellow lentils or pigeon peas (arhar/toover) in particular, generally made every day in middle-class households. A portion is kept plain (perhaps mashed and thinned out a little) to serve with rice. The rest is converted into amti.

Amti is generally thinner, seasoned with spices and flavoured with an acid (kokum, tamarind, etc). Confusingly, some people even call their thick amti 'varan', while occasionally a gravied vegetable dish is called amti! If that is not complicated enough, a kadhi (thickened with gram flour or rice flour) is actually 'amti' made with buttermilk! Katachi amti (p. 352) is made with leftover split, husked Bengal gram after making puran poli.

Lentil flour is used in dry and gravied dishes like jhunka and pithla. It is also shaped into dumplings or squares and served in a gravy, and made into sweets. The possibilities are simply endless.

Split, Husked Lentils

SADHA VARAN
Everyday Lentils
Serves: 4   Time: 20 minutes

Turichi dal (yellow lentils/split, husked pigeon peas) is probably the most commonly cooked lentil in Maharashtra. Many even eat varan with sugar or jaggery, scooped up in bread! This is the basic recipe. You can season it or not, as you choose.

Varan:
1 cup yellow lentils (arhar/toover), cleaned and rinsed
1 tsp vegetable oil
A pinch of asafoetida powder (hing)
¼ tsp turmeric powder
1 tsp salt
A pinch of sugar

Seasoning:
1½ tsp vegetable oil
½ tsp cumin seeds
¼ tsp red chilli powder

• If possible, soak lentils in water for 30 minutes. Pressure-cook lentils with oil, asafoetida and turmeric with water to cover for 7-10 minutes after the cooker reaches full presure (3 whistles) or cook on the stove top with 2½ cups water over medium heat for 30-45 minutes, till very soft. For stove-top cooking, stir occasionally and add more water if needed.

• Churn or mash the cooked lentils smooth, adding warm water for the desired consistency. Add salt and sugar. You can make varan in advance and gently reheat before serving.

- Heat oil for seasoning in a small wok. Add cumin seeds and let them pop. Stir in the chilli powder.
- Mix the seasoning into the lentils.
- Serve with white rice, tup, salt and lime wedges for a traditional first course.

Note: You could add cumin powder and red chilli powder to the cooked dal instead of a seasoning.

TURICHYA DALICHI AMTI
Savoury Lentils with Tamarind
Serves: 4   Time: 30 minutes

Most Marathi people like to sip amti during a meal. This tart-sweet Konkanastha amti is made from unseasoned sadha varan (opposite).

1 cup cooked yellow lentils (arhar/toover – opposite)
1-2 tbsp tamarind pulp (p. 27)
1 tbsp grated jaggery
1 cup diced vegetables of choice (optional)
1 tsp goda masala (p. 48)
1-1½ tsp salt

Seasoning:
1½ tbsp vegetable oil or tup (ghee)
1 tsp mustard seeds
2-3 curry leaves
2 green chillies, sliced or ¾ tsp red chilli powder

- Churn or mash the cooked lentils smooth.
- Heat the fat for seasoning in a large pan to almost smoking.

- Add mustard seeds and let them pop. Add curry leaves, reduce heat slightly and stir in chillies or chilli powder.

- Pour the lentils over the seasoning. Stir briskly, add 1 cup water, bring to a boil and cook for 5-7 minutes.

- Add tamarind, jaggery and vegetables (if used). Stir in goda masala.

- Add salt and more water if needed. Boil over low heat for 10-15 minutes, till it reaches the desired consistency.

- Serve with white rice, polis or bhakri.

AMBAT VARAN
CKP Sour Lentils
Serves: 4   Time: 30 minutes
Contributor: Sheela Pradhan

1 cup yellow lentils (arhar/toover)
$^{1}/_{3}$ cup grated fresh or dried coconut (kopra)
2-3 green chillies, sliced
$^{1}/_{3}$ cup chopped onion
¼ tsp turmeric powder
½ tsp red chilli powder
1 tbsp tamarind pulp (p. 27)
1 tsp grated jaggery
1 tsp salt
5-6 sprigs of coriander leaves, finely chopped

Seasoning:
1 tbsp vegetable oil
3-4 small cloves garlic, finely chopped
A pinch of asafoetida powder (hing)

- Clean, rinse and soak lentils in 1½ cups water for 15-20 minutes before draining.

- Grind coconut into a fine paste with a little water.

- Cook the lentils in a pan over medium heat with chillies, onion, turmeric, chilli powder and 2½ cups water for about 30 minutes, till tender. Mash the lentils smooth.

- Add enough water to liquefy the lentils. Bring to a boil and simmer for about 10 minutes.

- Stir in tamarind, jaggery, salt and coconut paste. Simmer for 7-10 minutes. Sprinkle coriander leaves over the dal.

- Heat oil in a wok and sauté the garlic for 1-2 minutes, till aromatic. Stir in asafoetida. Mix the seasoning into the lentils.

- Cover briefly before serving hot with rice.

DAL-METHI
Fenugreek Lentils
Serves: 4   Time: 2 hours soaking + 35-50 minutes cooking

Distinctively flavoured fenugreek seeds add a unique taste to Marathi vegetables, pickles, jams and legumes. This is the recipe of Sudhatai Kale, the paternal grandmother of my cousins, Ram, Arjun and Radhika.

1 cup yellow lentils (arhar/toover), cleaned and washed
½ tsp fenugreek seeds (methi), cleaned and washed
2 medium onions, finely chopped
1 green chilli, slit
1 tsp red chilli powder
¼ tsp turmeric powder
1 tsp salt
1 tsp grated jaggery or brown sugar
2 tsp tamarind pulp (p. 27)

Seasoning:
2 tbsp vegetable oil
½ tsp mustard seeds
½ clove garlic, crushed

Garnish:
5-6 sprigs of coriander leaves, finely chopped

- Soak lentils and fenugreek together in 1 cup water for at least 2 hours. Drain well. Pressure-cook lentils and fenugreek with onions, chilli, chilli powder, turmeric, salt, jaggery and enough water to cover (p. 206) or cook on the stove top in 4 cups water for 30-40 minutes. Churn or mash lentils till smooth.

- Heat oil for seasoning in a medium wok or pan. Add mustard seeds and let them pop. Add garlic and sauté briefly.

- Stir in lentils and tamarind. Simmer for 7-10 minutes.

- Serve hot garnished with coriander leaves.

GOLE SAMBAR/GOLYACHI AMTI
Bengal Gram Dumplings in Gravy
Serves: 4   Time: 4 hours soaking + 1 hour cooking
Special equipment: paper-lined platter
Contributor: Susheelabai

Sambar is a thickish side dish especially enjoyed in the Kolhapur-Sangli region during Shravan. There are many recipes for spicy lentil or lentil flour-dumplings or cakes cooked in a water-based gravy, such as usal-vada—lentil stew with rice-black gram dumplings; pat vadi rassa—gram flour squares in a gravy, etc.

8 tbsp split, husked Bengal gram (chana dal)
A pinch of turmeric powder
Red chilli powder to taste

1-1½ tsp salt
Up to 1 litre vegetable oil for deep frying
¾-1 cup grated fresh coconut
2 medium onions, chopped
1" piece of ginger
7-8 cloves garlic
2 small or 1 large bunch of coriander leaves, chopped

Seasoning:
2 tbsp vegetable oil
1 tsp mustard seeds
A pinch of asafoetida powder (hing)
½ tsp turmeric powder
6-8 curry leaves

- Clean, rinse and soak the gram in 1 cup cool water for about 4 hours. Drain well. Grind to a thick firm paste without water. Mix in pinches of turmeric, chilli powder and salt. Form small marble-sized balls (gole), setting them aside on a platter.

- Heat 2 tbsp oil in a skillet. Sauté coconut and onions till golden and aromatic. Grind them with the ginger, garlic and coriander leaves. Set aside covered.

- Heat 1-2 cups oil in a medium wok, till very hot. Deep-fry 5-8 gole at a time for 1-2 minutes, till golden brown. Drain well and place on the paper-lined platter.

- Heat oil for seasoning in a deep pan. Add mustard seeds and let them pop. Add asafoetida and turmeric. Add curry leaves.

- Stir in the coconut-onion paste and sauté till the oil begins to separate from it. Add 400-500 ml of hot water and the remaining salt. Bring to a boil and cook for 7-10 minutes.

- Float the dumplings in the gravy. Bring to a boil 3-4 times.

- Serve hot with rice.

PACH DALINCHI AMTI

Five-Lentil Stew

Serves: 6-10   Time: 1 hour soaking + 1-1½ hours cooking
Contributor: Dhanashree (Dadhe) Marathe

This hearty stew combines five kinds of lentils. Here I recommend
pressure-cooking them because of the sheer quantity.

1¼ cups yellow lentils (arhar/toover)
1¼ cups split, husked green mung (mung dal)
1 cup split, husked red lentils (masur dal)
4 tbsp split, husked Bengal gram (chana dal)
2 tbsp split, husked black gram (urad dal)
6-8 kokum (amsul – optional)
3 green chillies, sliced
2 medium onions, chopped fine
3-3½ tsp salt
3 tsp grated jaggery (optional)

Seasoning:

3 tbsp vegetable oil
1½ tsp mustard seeds
¼ tsp asafoetida powder (hing)
1 tsp turmeric powder
15-20 curry leaves

Garnish:

½ bunch of coriander leaves, finely chopped

- Clean the dals, rinse well and soak together for 1 hour.

- Pressure-cook the dals with just enough water to cover for
  10-15 minutes after cooker reaches full pressure (3-4 whistles)
  or cook on the stove top for 45-60 minutes, till soft in 10½
  cups water. Mash the dal till broken up but not smooth. Soak
  kokum in 2 tbsp warm water for 15 minutes (p. 27).

- Heat oil for seasoning in a deep pan. Add mustard seeds and let them pop. Add asafoetida, turmeric and curry leaves.

- Add chillies and onions and sauté for about 5 minutes, till onions are aromatic and golden. Add the dal and some water to thin it down. Bring to a boil and cook for 10-12 minutes.

- Add salt, jaggery and kokum with its soaking liquid. Cook for 7-15 minutes more.

- Stir and serve hot, garnished with coriander leaves.

Variation: A finishing hot-oil-and-garlic seasoning is delicious too (p. 22).

Whole Lentils

HARBHARYACHI USAL
Fresh Green Gram
Serves: 4-6   Time: 8 hours soaking + 30 minutes cooking
Contributor: Sudhakar Marathe

Fresh green gram (November-January) is very flavourful. Dad recalls, 'When women attended a haldi-kunku, the hostess would give them fresh harbhara, or dried harbhara soaked overnight in water, in a leaf bowl to take home. They would make "instant" usal out of it: a quick phodni and brief sautéing. When we knew our mother had gone to a haldi-kunku, we would hop around saying, "Ai (Mom) is coming home, we'll have usal today."'

Try this usal if you get green harbhara at the market. Shell the pods just before cooking. They require minimal water and time to cook. Or use rehydrated green/brown gram.

3 cups fresh, green, shelled Bengal gram (harbhara) or 1 cup dried
whole Bengal gram, soaked overnight
1 tsp coriander seed powder
½ tsp cumin powder
1-2 tsp salt
A marble-sized ball of jaggery, grated
½ cup grated fresh or dried coconut (kopra)
3 tbsp tamarind pulp (p. 27)

Seasoning:
1½ tbsp vegetable oil
¾ tsp mustard seeds
1 tsp ginger or garlic paste (optional)
¼ tsp asafoetida powder (hing – optional)
¼ tsp turmeric powder

1 tbsp grated fresh or dried coconut
5-6 sprigs of coriander leaves, finely chopped

- Pick over the rehydrated gram to remove debris or hard beans. Cook covered with 3 cups water and a pinch of salt for 15-25 minutes, till tender. Drain and set aside. Rinse fresh gram briefly under cold water.

- Heat oil for seasoning over medium-low heat in a large pan till almost smoking. Add mustard seeds and let them pop. Stir in ginger or garlic and asafoetida (if used), and turmeric.

- Add gram and sauté briefly. Pour in 3-4 tbsp water for fresh gram and ¼ cup for the rehydrated ones. Cook covered, stirring occasionally, for 10-12 minutes.

- Mix in coriander and cumin powders, salt and jaggery. Cook covered for 5-10 minutes.

- When the jaggery melts, add coconut and tamarind. Cook partially covered for 5-7 minutes more. Add some water if necessary. The usal is ready when the beans are very tender but unbroken.

- Serve hot garnished with coconut and coriander leaves.

Note: Use harbhara for a delicious snack like misal (p. 217)

MASURICHI USAL

Vahini Aji's Brown Lentils
Serves: 2   Time: 30 minutes
Contributor: Surekha Sirsikar

1 cup whole brown lentils (sabut masur), cleaned and washed
2 medium onions, finely chopped
1-1½ tsp salt
2 tbsp vegetable oil
1 tsp goda masala (p. 48) or garam masala powder
½ tsp turmeric powder
1 tsp red chilli powder
½ tsp coriander seed powder
Tamarind pulp from 2-3 dried pods (p. 27)
2 tbsp grated fresh coconut

Seasoning:
1 tbsp vegetable oil
½ tsp mustard seeds

Garnish:
A few sprigs of coriander leaves, finely chopped

- Cook lentils with 1 onion, a pinch of salt and 2½ cups water in a heavy-bottomed pan for 30 minutes or pressure-cook for 5 minutes after the cooker reaches full pressure (2 whistles).

- Heat 2 tbsp oil in a deep pan. Brown the remaining onion for 3-4 minutes. Add goda or garam masala, turmeric, chilli powder and coriander powder.

- Stir in cooked lentils, tamarind, coconut and remaining salt. Simmer for 5-7 minutes, adding water for more gravy.

- Heat oil for seasoning in a small wok. Add mustard seeds and let them pop. Stir seasoning into the lentils.

- Serve garnished with coriander leaves.

MATKICHI USAL AND MISAL
Spicy Brown Mung Stew and Party Mix
Serves: 6 as a meal, 10-12 as a snack
Time: 2 days soaking and sprouting + 30 minutes cooking

This hearty usal is a main course dish but topped with fresh coconut, onion, tomato, coriander and crunchy snacks (chivda, shev, etc.), it becomes a tasty snack called misal (mixture).

Keya's fourth birthday party had an 'Indian' theme. The guests wore Indian clothes, listened to Indian music and played Indian games. I served misal, a great party dish because you can make it in advance. Your guests choose their own toppings. It is great for kids: the beans are nutritious and can be cooked bland since the condiments add spice!

Usal:
400 gms whole brown mung (matki)
¼ tsp turmeric powder
2-2½ tsp salt
2 tsp ginger paste
2 tsp garlic paste
1 large white onion, finely chopped
2 green chillies, sliced or 1 tsp red chilli powder (optional)
½ cup tamarind pulp (p. 27)
2" cube jaggery, grated or 2 tsp brown sugar
1 cup grated fresh coconut
1 small bunch of coriander leaves, finely chopped

Seasoning:
2 tbsp vegetable oil
1 tsp mustard seeds
A pinch of turmeric powder
½ tsp asafoetida powder (hing)
10-15 curry leaves

Toppings for misal (party mix):
500 gms Laxmi Narayan chivda

500 gms fine gram flour strings (sev/shev)
500 gms yogurt
1 cup garlic chutney (p. 278 – optional)
1 cup tamarind chutney (optional)
1 cup coriander chutney (p. 277 – optional)
3 potatoes, boiled and finely diced
3 medium white onions, finely chopped
2 tomatoes, finely diced
1 bunch of coriander leaves, finely chopped
1 cup grated fresh coconut

Usal:

- Two nights before you want to serve the usal, clean, rinse, soak and sprout the gram (p. 54).

- Cook cleaned sprouts in 1 cup of water with turmeric and a pinch of salt for 12-15 minutes, till tender.

- Heat oil for seasoning in a large pan over medium heat till almost smoking. Add mustard seeds and let them pop. Reduce heat to low. Add turmeric and asafoetida. Stir in curry leaves.

- Raise the heat and add the ginger and garlic pastes. Sauté for 2 minutes, till golden. Add onion and chillies or chilli powder (if used) and sauté for 3-4 minutes.

- Mix in the cooked gram with its cooking liquid and salt. Stir well. Bring to a boil.

- Add tamarind and sweetener. Cook for 5-7 minutes, adding more water if needed. Mix in half the coconut and coriander leaves.

- Sprinkle with the remaining coconut and coriander leaves.

Misal:

- Serve misal at room temperature (hot usal makes the crunchy accompaniments soggy) with the toppings served alongside.

- With bread, the dish is called misal-pav.

MUGACHI USAL

Green Mung Bean Stew

Serves: 6 Time: 2 days soaking/sprouting + 30 minutes cooking

Contributor: Vimal Tai Laud

400 gms green mung beans (sabut mung)
½ tsp turmeric powder
½ tsp asafoetida powder (hing)
½ tsp mustard seeds
1 tsp vegetable oil
6 curry leaves
½ cup tamarind pulp (p. 27)
1 tsp salt

Coconut paste:
½ fresh coconut, grated
2-3 green chillies

Seasoning:
1 tsp vegetable oil
½ tsp mustard seeds
6 curry leaves
½ tsp asafoetida powder (hing)
¼ tsp turmeric powder

- Soak and sprout the beans 2 days before cooking (p. 54).

- Grind coconut paste ingredients fine.

- Immerse the sprouts in fresh water and rinse to remove their tough skins.

- Boil the sprouts in 1 cup of fresh water for 4-5 minutes. Add turmeric, asafoetida, mustard seeds, oil and curry leaves. Stir and cook for 15 minutes, till tender.

- Add tamarind and salt. Cook for 5-7 minutes. Mix in coconut paste and bring usal to a boil.

- Heat oil for seasoning in a wok. Add mustard seeds and let them pop. Add curry leaves, asafoetida and turmeric. Stir the seasoning into the gram.
- Serve hot with rice or bread.

Variation: Try this usal with brown mung (matki).

Beans, Nuts & Lentil Flour

VALACHI USAL
Gravied Bitter Beans
Serves: 2   Time: 8-12 hours soaking + 40 minutes cooking

Fresh green and dried bitter beans are a delicacy and an acquired taste. They are often served at wedding feasts. Also try them in masalé bhat (p. 128) or mugachi khichadi (p. 127).

300 gms bitter beans (val)
1 tbsp garlic paste
A little jaggery or sugar (optional)
1-1½ tsp salt

Spice paste:
1 tsp cumin seeds
2 green chillies or 1½ tsp red chilli powder
1 tsp ginger paste
2 tbsp grated fresh coconut

Seasoning:
3-4 tbsp vegetable oil or tup (ghee)
½ tsp mustard seeds
A pinch of asafoetida powder (hing)
¼ tsp turmeric powder

- Soak and sprout the beans for 8-12 hours (p. 54). Rinse and skin the beans.

- Grind the spice paste ingredients fine.

- Heat oil for seasoning in a medium pan. Add mustard seeds and let them pop. Add asafoetida and turmeric.

- Add beans and sauté briefly. Stir in garlic paste. Pour in twice the volume of water as beans and cook covered for 10-15 minutes.

- Mix in sweetener and salt and cook for 10-15 minutes, till beans are tender. Test a bean with your nail. If it breaks easily, it is done.

- Serve with puris, hot white rice or masalé bhat and tup.

KONKANASTHA MATARCHI USAL
Konkanastha Green Peas
Serves: 2   Time: 30 minutes

Serve usal with hot polya. Make tasty wrap-sandwiches by stuffing leftover usal into polya, nan or pita bread. Or top peas with chopped onions, tomatoes, shev and yogurt for a quick 'bhel'.

2 cups shelled tender fresh or frozen green peas
½ tsp sugar or jaggery
1 tsp salt

Spice paste:
3 tbsp grated fresh coconut
1 tbsp grated ginger
2 green chillies
1 tsp cumin seeds

Seasoning:
1½-2 tbsp vegetable oil or tup (ghee)
½ tsp mustard seeds
A pinch of asafoetida powder (hing)
¼ tsp turmeric powder

- Grind the spice paste ingredients fine.

- Heat the fat for seasoning in a skillet. Add mustard seeds and let them pop. Stir in asafoetida and turmeric.

- Raise heat and add green peas. Sauté for 2-3 minutes. Mix in spice paste. Cook covered for 7-10 minutes, stirring in the sweetener halfway through. Add salt, stir again and turn off the heat.

Note: For mature peas, add a little water and more sugar with the coconut paste.

SHENGDANYACHI AMTI

Peanut Sauce
Serves: 2-4   Time: 30 minutes

Serve this fasting day sauce with steamed varyacha bhat (p. 122). Do not use turmeric.

100 gms peanuts, coarsely ground
A pinch of sugar
1-1½ tsp salt

Spice paste:
2 green chillies
1½ tbsp grated fresh coconut
1 clove
½" stick cinnamon

Seasoning:
2 tbsp tup (ghee)
1 tsp cumin seeds
1 dried red chilli

- Grind the spice paste ingredients fine.
- Heat tup for seasoning in a pan. Add cumin seeds and let them pop. Add the red chilli.

- Stir in peanuts and sauté briefly. Mix in the spice paste and 2 cups water.

- Cook for15-20 minutes, till peanuts are tender and the water has reduced to a sauce.

JHUNKA-PITHLA-KADHI

Lip-Smacking Gram Flour Trio with Buttermilk
Contributors: Sudhakar & Meera Marathe

Jhunka, pithla and kadhi are made with gram flour and buttermilk in varying proportions. Jhunka, flavoured with mustard, chillies and ajwain/carum, often with tomatoes and onions thrown in, is thick but dry or moist. 'With fresh or stale sorghum roti, jhunka is delicious,' Dad says. 'Often country folk eat it cold, sometimes a day-old with crumbling stale bhakri.'

Jhunka is always drier than pithla, which is thick but definitely liquidy. Jhunka is also called korda or dry pithla! Similarly, pithla could be termed moist jhunka. Its consistency ranges from cake-batter-like to soup-like. Eat it with hot rice and tup or polya or bhakris.

Kadhi is a very popular thin, buttermilk soup, for which gram flour is the stabilizer and thickener.

JHUNKA

Gram Flour Topping with Seasoning
Serves: 4 Time: 20-30 minutes

200 gms gram flour (besan)
3 tbsp or more buttermilk or yogurt
1 tsp salt
½ tsp cumin powder
½ tsp red chilli powder
1 onion, finely chopped (optional)
2-3 small cloves garlic, finely chopped (optional)
1 tomato, finely chopped (optional)
1 tbsp vegetable oil

Seasoning:
1-2 tbsp vegetable oil
½ tsp mustard seeds
A pinch of asafoetida powder (hing)
½ tsp turmeric powder

Garnish:
4-5 sprigs of coriander leaves, finely chopped

- Put the gram flour into a bowl. Slowly whisk in buttermilk or yogurt and 1 cup of water till smooth. Add salt, cumin powder and chilli powder.

- Heat oil for seasoning in a deep skillet. Add mustard seeds and let them pop. Add asafoetida and turmeric.

- Add onion and garlic (if used) and sauté over high heat for 3-4 minutes. Add tomato (if used) and stir well.

- Reduce heat. Slowly pour in the gram flour-buttermilk mix, stirring continuously. Cook, stirring frequently for 5-7 minutes, till steam rises from the pan. The gram flour will thicken.

- Mix in 1 tbsp oil. Cook jhunka as dry as you like, stirring often.

- Serve hot or cold, garnished with coriander leaves.

PITHLA

Moist Gram Flour Topping with Buttermilk
Serves: 4   Time: 20-30 minutes

Up to 1 cup gram flour (besan)
700 ml thin, tart buttermilk or 1 cup yogurt whisked with 2 cups
warm water
½ tsp salt
A pinch of sugar
1 medium onion, finely chopped (optional)
1 large tomato, finely chopped (optional)
1 tsp red chilli powder (optional)

Seasoning:
3-4 tbsp vegetable oil
½ tsp mustard seeds
A pinch of asafoetida powder (hing)
¼ tsp turmeric powder
1-2 small cloves garlic, finely chopped (optional)
1 green chilli, sliced
5-7 curry leaves

Garnish:
4-5 sprigs of coriander leaves, finely chopped

- In a pan, heat 1 cup water till warm. Off the heat, slowly stir in ¾ cup gram flour (add more for thick pithla), whisking continuously to prevent lumps. Mix in buttermilk or liquified yogurt, salt and sugar. Set aside.

- Heat oil for seasoning in a deep pan. Add mustard seeds and let them pop. Add asafoetida and turmeric. Add garlic (if used) and sauté till fragrant. Stir in the chilli and curry leaves.

- Add onion (if used) and sauté over medium heat for 3-5 minutes, till golden. Mix in the tomato and chilli powder (if used) and sauté briefly. Raise heat to medium-high.

- Slowly pour in the gram flour-buttermilk mix, stirring continuously.

- Reduce heat to medium and stir for 10-15 minutes, to cook the pithla and thicken the sauce. Cook for another 5-7 minutes to thicken it further.

- Taste and add more salt if needed. Sprinkle generously with coriander leaves.

- Serve hot with rice and tup.

Note: Pithla thickens as long as it is being cooked and when it cools. To thin it out, add a little water and reheat briefly. Or mix buttermilk into your rice. Check the salt.

KULTHACHI PITHI
Vetch Flour Topping with Coconut Milk
Serves: 4   Time: 20-30 minutes

In the Konkan, pithla is sometimes made with vetch (horse gram) flour (kulthacha pith), which has a unique flavour. Konkani Hindus and Muslims eat kulthachi pithi with rice and roasted dry mackerel.

Use the quantities of ingredients given for pithla (opposite) for this variation. Season hot oil with cumin and chillies. Sauté finely chopped onion in it. Combine vetch flour and water, add it to the oil and cook, stirring. Thicken slightly before adding kokum, and coconut milk to replace the water.

DUDHACHA PITHLA

Gram Flour Topping Cooked in Milk
Serves: 4   Time: 20-30 minutes
Contributor: Prabhavati Gopalrao Deshpande

'This pithla may be special to our district. It uses dairy milk and the seasoning needs a little extra oil. Add as much gram flour to the milk as needed for your desired consistency. Serve immediately with bhakri.'

1 tbsp vegetable oil
½ tsp turmeric powder
A pinch of asafoetida powder (hing)
500 ml milk
4-5 large dried red chilli pieces
1-1½ tsp salt
1-1½ cups gram flour (besan)

* Heat oil in a wok over medium heat. Add turmeric and asafoetida. Stir and add milk, chillies and salt.

* Bring to a boil over medium heat and boil for 4-7 minutes. Stir and reduce heat to low.

* Slowly add the gram flour, stirring continuously to prevent lumps. Raise the heat slightly. Cook, stirring continuously for 7-10 minutes.

KADHI
Buttermilk-Gram Flour Sauce
Serves: 4   Time: 20-30 minutes

1 litre buttermilk or 2 cups yogurt whisked with 2 cups water
3-4 tbsp gram flour (besan) or more for a thicker kadhi
1-1½ tsp salt
A pinch of sugar (optional)

Seasoning:
2 tbsp tup (ghee) or vegetable oil
1 tsp cumin seeds
5-6 curry leaves or to taste
1-2 green chillies, sliced
1" piece of ginger, crushed
½ tsp turmeric powder

- Whisk the buttermilk or liquefied yogurt with gram flour, till smooth. Press out lumps.

- Heat tup or oil for seasoning in a deep pan till almost smoking. Add cumin seeds and let them pop. Add curry leaves, chillies and ginger. Stir in turmeric.

- Pour in gram flour-buttermilk mix, stirring continuously. Add salt and a pinch of sugar if the sauce is too tart.

- Simmer for 5-7 minutes. Taste and cook for 5-10 minutes more till the gram flour is cooked and the sauce is as thick as desired. The more you cook it, the more it thickens.

- Serve hot with white rice or mugachi khichadi (p. 127), papad and pickle.

Note: You can reheat kadhi before serving but connoisseurs will discern the flavour difference.

Poultry, Meat & Seafood

These recipes are gathered from all over Maharashtra, from the seafood-loving coast to the Kolhapur region famed for its mutton. Most recipes in the poultry section are for chicken, which is, interestingly enough, indigenous to India! There is one recipe for duck – East Indians serve it at weddings.

The meat section largely features 'mutton' (the Indian term for goat's meat) since that is the only meat many Indian Hindus eat, beef being taboo. Muslims and Christians do consume beef and it can easily replace mutton, as can lamb. East Indians do eat pork, forbidden to Muslims and generally eschewed by the Hindus. I include one East Indian pork dish because it is a great favourite.

The variety of local seafood is endless; however, since it may not be accessible to my readers, I simply introduce you to classics like fried pomfret or seafood in coconut-based gravies.

Unlike some cuisines, in which meat holds pride of place and is served in large portions, in India generally speaking, it is only one of several dishes eaten with the carbohydrate staple. One reason is that in Maharashtra, as in several other parts of India, a vegetarian diet has been specially valorized. The other is that in its hot climate, eating large quantities of meat was neither good for health nor essential for calories. Since meat was not raised for widespread consumption, it was largely unaffordable. So it was eaten sparingly on special occasions.

Also, before the time of refrigeration and preservatives, meat could not be stored so was cooked in small quantities and consumed the same day. A family of 4-6 would be thrilled to have 500 gms of meat to share at a meal (compared to the quarter to half pound or more individual servings offered in American homes or restaurants).

In order to overcome the problem of quantity and preservation, Indians treated meat like most of their other foods. They cooked it in spices after marinating it to flavour and tenderize it. (If marinating more than an hour, refrigerate meat, bringing it back to room temperature before cooking.) Often it was cooked in gravies, to spread flavour through the dish for everyone to relish. One or two pieces of meat were sufficient to satisfy each person.

In coastal regions with plentiful seafood (except in the monsoons when it was dangerous for fishing boats to venture out), people ate some every day. But again, for poor folk, consumption meant just a piece of fried fish or a little shrimp in gravy.

Like vegetables and fruit, seafood was dehydrated or pickled for use in lean periods: for example, the famous Bombay Duck (bombil, bummalo or lizardfish) a slim, long fish native to the waters off the Mumbai coast is cooked fresh and also dried (sukad bombil).

With most seafood, rice is the preferred staple. For meat and poultry, breads like poli and puri work fine. Digestive soups like solachi kadhi (p. 198) or molly (p. 199) traditionally accompany the meal.

Note: Avoid seafood during the monsoon. Shrimp can cause allergic reactions if not properly deveined. Wash, clean and devein it carefully.

Poultry

KHUDI
Sautéed East Indian Chicken
Serves: 4-6   Time: 1-1¼ hours
Contributors: The D'Penha family

The spice paste for this dish is also called khudi. You can make
mutton in this manner too.

1 kg chicken
2 tbsp vegetable oil
1 tbsp bottle masala (p. 51)
1-2 tsp salt
1-2 tsp tamarind pulp (p. 27) or lime juice
1 tsp garam masala powder (optional)
1-2 large potatoes, thickly sliced or quartered (optional)
2 tbsp tup (ghee) for potatoes (optional)

Khudi spice paste:
4 medium onions, finely sliced
4 green chillies, sliced
¼ fresh coconut, chopped or grated
2" piece of ginger
8 small cloves garlic

- Wash chicken, pat dry and cut into 1" or serving-size pieces.
- To make khudi spice paste, toast onions, chillies and coconut
  on a hot griddle for 7-10 minutes, stirring often, till soft and
  nearly golden brown. Grind into a paste with ginger and garlic.

- Heat oil in a large pan. Sauté the khudi paste for 5-7 minutes, till aromatic and slightly crisp. Stir in bottle masala.

- Add chicken and sauté over high heat for 5-7 minutes, till it begins to brown. Add 1-2 cups water and salt. Cook covered over low heat for 20-30 minutes till the chicken is tender. Stir occasionally. Sprinkle chicken with tamarind or lime juice and garam masala.

- Shallow-fry potatoes (if used) in 2 tbsp tup for 7-10 minutes, till almost tender. Add to chicken and heat for 2-3 minutes.

- Serve with rice or bread.

KOMBDI, JIRA GHALUN
Cumin-Scented Chicken
Serves: 4   Time: 1 hour marinating + 30 minutes cooking
Contributor: Anuradha Samant

Since cumin is added to the chicken just before serving, its fresh aroma and flavour is intense. Make this dish an appetizer, by reducing the gravy. Serve chicken on toothpicks, garnished with coriander and vinegar-marinated onions.

500 gms boneless, skinless chicken breast or bone-in drumsticks
4 tbsp vegetable oil
1½ medium onions, minced
1 medium tomato, finely chopped
3 tbsp cumin seeds, freshly roasted and powdered

Marinade:
2 tbsp yogurt
2 tbsp ginger-garlic paste
1 tbsp red chilli powder
1 tsp salt

Garnish:
4-6 sprigs of coriander leaves, finely chopped

- Wash chicken and pat dry. Cut chicken breasts (if used) into 1½" cubes (for an appetizer) or 3" chunks (for an entrée). Leave drumsticks (if used) whole.

- Combine the marinade ingredients together. Rub the paste into the chicken. Marinate covered for at least 1 hour.

- Heat oil in a deep pan. Brown the onions for 3-4 minutes. Add the tomato and sauté briefly.

- Add chicken and 2 cups hot water. Cook over medium heat for 12-15 minutes, stirring occasionally, till the chicken is tender and the water has reduced. To reduce the gravy further, increase the heat and cook for 5-10 minutes more.

- Stir cumin powder into the chicken. Garnish with coriander leaves and serve hot.

KOMBDI, KOTHIMBIR GHALUN
Coriander Chutney Chicken
Serves: 4-6 as a main course, 10-12 as an appetizer
Time: 2-8 hours marinating + 45 minutes cooking
Contributor: Surekha Sirsikar

1 kg chicken
2 tbsp vegetable oil or tup (ghee)
2 medium onions, minced

Chutney:
350-400 gms coriander leaves, stemmed
4-8 green chillies
6-8 small cloves garlic
4" piece of ginger

Juice of 1-2 limes
1½ tsp cumin powder
1½ tsp salt

• Wash chicken and pat dry. Cut chicken into 2" chunks (or 4-6 single serving pieces).

• Grind the chutney ingredients fine.

• Marinate the chicken in the chutney for 2-8 hours.

• Heat the fat in a large pan till bubbling hot. Brown the onions for 7-10 minutes.

• Add chicken pieces (reserve excess marinade) and sear them over high heat. Stir in the remaining marinade, reduce heat to medium-low and cook for 15-20 minutes, stirring occasionally. Thicken the gravy over slightly lower heat for 2-5 minutes.

• Serve hot with chapatti and batatyacha bharit (p. 145).

Variations: You can make this dish with mutton or fish (kingfish, monkfish, tilapia or halibut). Add 1 tsp each of turmeric and garam masala powders to the marinade for mutton. For fish, omit onions. Note that fish has a shorter cooking time than chicken.

KOMBDICHA RASSA

Chicken in Fragrant Gravy
Serves: 4-6   Time: 1 hour marinating + 1 hour cooking

1 kg chicken
4 small onions, minced
2 medium tomatoes, minced
4 tsp grated fresh coconut, ground to a smooth paste

Spice paste:
2" piece of ginger
12 small cloves garlic
2 green chillies
3 almonds

Marinade:
3 tbsp tart yogurt
1-1½ tsp red chilli powder
1 tsp turmeric powder
1½ tsp salt

Spice powder:
4 dried red Kashmiri chillies
10 black peppercorns
3 x 1" sticks cinnamon
3 cloves
2 green cardamoms
2 tsp poppy seeds (khus-khus)
2 tsp coriander seeds
1 tsp royal cumin seeds (shah jeera)
½ tsp fennel seeds (badi saunf)
¼ tsp freshly grated nutmeg (jaiphal)

Seasoning:
3 tbsp vegetable oil
2 bay leaves (tej patta)
1" stick cinnamon
1 black cardamom

Garnish:
6-10 sprigs of coriander leaves, finely chopped

- Wash chicken, pat dry and cut into 4" pieces.

- Grind the spice paste ingredients fine.

- Rub spice paste into chicken. Whisk the marinade ingredients till smooth and rub into chicken. Marinate chicken for 1-3 hours.

- To make the spice powder, toast spices separately on a hot griddle for 15-40 seconds each. Grind together into a dry powder.

- Heat oil for seasoning in a large pan to almost smoking. Reduce heat. Stir in bay leaves, cinnamon and cardamom. Raise heat to medium-high. Add the onions and brown for 4-5 minutes.

- Stir in spice powder. Add tomatoes and sauté for 4-5 minutes, till they release their juices and the oil begins to leave the edges of the pan.

- Raise heat to high, add chicken pieces and sear them for 4-5 minutes. Reduce heat to low. Cook covered for 10-15 minutes, stirring occasionally.

- Stir in coconut paste and, if needed, up to ¾ cup water. Cook covered for 10-15 minutes, till the chicken is tender and fragrant.

- Garnish with coriander leaves and serve hot.

Variation: To roast the chicken, rub it with the spice paste and marinate as above. Prepare the seasoning. Sear the chicken in it, browning on all sides. Stir in coconut and ¼-½ cup water. Cook covered for 10 minutes. Transfer to a roasting pan with all the juices. Bake at 180°C (350°F) for 30-40 minutes, till tender. Baste every 7 minutes or so with the juices. For the last 10 minutes, cover chicken with aluminium foil. Remove chicken from the oven and rest covered for 15 minutes. Heat pan juices on the stove to serve as gravy.

DUCK MOILE
East Indian Feast Day Duck
Serves: 4-6   Time: 1½-2 hours
Contributor: Iris D'Penha

East Indians traditionally make duck moile for feast days. A typical feast 'would also include sarpatel (p. 253), vindaloo, pork sausages, a stuffed chicken roast (for extra special occasions, a stuffed roast suckling pig), corned tongue (marinated in lime, salt and saltpetre for 2-3 days, cooked and sliced), served with boiled green peas, potato chops (p. 252), fugias (p. 110), chitaps (rice pancakes), wedding rice (pulao garnished with fried onions, cashews, plums and sliced boiled eggs) and a sliced beetroot, tomato, cucumber and onion salad.' Dessert would include bol marie (p. 319) and marzipan.

1 kg duck, plucked
2-4 tbsp wholewheat flour (atta)
1 tbsp + 3 tbsp white vinegar
1 tsp salt
3 tbsp tup (ghee)
2 tbsp sugar
500 gms onions, sliced in rings
½" piece of ginger, julienned
5-6 small cloves garlic, julienned
6 green chillies, slit and seeded
1 tbsp bottle masala (p. 51)
2 tsp garam masala powder
250 gms potatoes, thickly sliced or quartered (optional)
2 tbsp tup (ghee – optional)

• Rub the duck with flour to remove stubborn feathers. Cut into fairly large pieces—thighs, legs, etc. Mix 1 tbsp vinegar with 1 litre water. Wash the duck well with this liquid 2-3 times. Drain in a colander.

- Place the duck in a large pan with salt and ½ cup water. Cook covered over low heat for about 30 minutes, till the water is absorbed.

- Add 3 tbsp tup to the duck. Sauté for about 10 minutes, till light golden but not brown. Add sugar to glaze the meat. Sauté for 2-3 minutes.

- Transfer the duck, without the fat, to a bowl. Add onions to the pan containing the hot fat and sauté for 3-5 minutes, till soft and translucent. Add ginger, garlic and chillies and sauté briefly.

- Sprinkle in bottle masala and sauté for 4-5 minutes, adding 1 tbsp water to prevent it sticking. When it is browned and aromatic, add up to ½ cup water, depending on the bird's tenderness, and bring to a boil.

- Return duck to the pan. Cook covered over low heat for about 20 minutes, till tender.

- Mix in the remaining vinegar and simmer for about 10 minutes, till fat floats to the top. Add garam masala and cook for 15 minutes more, stirring occasionally. Shallow-fry potatoes (if used) in 2 tbsp tup for 7-10 minutes, till tender.

- Add to the duck and serve hot.

Note: Use the same recipe for beef or tongue (use slightly less meat, about 750 gms).

Meat

KOLHAPURI MUTTON: PANDHRA RASSA, TAMBDA RASSA, SUKA MUTNA, PULAVA
Kolhapur-Style Four Dish Meat Fiesta
Serves: 4   Time: 2-3 hours
Contributor: Anuradha Samant

The fame of Kolhapuri mutton stretches beyond the borders of Maharashtra. It is known to be hot, spicy, colourful and flavourful. But not many people know that Kolhapuri mutton actually consists of three dishes. Since meat was expensive, when a Kolhapuri family did buy it, they took one batch of meat through three cooking processes to make three rich dishes served with a fragrant mutton-spice rice. Plan to spend time and effort making this feast. Have the traditional Kolhapuri masala (p. 49) on hand to flavour the meat. Then invite friends over to share in the fruits of your labour. Here is the menu for a traditional meal:

The first Course: Pandhra rassa (white soup)
The second Course: Tambda rassa (red sauce) and sukha mutna (sautéed mutton) with chapatti, white rice and dahi-kanda (p. 148)
The third Course: Pulava (mutton-spice rice) with the above dishes.

BASIC STOCK

1 kg mutton or chicken
1" piece of ginger
4-6 small cloves garlic
2 tsp salt
1 tbsp vegetable oil (for chicken)

Poultry, Meat & Seafood   243

- Wash meat, pat dry and cut into 1½" cubes.

- Grind ginger and garlic into a paste. Rub paste and salt into the meat or chicken.

Mutton:

- Cover meat with 9 cups boiling water. Pressure-cook for 10-15 minutes after cooker reaches full pressure (4-5 whistles), or cook on the stove top for 1-1¼ hours, tightly covered over low heat, stirring occasionally, till the meat flakes easily. Add a little more water if needed.

Chicken:

- Heat oil in a large pan. Sauté chicken for 4-5 minutes, till aromatic and golden. Add boiling water and cook covered over low heat for at least 30 minutes, till tender.

Stock:

- When the mutton or chicken is cooked, strain the stock into another pan, retaining ½ cup with the meat.

PANDHRA RASSA
White Soup

Spice paste:
5 cashew nuts
5 black peppercorns
2 cloves
½" stick cinnamon
1 tsp rice grains
1 tsp poppy seeds (khus-khus)
1 tsp sesame seeds (til)
1 tsp seeds from dried red chillies

Soup:
1 cup thick coconut milk
Juice of ½ a lime
4 cups mutton or chicken stock (p. 243)
1 tbsp tup (ghee)
3 green cardamoms
2 dried red chillies
1 tsp salt

Garnish:
A few sprigs of coriander leaves, finely chopped

- Soak spice paste ingredients in water for 1 hour. Drain and grind into a fine paste. Stir the paste, coconut milk and lime juice into the stock.

- Heat tup in a pan to almost smoking. Add cardamoms and chillies. Reduce heat and pour in stock. Cook for 7-10 minutes, stirring continuously to prevent curdling. Add salt.

- Serve in small bowls, garnished with coriander leaves.

TAMBDA RASSA
Red Sauce

Spice paste:
1 tbsp vegetable oil
2 small onions, minced
½ cup grated fresh coconut
1 green chilli
2 small cloves garlic
4 black peppercorns
2 cloves
½" stick cinnamon
½ tsp poppy seeds (khus-khus)

Sauce:
4½ cups meat or chicken stock (p. 243)
2 tbsp vegetable oil
1 medium tomato, diced
1 tbsp sesame seeds (til), ground to a fine paste
2 tbsp Kolhapuri masala or to taste (p. 49)
Juice of ½ a lime
1-1½ tsp salt

Seasoning:
1 tsp vegetable oil
1 tsp coriander seeds

Garnish:
A few sprigs of coriander leaves, finely chopped

- Heat oil for spice paste in a small pan. Sauté onions, reserving 1 tbsp. Add the coconut, chilli, garlic, whole spices and poppy seeds and sauté for 3-5 minutes, till golden brown and aromatic. Grind into a fine paste.

- Meanwhile, bring the stock to a boil.

- Heat 2 tbsp oil in a large pan. Sauté the reserved onion. Stir in the tomato over medium-high heat. Add spice paste, sesame seed paste and Kolhapuri masala, stirring continuously.

- Pour in boiling stock. Bring back to a boil and cook for 4-5 minutes. Stir in lime juice and salt. Turn off the heat.

- Heat oil for seasoning in a small wok. When almost smoking, add coriander seeds and let them pop. Stir into the sauce.

- Garnish with coriander leaves and serve hot as a soup or a topping for white rice or pulava (p. 248).

SUKHA MUTNA
Sautéed Mutton

If you used chicken to make the basic stock (p. 243), use the cooked chicken for this dish.

Spice paste:
2 tbsp vegetable oil
1 large onion, minced
150 gms dried coconut (kopra), grated
7 black peppercorns
3 cloves
1" stick cinnamon
1 tbsp coriander seeds
1 tsp sesame seeds (til)
1 tsp poppy seeds (khus-khus)
½" piece of ginger
5 small cloves garlic

Mutton:
1 cup vegetable oil
2 large onions, minced
2 medium tomatoes, finely chopped
5 tbsp Kolhapuri masala (p. 49)
1 kg boiled mutton (p. 243)
½ cup meat stock (p. 243)
Juice of one lime

Garnish:
A few sprigs of coriander leaves, finely chopped
2 green chillies, slit

• Heat oil for the spice paste in a skillet. Sauté onion for 3-5 minutes, till golden. Add the remaining spice paste ingredients. Toast gently for about 5 minutes, till aromatic. Grind to a fine paste.

- Heat 1 cup oil in a large pan. Brown onions for 10-12 minutes over high heat. Add tomatoes and sauté for 3-5 minutes.

- Stir in the spice paste and Kolhapuri masala and sauté for 2-3 minutes till fragrant.

- Mix in meat. Pour in stock and simmer for 10 minutes, stirring often, till the liquid cooks out completely.

- Sprinkle the meat with lime juice and garnish with coriander leaves and chillies. Serve hot.

PULAVA
Mutton-Spice Rice

Pulava, traditionally served with Kolhapuri mutton, can be made separately from the rest of the feast.

Measure the rice after washing it. Use *exactly* 1½ times as much liquid as rice. Cook leftover rice grains as white rice.

250 gms mutton
1 tbsp ginger-garlic paste
1-2 tsp salt
2 tbsp vegetable oil
4 black peppercorns
2 cloves
1" stick cinnamon
1 green cardamom
4 dried red chillies
2 bay leaves (tej patta)
2 cups washed and drained small-grained rice
1 tsp garam masala powder
½ cup grated fresh coconut

Garnish:
A few sprigs of coriander leaves, finely chopped

- In a medium pan, combine 3 cups water, meat, ginger-garlic paste and salt. Cook covered over medium-low heat for 35-40 minutes, till tender. Strain and measure the stock (you need 3 cups. Reserve extra stock for another purpose). Check salt, adding more if needed.

- Heat oil in a large pan to almost smoking. Add whole spices, chillies and bay leaves. Stir for about 30 seconds, till aromatic.

- Add rice and sauté over medium-high heat. Mix in meat and sauté for 4-5 minutes.

- Stir in stock, garam masala and coconut. Cook covered for 15-20 minutes, till the rice is tender and fluffy.

- Serve hot garnished with coriander leaves.

LONVAS

East Indian Mutton with Bottle Gourd
Serves: 4   Time: 1 hour
Contributor: Iris D'Penha

You can substitute okra, cabbage or radish for the gourd and replace mutton with beef or shrimp.

500 gms mutton
½ tsp + ¾ tsp salt
2 tbsp vegetable oil
8 small cloves garlic, crushed
3 tbsp bottle masala (p. 51)
250 gms bottle gourd (lauki/ghia), washed, peeled and cut into 1" dice
½ cup coconut milk (p. 29)
¼ cup tamarind pulp or to taste (p. 27)

- Wash mutton and cut into 1" pieces.

- Cook mutton covered in a medium pan with ¼ cup water and ½ tsp salt for about 30 minutes, till tender (add up to ¼ cup more water if needed). Stir occasionally to prevent sticking. There should be some liquid left in the pan once the meat is cooked.

- Heat oil in another large pan. Sauté, but do not brown the garlic. Add bottle masala and sauté for 2-3 minutes.

- Stir in the gourd, meat and stock (if minimal, add a few tbsp water). Cook covered over medium-low heat stirring occasionally for about 15 minutes, till the gourd is tender.

- Mix in coconut milk and up to ¾ tsp salt. Cook for 5-7 minutes. Stir in tamarind and warm through.

- Serve immediately.

MALVANI MUTTON

Serves: 4   Time: 2-8 hours marinating + 1½ hours cooking

500 gms mutton on the bone
2 tbsp ginger-garlic paste
1-2 tsp salt
3 tbsp vegetable oil
2 medium onions, minced
1 small tomato, finely chopped
Red chilli powder to taste (optional)
¼ tsp turmeric powder
½ cup thick coconut milk (p. 29)

Spice paste:
2 tbsp vegetable oil
1 medium onion, finely sliced
3 small cloves garlic

4 dried red chillies
4 black peppercorns
3 cloves
1" stick cinnamon
1 tsp coriander seeds
1 tsp sesame seeds (til)
½ tsp poppy seeds (khus-khus)
¼ tsp royal cumin seeds (shah jeera)
1 cup grated fresh coconut

- Wash mutton, pat dry and cut into 1" pieces. Rub it with ginger-garlic paste and salt. Marinate covered for 2-8 hours.

- Heat oil in a medium pan. Brown the minced onions over medium heat for 5-7 minutes. Stir in tomato and cook for 3-5 minutes.

- Add mutton and sauté for 5-7 minutes. Cover pan with a lipped lid or metal plate and pour some water on it. Cook for 10 minutes over medium-low heat. Stir in warm water from the lid.

- Add chilli powder and turmeric. Cook covered for 30-40 minutes, till tender, stirring occasionally, adding water as needed.

- Meanwhile, heat oil for the spice paste in a skillet. Sauté the sliced onion over medium-high heat for 3-5 minutes, till golden.

- Add garlic and stir-fry for 2-3 minutes. Stir in remaining ingredients for spice paste except coconut. Sauté for 3-5 minutes, till aromatic. Add coconut and sauté for 2-3 minutes, till golden.

- Grind mixture into a fine paste.

- When the meat has cooked, stir in the paste. Bring to a boil and cook for 4-5 minutes.

- Add coconut milk and warm through before serving.

POTATO CHOPS

East Indian Meat and Potato Croquettes
Serves: 4-6   Time: 1 hour
Special equipment: paper-lined platter
Contributor: The D'Penha Family

2 tbsp tup (ghee)
2 large onions, finely minced
1" piece of ginger, finely minced
6 small cloves garlic, finely minced
2-3 green chillies, finely minced
500 gms minced or ground mutton or other meat
3 medium tomatoes, finely minced
1 tsp + ¾-1 tsp salt
½ tsp ground black pepper
½ tsp garam masala powder
Juice of 1 lime
3-4 mint leaves, finely minced
1 kg old potatoes, washed and boiled
1 egg
2 cups breadcrumbs
Up to 500 ml vegetable oil for shallow-frying

- Heat tup in a skillet. Sauté onions, ginger, garlic and chillies over medium heat for 3-5 minutes, till light brown. Raise heat slightly. Stir in ground meat, tomatoes and 1 tsp salt. Cook covered with 2 cups water for 12-15 minutes, stirring occasionally.

- When the meat is almost done, add pepper, garam masala, lime juice and mint. Cook for 2-3 minutes more. Cool completely.

- Peel and mash potatoes. Mix in ¾-1 tsp salt.

- Shape a handful of potato mash into a shallow cup against your cupped palm. Place 1 tbsp meat into the cup and cover with a little more mash. Smooth out the edges to seal the ball. The croquettes should be round but slightly flattened. Shape all the croquettes placing them on a plate, covered with a damp cloth.

- Whisk the egg in a bowl and place the breadcrumbs on a plate on the counter next to the croquettes. Dip each croquette in the egg, drain well and press it into the breadcrumbs till evenly covered.

- Heat a little oil in a skillet over medium-low heat. Shallow-fry 3-4 croquettes at a time for 2-3 minutes per side, till evenly brown and hot. Drain each croquettes well against the side of the pan. Place on the paper-lined platter. Replenish the oil and bring it to the right temperature before frying a fresh batch of croquettes.

- Serve hot with vinegar-marinated onions. For a quick lunch, make a chop sandwich!

SARPATEL

East Indian Pork in Vinegar
Serves: 4-6   Time: 1-1¼ hours
Contributor: Jeanne D'Penha

East Indian sarpatel is different from its Goan cousin of the same name, being made with dried spices and bottle masala rather than a fresh spice paste. For special occasions, East Indians make enough sarpatel to last a month. 'The vinegar pickles the pork and its taste improves with time.'

1 kg boneless pork, washed
250 gms pork liver, washed
½ tsp turmeric powder
1-2 tsp salt

1½ tbsp + 1½ tbsp bottle masala (p. 51)
2 tbsp vegetable oil
100 gms garlic, finely slivered
100 gms ginger, finely slivered
6-8 green chillies, slit and seeded
¼ cup white vinegar

Garnish:
A few sprigs of coriander leaves, finely chopped

- Wash the pork and liver.

- In a large pan, cook the pork, liver, turmeric, salt and 1½ tbsp bottle masala with 2 cups water for about 30 minutes. Drain and reserve stock (about 2 cups). Cool meat before cutting into small dice.

- Heat oil in a heavy-bottomed pan. Sauté garlic, ginger and chillies for about 3 minutes, till the garlic turns light pink. Add the remaining bottle masala and sauté over low heat for 2 minutes.

- Raise heat to medium-high. Sear the diced meat and stir in vinegar and reserved stock. Reduce heat to medium-low and simmer covered for about 30 minutes, till the gravy thickens and oil rises to the top.

- Stir in more salt if needed.

- Garnish with coriander leaves before serving the sarpatel hot or cold with bread or fugia (p. 110).

Seafood

BANGDA MASALA
Spicy Saraswat Mackerel
Serves: 3-4   Time: 3 hours marinating + 20-30 minutes cooking
Special equipment: paper-lined platter
Contributor: Maya Kale-Laud

Serve the mackerel with or without gravy.

Fish:
6 medium or 3 large mackerel, slit along the belly and gutted
10-12 small cloves garlic
1 tsp + 1 tsp salt
10 tbsp rice flour
4 tbsp semolina (sooji/rava – optional)
1 cup vegetable oil

Coriander paste:
1 bunch of fresh coriander leaves, stemmed
½ tsp turmeric powder
1 tbsp red chilli powder or to taste
½ tsp goda masala (p. 48) or garam masala powder
1 tsp vegetable oil
1-2 tsp white vinegar

Gravy:
1½ tbsp vegetable oil
1 tsp cumin seeds
½ tsp turmeric powder
1 tsp red chilli powder or to taste
2 medium onions, minced
Reserved coriander paste
1½ tsp salt or to taste

Garnish:
A few sprigs of coriander leaves, finely chopped

Fish:
- Slit the larger mackerel along the belly, parallel to the spine, to open and halve the fish, while keeping the two sides connected. Briskly wash the fish, pat dry and place on a platter.

- Make a coarse paste with garlic and 1 tsp salt. Smear this on the fish. Set aside for at least 30 minutes.

- Grind the coriander paste ingredients fine. Apply the paste on the fish, inside and out. Marinate covered for 2-3 hours. Reserve extra paste.

- Combine rice flour and semolina on a small plate. Press fish into it, coating both sides evenly.

- Heat some oil on a griddle. Shallow-fry 2-3 fish pieces at a time for 3-4 minutes per side (4-5 minutes for whole mackerel), till golden and crisp. Drain well and place on the paper-lined platter.

- Serve with lime wedges and freshly sliced onion.

Gravy:
- Heat oil in a deep pan till almost smoking. Add cumin seeds and let them pop. Add turmeric and chilli powder.

- Add onions and sauté for 5-7 minutes, till brown. Mix in reserved coriander paste and salt and cook for 1-2 minutes.

- Stir in 1½ cups water. Bring to a boil over medium-high heat. Cook uncovered for 5-7 minutes, till thickened.

- Add the fried fish and bring to a boil. Simmer for 5 minutes.

- Serve hot over hot white rice, garnished with coriander leaves.

BANGDYACHI KOSHIMBIR
Dried Mackerel 'Salad'

'Roasted dry bangda is very flavourful,' Mom recalls. 'My mother made a wonderful koshimbir with it.' Rehydrate sun-dried mackerel in water or rub a little oil on it and roast lightly on a griddle for 3-5 minutes. Chop it into small chunks. Add finely chopped onions, coriander leaves, a pinch of salt (remember, the fish is already salty) and red chilli powder. Squeeze fresh lime juice over. Stir and serve immediately.

POPLETCHI KADHI
Gravied Pomfret
Serves: 4 Time: 30-40 minutes
Contributor: Surekha Sirsikar

500 gms pomfret or other firm white fish fillets
1½-2 tsp salt
¾ large fresh coconut, grated
1 tsp rice flour or gram flour (besan)
½ cup tamarind pulp or to taste (p. 27)
1½ tbsp vegetable oil
2 large red onions, minced

Coconut-spice paste:
¼ large fresh coconut, grated
1 tsp coriander seeds
1 tsp red chilli powder or to taste
6-8 black peppercorns
A pinch of turmeric powder

Garnish:
6-7 sprigs of coriander leaves, finely chopped

- Wash fish and pat dry. Lightly sprinkle fish with salt.

- Extract milk from the coconut (p. 29). Stir in rice flour or gram flour, pressing out lumps.

- Grind ingredients for coconut-spice paste fine, with some tamarind pulp, if needed.

- Heat oil in a large pan. Sauté onions over medium-low heat for 2-4 minutes, till pink.

- Increase the heat to medium. Add fish fillets and sear on each side for 1-2 minutes. Add up to 2 tbsp water. Cover pan and steam the fish over low heat for 5-7 minutes.

- Gently stir in tamarind, coconut-spice paste and coconut milk. Bring the gravy to a boil and remove from heat immediately; do not cook it longer.

- Garnish with coriander leaves and serve immediately with hot white rice.

PATHARÉ-PRABHU BHARLELA POPLET
Stuffed Pomfret Patharé-Prabhu Style
Serves: 4   Time: 30-40 minutes
Contributors: Deepak & Ujwal Mankar

This pair of simple recipes is great for Indian or Western menus. Traditionally the fish was baked in a bhatti (oven). Use a conventional oven or pan-fry the fish.

2 medium whole pomfret, cleaned and slit down the centre or
500 gms thinly filleted fish (surmai, whitefish, red snapper, tilapia)
A pinch of salt
1 tsp vegetable oil, for pan-frying

½ fresh coconut, grated
1 packed cup coriander leaves
4–5 small cloves garlic
2 small green chillies
½ tsp salt
Juice of ½ a lime

Onion and tomato filling:
1 tsp vegetable oil
4–5 small cloves garlic, minced
1 green chilli, minced (optional)
1 small onion, minced
1 small tomato, minced
½ tsp salt
A handful of fresh coriander leaves, finely chopped

Garnish:
6-7 sprigs of coriander leaves, finely chopped

Chutney filling:

• Grind the chutney ingredients fine, without water if possible.

Onion and tomato filling:

• Heat oil in a small skillet (a larger one if pan-frying the fish).
  Sauté the garlic briefly. Add chilli (if used), onion and tomato
  and sauté for about 5 minutes. Mix in salt and coriander leaves.

• Lightly mash ingredients with the back of a spoon, retaining
  some texture.

Fish:

• Wash fish and pat dry. Sprinkle fish lightly with salt. Stuff
  whole fish with the filling of choice.

To bake fish:

• Bake whole stuffed fish in an oven preheated to 150°C (350°F)
  for 15-20 minutes.

- For fillets, spread a little stuffing on each. Carefully roll up the fillet, skewering it in place with a toothpick. Bake for 12-15 minutes.

To pan-fry fish:

- Heat oil in a skillet. Spread filling on one fillet and top it with another, pressing down gently to hold it in place.

- Pan fry the whole stuffed fish or the fillets over medium-low heat for 5-7 minutes on each side, flipping them over gently, ensuring no filling falls out

To serve:

- Garnish fish with coriander leaves. Serve immediately with hot white rice and molly (p. 199).

TALLELA POPLET
Fried Pomfret
Serves: 4   Time: 30 minutes marinating + 30 minutes cooking

Serve fried fish with lime wedges and lime-marinated, sliced onions. Fry fish just before serving. Try marinating shrimp this way too and deep or shallow-fry them

500 gms pomfret or firm white fish fillets
2 tsp salt
3 tsp turmeric powder
1 cup vegetable oil
50 gms fine rice flour
2½ tsp red chilli powder

Garnish:
Lime wedges

- Wash fish fillets and pat dry. Rub fillets with salt and turmeric 30 minutes before frying.

- Heat 2-3 tbsp oil on the griddle for 4-5 minutes, till very hot.

- Spread rice flour in a small plate. Sprinkle some chilli powder over each fillet. Transfer it to the rice flour, pressing down to coat both sides evenly.

- Shallow-fry 6-8 fillets at a time for 3-5 minutes per side. Drizzle a little oil around them. Turn fillets when the first side is firm and golden brown. Replenish oil as needed. Drain well before serving.

- Garnish with lime wedges and serve immediately.

Variations:

- **Meera's Version:** Mom marinates the fish in salt, turmeric, 1 tbsp lime juice, ½ tbsp ginger-garlic paste and 1 tsp red chilli powder.

- **Malvani Version:** Rub 1 tsp kokum extract into the fish before frying.

KHADKHADI

'Noisy' Shrimp

Serves: 2-4 Time: 30 minutes marinating + 30 minutes cooking

Contributor: Maya Kale-Laud

Tasty shrimp make a great snack on toast or an unusual pickle. Khadkhadné means to bubble and boil: that is what this dish does. Do not overcook the shrimp or they will taste tough.

250-500 gms shrimp
1½ tsp red chilli powder or to taste

¼ tsp turmeric powder
1½ tsp salt or to taste
2¼ tbsp vegetable oil
¼ tsp mustard seeds
3-4 tbsp thick tamarind paste (p. 27)

Coconut paste:
170 gms fresh coconut, grated
2 small cloves garlic

- Shell, devein and wash shrimp. Toss them in chilli powder, turmeric and salt, 30 minutes before cooking.

- Grind the coconut paste ingredients fine.

- Heat oil in a small skillet till almost smoking. Add mustard seeds and let them pop.

- Add coconut paste and sauté over low heat for 7-10 minutes, till pink. Add the shrimp and sauté briefly.

- Stir in tamarind and 1 cup water. Cook over medium heat for 7-12 minutes, stirring occasionally till the liquid evaporates.

- Serve hot or at room temperature.

Note: Refrigerate khadkhadi 'pickle' in a clean, airtight jar for up to 4-5 days.

MALVANI MASA/KOLAMBI KADHI

Malvan Fish/Shrimp with Sauce
Serves: 4-6 Time: 40 minutes
Contributor: Pragati Parkar

Sindhudurg borders northern Goa and though cross-cultural influences are par for the course, its cuisine is distinctly unique, known as Malvani, as opposed to Konkani or Goan. The Bhandari community there is well known for its non-vegetarian dishes, especially kombadi vadé (chicken and puri), and amboli. For this recipe, Pragati recommends pomfret, black pomfret (halwa), seer, salmon, shrimp, mackerel or silver barfish.

Some families vary the chillies used, adding Sankeshwari to the Bedgi, which subtly alters the taste. 'In the summer, when raw mango (kairi) is available, use it instead of kokum for a unique flavour.' The region's Muslims add ½ tsp cumin and use coconut milk instead of paste.

750 gms fish (6-7 fillets) or shrimp
1-1½ tsp salt
2 tbsp vegetable oil
1½ medium onions, finely chopped
½ tsp turmeric powder
4-5 kokum (amsul)

Spice paste:
1 tsp coriander seeds
7-8 dried red Bedgi chillies
4-5 black peppercorns
1 tsp rice grains
½ fresh coconut, grated
4-5 cloves garlic
½ medium onion

Garnish:
4-5 sprigs coriander leaves, washed and finely chopped

- Shell and devein shrimp if used. Wash fish or shrimp and pat dry. Sprinkle with salt.

- To make the spice paste, soak coriander seeds, chillies, peppercorns and rice grains in water for 15 minutes. Drain. Grind all spice paste ingredients fine.

- Heat oil in a large pan to almost smoking. Sauté the chopped onions for 2-3 minutes, till golden.

- Add the spice paste and turmeric and sauté for 2-3 minutes. Stir in 1-1½ cups water and kokum. Simmer over low heat for 10-15 minutes.

- Slide in the seafood. Cook for 8-10 minutes, till tender. Add more salt if needed.

- Garnish with coriander leaves and serve immediately with hot white rice, fried fish and solachi kadhi (p. 198).

Note: For mackerel and silver barfish, use 8-9 Goa spiceberries (triphala). Remove their seeds, soak in water for 2-3 minutes and add along with kokum.

MUSTARD SHRIMP

East Indian Shrimp with Ground Mustard Seeds
Serves: 4
Time: 1 hour soaking + 30 minutes marinating +
20 minutes cooking
Contributor: Iris D'Penha

'Mom makes this dish with fresh white, sweet prawns, which are great with the spicy masala,' says Jeanne. 'She leaves the heads and skin on. They are quite tasty this way.' If you prefer, shell the prawns.

500 gms large shrimp
2 tbsp vegetable oil

Spice paste:
3 tbsp mustard seeds
6-8 dried red chillies
6 small cloves garlic
2" piece of ginger
½ tsp turmeric powder
A pinch of sugar
1 medium onion
1½ tbsp sea salt
100-150 ml white vinegar

- Shell and devein the shrimp. Wash them and pat dry.

- Soak mustard seeds in ½ cup water for 1 hour. Drain, reserving the soaking water. Grind all spice paste ingredients fine. Add a few drops of the reserved water if needed.

- Marinate shrimp in the paste for 30 minutes.

- Transfer shrimp with the marinade to a small pan. Add oil and mix well. Simmer covered for 15-17 minutes, till cooked.

- Add reserved soaking water, if needed, for the gravy. Raise the heat, bring to a boil and turn off the heat.

MUSTARD SHRIMP

East Indian Shrimp with Ground Mustard Seeds

Serves 4

Time: 1 hour soaking + 30 minutes marinating +
20 minutes cooking

Contributor: Irsy Toth

Mom makes this dish with fresh white, sweet prawns, which are great with the spicy masala, an edge/taste. She leaves the heads and skin on. I buy quite easy that way. I buy prawns, shell the prawns.

500 g/large shrimp
3 tbsp vegetable oil

Spice paste:
3 tbsp mustard seeds
4-8 dried red chillies
6 small cloves garlic
2" piece of ginger
½ tsp turmeric powder
A pinch of sugar
1 medium onion
1½ tbsp sea salt
100-125 ml white vinegar

- Shell and devein the shrimp. Wash, pat and pat dry.

- Soak mustard seeds in ¼ cup water for 1 hour, then, reserving the soaking water. Grind all spice paste ingredients, fine. Add a few drops of the reserved water if needed.

- Marinate shrimp in the paste for 30 minutes.

- Transfer shrimp with the marinade to a small pan. Add oil and mix well, simmer covered for 15-17 minutes, till cooked.

- Add reserved soaking water, if needed, for the gravy. Raise the heat, bring to a boil and turn off the heat.

Chutneys, Raitas, Pickles & Preserves | 285

Chutneys, Relishes, Pickles & Preserves

One of the reasons chutneys and pickles are so popular in Maharashtra is that people want a tart-spicy-sweet taste to perk up their meal. Historically, condiments were also an important source of vitamins and minerals, and even some proteins. Even today, millions of mainly rural working people often eat their bread just with some chutney. For many, the expression 'chutney-bhakar' means a meal.

In the West, chutney is generally 'a spicy condiment made of fruits or vegetables with vinegar, spices, and sugar.'[28] Noted Indian food historian, K. T. Achaya writes: 'In colonial times [chutney] was used to denote a preserve, usually of mango slices, slightly spiced and placed in sugar syrup. These were manufactured ... mostly for export to England (like Major Grey's and Bengal Club chutneys).'[29]

But the original Indian range of chutneys implied chilli-hot, sometimes slightly sweet condiments made of finely ground or powdered, even roughly smashed ingredients, to be eaten fresh or within a few days (occasionally weeks) of preparation. Chutney might be a dry or moist, 'freshly ground relish . . . of ingredients such as the coconut, sesame, groundnuts, puffed Bengal gram, several dhals, raw mangoes, tomato, mint leaves . . .'[30] Marathi chutneys are many, utilizing unusual ingredients from curry leaf to bitter gourd.

While a chutney can be made on the spur of the moment, Indian pickles, generally preserved in oil, take more effort and planning and generally last longer (though there are some fresh pickle-like chutneys in oil). They are made once or twice a year, in large quantities.

Fruits are conserved in sugar or jaggery syrup and most are eaten like a jam with bread, others are considered tonics: gulkand (rose petal preserves) or moravla (preserved gooseberries, p. 296). Pickles and preserves are notoriously tricky to make successfully. Read more (p. 287 and in other sources) before attempting them.

Store chutneys, pickles and preserves in airtight jars, in a cool place.

Chutney Powders

DANYACHI CHUTNEY
Peanut Chutney
Makes: about 250 gms   Time: 20 minutes
Special equipment: winnowing fan

Peanut chutney, in various forms, is common across Maharashtra.
It is great to have on hand when food needs a little pick-me-up!

250 gms raw peanuts
¼ tsp sesame or peanut oil
4-5 dried red chillies
1½ tsp cumin seeds
1 tsp sugar
¾ tsp salt

- Roast peanuts on a griddle for 8-10 minutes stirring often, till
  their skins darken and peel off easily when rubbed (roast
  skinned peanuts for 5-7 minutes, till golden). Cool slightly on
  a platter. Rub nuts to loosen skins and remove by hand or
  with a winnowing fan

- Oil the same hot griddle. Toast chillies for 2-3 minutes, till
  crisp. Toast cumin for 2-3 minutes, stirring frequently, till
  aromatic.

- Carefully pound half the peanuts with chillies, cumin, sugar
  and salt (pulse on a food processor), making a dry, powdery
  chutney. Toss ingredients occasionally. Add the remaining
  peanuts and powder well.

KADHILIMBACHI CHUTNEY
Curry Leaf Chutney
Makes: 1 cup   Time: 20 minutes

1 tbsp vegetable oil
2 tbsp split, husked Bengal gram (chana dal)
2 tbsp split, husked black gram (urad dal)
1 packed cup fresh curry leaves, washed and thoroughly wiped dry
7-8 green chillies
1-1½ tsp salt

- Heat and oil a griddle. Gently and briefly roast the gram for 30-40 seconds, till golden. Set aside.

- On the same griddle, toast curry leaves and chillies for 4-6 minutes, till brittle.

- Cool. Add salt and blend or grind the ingredients to a fine dry powder.

KARLYACHI CHUTNEY

Bitter Gourd Chutney
Makes: about 400 gms   Time: 30 minutes

This slightly bitter chutney lasts about a month and is often taken on journeys.

250 gms bitter gourd (karela) washed, dried and peeled
Up to 1 tbsp vegetable oil
100 gms sesame seeds (til)
50 gms cumin seeds
10 dried red chillies
2 tbsp grated dried coconut (kopra – optional)
3" piece of soft tamarind, without seeds and fibres
A pinch of sugar
1-1½ tsp salt

- Halve or quarter the gourds.

- Heat and oil a griddle, using ½ tbsp oil. Sauté the gourds for 5-10 minutes, till quite dry. Set aside.

- Lightly toast sesame and cumin seeds for 5-7 minutes, till golden.

- Re-oil the griddle with ¼ tbsp oil and toast chillies for 3-4 minutes.

- Add ¼ tbsp oil to griddle and toast coconut (if used) for 1-2 minutes, stirring often.

- Mix the toasted ingredients, tamarind, sugar and salt with the gourd. Grind to a dry powder, adding more salt if needed.

Note: Refrigerate chutney containing coconut.

LASNICHI CHUTNEY

Garlic Chutney
Makes: about 1½ cups   Time: 20 minutes
Contributor: Surekha Sirsikar

¼ cup soft, sweet tamarind, without seeds and fibres
1 head (10-15 small cloves) garlic, coarsely chopped
1 cup grated dried coconut (kopra)
2-3 dried red chillies
½ tsp sugar
1-1½ tsp salt

- Tear tamarind into small pieces.

- Roast garlic on a hot griddle for 1 minute, till golden and fragrant.

- Toast coconut for 2-3 minutes, till aromatic and crisp. Cool both for 5 minutes.

- Grind tamarind, garlic, coconut and chillies till well mixed. Add sugar and salt. Grind again.

- Use it quickly, as it won't last long.

Variation: **Khevda (Garlic-Peanut Chutney)**: Use the above method, substituting green chillies for the red and adding 50 gms raw peanuts and a pinch of asafoetida.

Chutney Pastes

BHOPLYACHYA SALACHI CHUTNEY
Red Pumpkin Rind Chutney
Makes: about 100 gms   Time: 20-30 minutes

One of this book's recurring themes is Marathi frugality. This recipe embodies it. Its main ingredient is pumpkin rind.

100 gms red pumpkin (kaddu) rind
2-3 dried red chillies
1 tbsp sesame seeds (til)
3 tbsp grated fresh coconut
4 dried tamarind pods, without seeds and fibres
2 tsp grated jaggery
1½ tsp salt or more

Seasoning:
3 tbsp vegetable oil
½ tsp mustard seeds
¼ tsp asafoetida powder (hing)
¼ tsp turmeric powder

- Peel the rind thickly off a very ripe pumpkin (reserve the pumpkin flesh for another use). Cut it into manageable, 4"x 2" strips.

- Heat oil for seasoning in a medium skillet to almost smoking. Add mustard seeds and let them pop. Add asafoetida and turmeric. Stir well.

- Add pumpkin rind and sauté for 7-10 minutes, till soft. Stir in chillies, sesame seeds and coconut. Sauté for 5 minutes. Turn off the heat.

- Mix in tamarind, jaggery and salt and grind to a fine paste.
- Taste and add more tamarind, jaggery or salt if needed.

Dad's Variation: Sauté sun-dried pumpkin rind in oil till crisp. Powder fine with grated dried coconut, sesame, chillies, salt and tamarind.

KANDYACHI CHUTNEY
Mouth-Watering Onion Chutney
Makes: about 250 gms   Time: 15 minutes
Contributor: Shubhangi Vaze

Serve this chutney plain or seasoned.

150 gms raw peanuts, ground
2 large onions, minced or grated
1 tsp red chilli powder or to taste
1-2 tsp salt
1½ tsp cumin seeds
2" piece of ripe tamarind, without seeds and fibre
1 tbsp grated jaggery
6-7 sprigs coriander leaves

Seasoning (optional):
1 tbsp vegetable oil
½ tsp mustard seeds
A pinch of asafoetida powder (hing)
¼ tsp turmeric powder

- Combine peanuts with onions, chilli powder, salt, cumin,

tamarind, jaggery and coriander leaves. Grind fine with a touch of water.

- For a 'really mouth-watering chutney', heat oil in a wok. Add mustard seeds and let them pop. Stir in asafoetida and turmeric. Mix seasoning into the chutney.

- Serve with bread.

KOLHAPURI KHARDA
Chilli-Onion-Tomato Chutney
Makes: 1-1½ cups   Time: 20-25 minutes
Contributor: Anuradha Samant

Kharda is a tasty condiment with any staple, but Marathi people think of sorghum bhakri and kharda in the same breath. In fact, kharda, yogurt and bhakri make up a typical farmer's lunch in many parts of Maharashtra. For a really hot chutney, omit onion.

1 tbsp vegetable oil
20 green chillies, washed and dried
1 small onion, minced
1 head (20 small cloves) garlic
1 green (raw) tomato, minced
1-2 tsp salt

- Heat oil in a small skillet. Sauté chillies for 5-6 minutes, till crisp and golden.

- Add onion and sauté for 2-3 minutes. Reduce heat to low, add garlic and tomato and sauté for 5 minutes. Cool.

- Pound into a slightly thick paste with salt.

ARUNA'S KHARDA

Green Chilli-Garlic Chutney
Makes: about 250 gms   Time: 20-25 minutes

1-2 tsp vegetable oil
100 gms green chillies, washed and dried
1 tsp cumin seeds
75 gms garlic, crushed
4-5 curry leaves
4-5 mint leaves
Rock salt or table salt to taste
4 tbsp peanuts, ground
Juice of ½ a medium lime
1 tbsp coriander leaves, finely chopped

- Heat oil in a shallow pan. Sauté chillies. Stir in cumin, garlic, curry leaves and mint.

- Remove from heat and grind, with the bottom of a vati or metal bowl, or in a wide-mouthed mortar. Add salt and peanuts. Grind thoroughly. Mix in lime juice and coriander leaves.

- Return chutney to pan and sauté again over medium heat for 2-3 minutes.

- Eat with bhakri or as a sandwich topping.

KOTHIMBIRICHI CHUTNEY

Meera's Coriander Chutney Trio
Makes: about 250 gms   Time: 15-20 minutes

250 gms coriander leaves, stemmed
3-5 green chillies, coarsely chopped
1-1½ tsp cumin powder

Chutneys, Relishes, Pickles & Preserves   277

2-3 small cloves garlic, peeled (optional)
1 tsp salt or more
Juice of 1 lime
A pinch of sugar (optional)

- Grind coriander leaves, chillies, cumin, garlic (if used) and salt into a fine, soft paste, using minimal water.

- Add lime juice, sugar (if used) and more salt as needed.

- Use chutney within 3-4 days or freeze for up to 2-4 weeks.

Variations:

- **Coriander-Tomato Chutney:** Add 2 coarsely chopped tomatoes to the basic recipe.

- **Coriander-Onion Chutney:** Add 1 rough-chopped onion to the basic recipe.

LASNICHI OLI CHUTNEY
Vahini Aji's Super Moist Garlic Chutney
Makes: 2-3 cups   Time: 15-20 minutes

This is my all-time favourite chutney.

1 head (10-15 small cloves) garlic
1 fresh coconut, grated
2-3 dried red chillies
4 tbsp thick tamarind paste (p. 27)
1 tsp cumin seeds (optional)
¼-½ tsp sugar
1½ tsp salt

- Grind garlic, coconut and chillies into a fine paste with some tamarind paste to moisten it.
- Add cumin, sugar, salt and leftover tamarind paste.
- Grind fine into a chutney thick enough to press into a lump.
- Serve immediately or refrigerate covered for up to 2-4 days.

Note: Mom adds finely chopped onion for immediate-use chutney.

KHOBRYACHI CHUTNEY – I
Meera's Coconut Chutney
Makes: 350-400 gms   Time: 15-20 minutes

250 gms coriander leaves, stemmed
1 cup grated fresh coconut
¼ cup grated green mango (optional)
3-5 green chillies
1 tsp cumin seeds
1-1½ tsp salt
Juice of 1 lime

- Grind ingredients into a fine paste with minimal water.
- Serve immediately or refrigerate for up to 4 days.

KHOBRYACHI CHUTNEY – II
Anuradha's Coconut Chutney
Makes: about 2 cups   Time: 15-20 minutes

Serve this with batata vada (p. 87).

1 tsp tup (ghee)
3 green chillies
3 small cloves garlic
1 tsp peanuts
1 cup grated fresh coconut
½ cup yogurt
1 tsp grated jaggery
1-1½ tsp salt

Seasoning (optional):
1 tsp tup (ghee)
¼ tsp mustard seeds
¼ tsp cumin seeds
4-5 curry leaves

- Heat tup in a small skillet. Stir-fry chillies, garlic and peanuts for 3-4 minutes, till golden.

- Grind to make a smooth paste with coconut, yogurt, jaggery and salt.

- Serve, or season first. Heat tup in a small wok. Add mustard seeds and let them pop. Reduce heat and add cumin and curry leaves. Stir the seasoning into the chutney.

THECHA
Pounded Chilli & Lime Chutney
Makes: 600-650 gms   Time: 30 minutes

10 green chillies, washed, dried and roughly chopped
½ cup salt
6 limes or small lemons, washed, dried and cut into eighths
½ cup jaggery or sugar
¼ tsp asafoetida powder (hing)
½ tsp fenugreek seeds (methi), lightly toasted
½ cup grated ginger (optional)

Seasoning:
¾ tbsp vegetable oil
¼ tsp asafoetida powder
½ tsp turmeric powder

- Pound chillies with salt.

- Add limes or lemons, sweetener, asafoetida, fenugreek and ginger (if used) at regular intervals, pounding till well mashed.

- Heat oil in a wok. Add asafoetida and turmeric. Stir immediately into the thecha.

Relishes

CHUTPUT/MHADYA
Peanut-Onion Relish
Makes: about 150 gms   Time: 15 minutes
Contributor: Aruna Karande

Chutput has a longer life than most fresh chutneys. 'Villagers often carry it with bhakri in a cloth bundle to eat when travelling. It will not go bad for several days and doesn't need refrigeration.'

1 medium onion, minced
100 gms peanuts, roasted and coarsely ground
1-2 tsp salt

Seasoning:
3½ tbsp vegetable oil
½ tsp mustard seeds
½ tsp cumin seeds
¼ tsp asafoetida powder (hing)
¼ tsp turmeric powder
4-5 tsp dark red chilli powder (kala tikhat)
3-4 small cloves garlic, finely sliced

Garnish:
4-5 coriander leaves, finely chopped

- Heat oil for seasoning in a shallow iron pan. Add mustard and cumin seeds and let them pop. Stir in asafoetida, turmeric, chilli powder and garlic.

- Add onion and brown slowly for 4-5 minutes.

- Pour in 300 ml water and bring to a boil. Add peanuts and simmer for 7-10 minutes, till the water evaporates.

- Stir in salt. Turn off heat when a thin layer of oil begins to rise from the mixture.

- Serve at room temperature, garnished with coriander leaves.

KAIRI SASAV

Green Mango-Coconut Relish
Makes: about 500 gms   Time: 40 minutes
Contributor: Laxmibai Sirsikar

2 near-ripe mangoes, washed
4" piece of jaggery, grated
6-8 tbsp grated fresh coconut
1 green chilli, minced
¾ tsp salt

Seasoning:
1½ tsp vegetable oil
½ tsp mustard seeds
A pinch of asafoetida powder (hing)

- Boil mangoes in 2 cups water for 10-15 minutes, till soft. Peel and squeeze flesh into a bowl. Mash well.

- Mix in jaggery and stir till dissolved.

- Add coconut, chilli and salt.

- Heat oil in a small wok. Add mustard seeds and let them pop. Add asafoetida. Immediately mix the seasoning into the chutney.

KOCHKAI

Grated Green Mango Relish
Makes: about 2 cups   Time: 15 minutes
Contributor: Meera Marathe

2-3 medium green mangoes, washed, peeled, stemmed and grated
½-1 tsp salt

Seasoning:
2 tbsp vegetable oil
½ tsp mustard seeds
½ tsp cumin seeds
A pinch of asafoetida powder (hing)
¼ tsp fenugreek seeds (methi)
½ tsp turmeric powder
1 tsp red chilli powder or more

- Salt the mangoes.

- Heat oil in a small wok to smoking. Reduce heat, add mustard seeds and let them pop. Add cumin, asafoetida and fenugreek. Turn off the heat. Stir in turmeric and chilli powder. Cool completely.

- Mix seasoning into the mangoes with your fingers.

- Store in an airtight container for up to a week.

KOL ANI CHUTNEY

Spiced Coconut Sauce & Relish
Serves: 4-6
Time: 30 minutes for the kol + 15 minutes for the chutney

Fresh coconut milk is used to make kol, a rich sauce eaten with hot rice. The flesh is recycled into a delicious chutney.

Kol:

1 large fresh coconut, grated
2-3 green chillies
½" piece of ginger
1" piece of tamarind, without seeds and fibres
1-2 tsp salt
1" piece of jaggery, grated (optional)

Seasoning:

¾ tbsp tup
¾ tsp cumin seeds
½ tsp asafoetida powder (hing)

Chutney:

½ cup raw peanuts
3 green chillies, chopped
1-1¼ tbsp vegetable oil
½ tsp asafoetida powder (hing)
1 head (10-15 small cloves) garlic, finely minced
¾-1 tsp salt
Reserved coconut residue from the kol

Kol:

- Grind coconut, chillies, ginger, tamarind and salt into a smooth, fine paste.

- Squeeze a handful of paste at a time into another bowl to express the thick, milky coconut liquid.

- Mix ½ cup warm water into the paste. Extract the milk into a separate bowl. Reserve the residue paste for the chutney.

- For thick sauce, do not combine the two batches of milk (reserve dilute milk for another use) but do so for a thinner sauce. Stir in jaggery. Add more salt if needed.

- Heat tup in a wok. Add cumin and asafoetida. Pour over the kol, stir once and keep covered for 2-3 minutes.

- Stir and serve immediately.

Chutney:

- Pound peanuts and chillies coarsely. Heat oil in a skillet. Add asafoetida, stir in garlic, peanut-chilli powder, salt and coconut.

- Stir-fry for 8-10 minutes, till dry and crisp.

- Refrigerate chutney for up to 2-3 days.

PANCHAMRUT
Tangy Capsicum Relish
Makes: about 2 cups   Time: 20 minutes

8-10 slivers (1" long) dried coconut (kopra)
2 capsicums, washed, dried and chopped into ½" bits
1½ tsp peanuts, ground
1½ tsp sesame seeds, finely ground
1½ tsp grated fresh coconut (optional)
A small marble-sized ball of jaggery or more, chopped
1½ tsp thick tamarind paste (p. 27)
1-1½ tsp salt

Seasoning:
1 tbsp vegetable oil
½ tsp mustard seeds
A pinch of asafoetida powder (hing)
A pinch of turmeric powder

- Heat oil for seasoning in a small pan. Add mustard seeds and let them pop. Stir in asafoetida and turmeric.

- Add dried coconut slivers and sauté briefly till crisp. Add capsicums, peanuts, sesame powder and grated fresh coconut. Sauté for 5 minutes.

- Stir in jaggery, tamarind and salt. Cook for 3-7 minutes, till soft and brownish, with the capsicum still distinguishable.

- Serve at room temperature.

Pickles

Pickle making is an art; cooks spend years honing their techniques. Some pickles are eaten fresh. Some last months or years and usually require more oil and care. Their flavour improves with age. They take preparation, planning and time.

Here are some tips to making a good pickle:

- Ensure that pans, utensils, jars and ingredients are washed clean and thoroughly dried before you start. The slightest hint of moisture or dirt can ruin an entire batch of pickle. Make pickles on a dry day so humidity will not affect the ingredients.

- Store pickles in airtight ceramic (or glass) jars. Ceramic reduces the effects of temperature changes. Sun-dry the jars a few days before you fill them.

- Do not stint on salt during pickling. It helps preserve pickles. Insufficient salt leads to odd-smelling, unsalvageable pickles.

- Fenugreek seeds flavour pickles and help thicken their khar (juice). They should be well sautéed or they will taste slimy, spoil the pickle and make it bitter. Sauté over very low heat till just reddish brown.

- Sauté turmeric briefly to eliminate its raw smell and taste.

- Good quality red chilli powder gives pickles a deep red hue.

- Oil is often heated and cooled twice before being added to pickles. After making a seasoning, cool oil completely before pouring it over the ingredients.

- When filling pickles in a jar, press down on them occasionally with a spoon to reduce trapped air. The less air, the less chance of spoilage. Fill pickle up to the neck of the jar. Many pickles require a layer of rock salt over the top. Spread it and close the lid tight.

- Store in a cool, dry place.

Fruits like mangoes, avlas and guavas are often preserved in sugar syrups and flavoured with fenugreek, red chilli powder, cardamom and saffron. Sweet preserves are eaten with bread while the spicier ones, like methamba, are frequently treated like pickle.

Use pickle-making tips for preserves too. Watch preserves carefully during cooking so the fruit does not overcook. Make sure syrups do not overcook either, or they will crystallize, resulting in hard or overly thick preserves and fruit with a flaky, sugary coating.

AMBYACHA LONCHA
Green Mango-Mustard Pickle
Makes: 1-1½ kg   Time: 1-1½ hours

This oil-free loncha is great for dieters. Its distinctly Marathi taste comes from ground mustard seeds. Make it when mangoes are in season with their stones set. One batch lasts for up to 2-3 months. Double the quantities if you like.

12 large green mangoes, washed and dried
1½ cups salt
1 cup red chilli powder
1 cup ground yellow mustard seeds
3 tsp turmeric powder
2 tsp finely ground asafoetida (hing)
¼ tsp vegetable oil
1 tsp fenugreek seeds (methi)

- Remove mango stems (p. 27). Halve the fruits and remove their stones. Cut the unpeeled mangoes into 1½" chunks. Combine them with salt, chilli powder, mustard, turmeric and asafoetida.

- Heat and lightly oil a griddle. Toast fenugreek seeds lightly for 1-2 minutes before powdering. Stir it into the pickle mix.

- Transfer pickle to jars, packing it in tight.

- Shake jars daily to redistribute the spices and juices (khar). The pickle is ready in 2-3 days but softens more with time.

AVLYACHA LONCHA
Indian Gooseberry Pickle
Makes: about 100 gms   Time: 30 minutes

100 gms Indian gooseberries (rai avla/amla), washed, dried and seeded
1½ tbsp mustard seeds
1 tbsp grated jaggery
½ tsp fenugreek seeds (methi), lightly toasted and powdered
½ tsp asafoetida powder (hing)
1-1½ tsp salt
Up to ¼ tsp vegetable oil
2-3 green chillies, minced

- Sliver the avlas.

- Grind mustard seeds fine, add jaggery and a touch of water. Grind again till the mustard froths and become aromatic.

- Combine avlas, fenugreek, asafoetida, salt and mustard with oil. Mix in chillies.

- Serve fresh with rice or poli. Refrigerate for up to 3-5 days.

EAST INDIAN CARROT PICKLE

Makes: 500 gms   Time: 3-4 hours sunning + 1 hour cooking
Contributor: Iris D'Penha

500 gms carrots, washed, dried and peeled
1 tbsp salt
120-150 ml mustard oil
5-6 curry leaves
½ cup sugar

Spice paste:
10 small cloves garlic
1" piece of ginger
1 tsp mustard seeds
1 tsp cumin seeds
1 tsp fenugreek seeds (methi)
1 tsp turmeric powder
3 tsp red chilli powder
1 cup white vinegar

- Slice carrots into thin rounds or matchsticks. Place on a large platter, sprinkle with salt and set in the sun for 3-4 hours.

- Squeeze the carrots out over the sink, draining excess liquid.

- Grind the spice paste ingredients fine.

- Heat oil in a deep pan till almost smoking. Turn off the heat and cool completely.

- Reheat oil, sauté curry leaves and add spice paste. Mix in carrots and sugar. Simmer over medium heat for 15 minutes.

- Cool completely. Transfer to a jar. Store refrigerated.

- This pickle can be served immediately but tastes best after 5-7 days.

TAJYA GAJRACHA LONCHA
Fresh Carrot Pickle
Makes: 500 gms   Time: 25 minutes + 3-4 hours marinating
Contributor: Meera Marathe

This is a quick, easy-to-make condiment that also works well with mangoes, cauliflower, seeded avlas and firm apples, peeled ginger or slightly under-ripe pears. It is best eaten fairly fresh but lasts 7-10 days, refrigerated. To prevent spoilage, occasionally mix in some fresh oil.

3-4 medium carrots, washed and thoroughly dried
1-2 tsp salt

Seasoning:
4 tbsp vegetable oil
½ tsp asafoetida powder (hing)
½ tsp mustard seeds or ground yellow mustard seeds
1 tsp turmeric powder
1 tsp red chilli powder or more
A few fenugreek seeds (methi)

- Peel carrots and cut into fine dice, less than ¼" thick.

- Heat oil well in a small wok. Add asafoetida. Turn off the heat. Immediately add mustard, turmeric, chilli powder and fenugreek. Stir briskly. Cool completely.

- Mix the seasoning with the carrots. Stir in salt.

- Marinate covered for 3-4 hours, before serving.

Ai Aji's Variation: Combine prepared vegetable with ½ cup grated jaggery, 1 tsp chilli powder, ½ tsp turmeric powder, ½ tsp salt, ¼ tsp toasted fenugreek seeds and a pinch of asafoetida. Briskly whisk 2 tsp ground mustard seeds with 1-2 tbsp water in a bowl. When it froths, mix it into the pickle. Marinate for 30 minutes before serving.

KARLYACHA LONCHA
Bitter Gourd Pickle
Makes: 750 gms   Time: 2 hours draining + 1 hour cooking
Contributor: Aruna Karande

These days, people are downing bitter gourd juice or popping bitter gourd in supplement form to make the most of its health benefits. I would rather eat it myself!

500 gms tender bitter gourd (karela), washed, dried and peeled
2 tsp turmeric powder
80 gms salt
100 ml lime juice
100 ml vegetable oil

Seasoning:
100 ml vegetable oil
2 tsp mustard seeds
1 tsp asafoetida powder (hing)
50 gms garlic, crushed
50 gms ginger, grated
8-9 green chillies, sliced
100 gms ground yellow mustard seeds

- Cut the gourd into short vertical strips. Rub with turmeric and salt. Rest for 2 hours, then drain and discard the bitter juices released. Dry the gourd well. Place in a clean, dry bowl.

- Heat oil for seasoning in a small wok. Add mustard seeds and let them pop. Add asafoetida.

- Mix in garlic, ginger and chillies and sauté for 2-3 minutes. Add ground yellow mustard seeds and sauté for 2 minutes.

- Cool completely. Pour over the gourd. Stir in lime juice.

- Heat oil in a small pan to almost smoking. Cool completely. Pour oil over the bitter gourds. Mix well.

- Transfer to a jar. After 4 days, stir well and serve.

LIMBACHA PAKATLA LONCHA

Lime Pickle in Syrup

Makes: 2-2½ kg   Time: 2 hours over an 8-day period

Contributor: Aruna Karande

Without asafoetida, fenugreek and turmeric, this pickle works for fasts.

> 25 medium limes, washed and dried
> 2 tsp turmeric powder
> 100 gms + 100 gms salt
> 1 kg sugar
> 1 tsp fenugreek seeds (methi)
> A touch of vegetable oil
> 2 tsp asafoetida powder (hing)
> Red chilli powder to taste

- Cut limes into eight wedges each and set aside.

- Mix turmeric and 100 gms salt into the lime wedges. Rest in a jar for 4 days.

- Using the same container (vati, cup or small bowl), measure 4 parts sugar and 3 parts water into a large pan. Cook for 8-10 minutes to make a thick syrup. Carefully press a drop of syrup between thumb and index finger. When you pull your fingers apart, it should stretch to 2-3 strands.

- Toast fenugreek seeds on a hot, oiled griddle before powdering it fine.

- Mix fenugreek, 100 gms salt, asafoetida and chilli powder into the syrup. Turn off the heat.

- Stir in the limes and their residual juices.

- Cool completely. Transfer to jars. Stir well after 4 days.

MA-IN MULYACHA LONCHA
'Ma-In' Radish Pickle
Makes: 650-750 gms Time: 2 hours over a 5-day period
Contributor: Aruna Karande

Aruna learnt this recipe from her friend, Mrs Jadhav. 'Some say this pickle has medicinal value. If you are under the weather, it will refresh you.' Ma-in mula is a regional speciality. If unavailable, use white radish.

500 gms 'Ma-in' radish, washed, dried and peeled
100 ml lime juice
5 packed tbsp red chilli powder
50 gms salt
2 tsp whole fenugreek seeds (methi)
50 gms split yellow mustard seeds
3 tsp turmeric powder

Seasoning:
150 ml vegetable oil
1 tsp mustard seeds
1 tsp asafoetida powder (hing)
1 tsp ground fenugreek seeds

• Dry peeled radish with a clean cloth. Slice into long strips. Sprinkle with lime juice to prevent darkening.

• Heat oil for seasoning in a small wok. Add mustard seeds and let them pop. Stir in asafoetida and ground fenugreek. Pour the seasoning over the radish.

• Mix in chilli powder, salt, whole fenugreek, split yellow mustard and turmeric. Stir thoroughly.

• Transfer cooled pickle to a jar. Stir every other day for a week before serving.

VANGYACHA LONCHA
East Indian Aubergine Pickle
Makes: 2-2½ kg   Time: 1 hour
Contributor: Iris D'Penha

2 kg aubergines (baingan), washed, dried and stemmed
1 tbsp salt
225 gms sugar
500 ml vinegar
500 ml mustard oil
3 sprigs curry leaves
1 tbsp black peppercorns
10 small green chillies, coarsely chopped
2 x 2" pieces of ginger, chopped
½ small head garlic, sliced

Spice paste:
20 gms dried red Kashmiri chillies
1 small head garlic
3 tbsp turmeric powder

Spice powder:
1 tbsp cumin seeds
1 tsp fenugreek seeds (methi)
1 tsp mustard seeds

- Cut aubergines into 1" cubes. Place them in a colander, salt them and set aside to drain for 30 minutes.

- Meanwhile, grind spice paste ingredients with a little of the measured sugar and vinegar.

- Coarsely grind the spice powder ingredients.

- Heat oil in a deep pan till almost smoking. Cool for 2-3 minutes. Reheat oil. Sauté curry leaves, peppercorns, green chillies, ginger and garlic for 1-2 minutes.

- Add spice paste and sauté for 2-3 minutes.

- Stir in aubergines and sprinkle in spice powder and the remaining sugar and vinegar. Mix well. Simmer for 15-17 minutes, till aubergines are tender but still firm.

- Cool well. Transfer to jars.

METHAMBA

Mango Preserve with Fenugreek Seeds
Makes: 1 kg   Time: 1 hour preparation + 24 hours resting

Enjoy methamba as a pickle or jam.

500 gms large green mangoes, washed and dried
½-1 tsp salt
500 gms jaggery, grated or chopped
7-8 cloves, powdered
2-3 x 1" sticks cinnamon, powdered

Seasoning:
6-8 tbsp vegetable oil
1 tsp mustard seeds
½ tsp fenugreek seeds (methi)
A pinch of asafoetida powder (hing)
5-6 dried red chillies

- Carefully remove mango stems (p. 27). Peel and cut mangoes into ½"-1" pieces (reserve pits for another use) and mix with salt. Transfer to a large jar (or two) to rest for 24 hours. Drain off any liquid.

- Heat oil in a large pan. Add mustard seeds and let them pop. Add fenugreek, asafoetida and chillies and sauté for 1-2 minutes, till fragrant.

- When the chillies begin to darken, add mango. Sauté for 2-3 minutes. Mix in jaggery and cook for 10-15 minutes, till completely melted.

- Stir in cloves and cinnamon. Cook for 5 minutes till the jaggery thickens ever so slightly.

- Cool completely before storing.

Meera's Speed-of-Light Methamba: For immediate use, follow the above method without salting the fruit.

Preserves

KAIRICHA MORAMBA

Green Mango Preserve
Makes: about 3 cups   Time: 1½ hours

2 cups grated flesh of washed, dried and peeled raw mangoes
2 cups crushed sugar or jaggery
1 tsp powdered green cardamom

- Combine mango, sweetener and cardamom in a heavy-bottomed pan. Bring to a boil over medium heat. Reduce heat to low and cook for about 1 hour, stirring occasionally.

- The sweetener will melt, becoming liquidy. The mango will turn translucent. The moramba is ready when the mango turns transparent.

- Cool completely before storing. Refrigerate if needed.

MORAMBA
Ripe Mango Jam
Makes: about 400 gms   Time: 1 hour

Use good quality (Alphonso) mangoes. You will appreciate their fine flavour in the preserve.

2 ripe but firm, un-bruised Alphonso mangoes, washed, dried and peeled
250 gms sugar

- Cut mangoes into 1" chunks.

- Cook sugar and ¾ cup water in a deep pan for 3-4 minutes to make simple syrup.

- Add the mangoes. Cook for 5-7 minutes till the syrup thickens slightly.

- Cool completely before storing.

MORAVLA

Indian Gooseberry Preserve
Makes: 1¼-1½ kg   Time: 1½ hours over a 2-day period

Moravla is excellent for people with stomach ailments. The large variety (dongri avla) is preserved in sugar to make this sweet-astringent preserve-tonic. Alum helps preserve the fruit and maintain crispness. Lime neutralizes excess acid.

500 gms Indian gooseberries (dongri avla/amla), washed
A small piece or pinch of alum
A peanut-sized ball of edible lime (chunam)
1 kg sugar
3-4 green cardamoms, powdered
6-7 saffron strands

- Prick avlas all over with the point of a knife.

- Pour 2 litres water in a deep pan, add alum and lime, and soak the avlas for 24 hours.

- The next day, bring 2 litres of fresh water to a boil. Drain avlas and wipe them dry. Add to the boiling water and cook for 3-4 minutes, till tender. Drain again and spread avlas on a clean cloth to air-dry.

- In a large pan, cook sugar with 3 cups water for 7-8 minutes to make a syrup.

- Add the avlas. Cook for 7-8 minutes, till the syrup thickens. Mix in cardamom and saffron.

- Cool completely before storing.

Desserts & Sweets

At a Marathi feast, desserts are the attraction and, frequently, the main course. Such meals might be named after the dessert of choice: jilebiché jevan (the jilebi meal), puran policha jevan (the puran poli meal), etc. On these occasions, savoury dishes play a secondary or supporting role.

The term 'sweets' in this book encompasses treats meant for eating outside of a meal, like karanjis and ladus. Traditionally, these are made for festivals, pujas and rituals. Some are associated with specific occasions. For instance, around March, children sing: 'Holi re Holi, puranachi poli' (Holi's coming, puran polis to eat!) in anticipation of the sweet chickpea-stuffed breads to come. Rich, sweet Satyanarayanacha shira (p. 71), similar to Punjabi or Sindhi kada prashad, is always made for Satyanarayana pujas. Other shiras are made from semolina (gode shira, p. 69), rice, sweet potato, bananas (kelyacha shira, p. 308), even mung.

Among Maharashtra's favourite sweets are also gulachi poli, a vast array of kheers and ladus, anarsé, dudhi and gajar halwa, jilebi. Since the last two are made across India, they are not represented here.

Marathi Muslims make many of the same sweets as the Hindus but also eat the specialties of pan-Indian Muslim culture. Similarly, East Indians have certain special sweets reflecting their Anglo-Portuguese influences and indigenous ingredients.

Here is a glimpse at the Marathi year through sweets:

Gudhi Padva (Marathi New Year): Shrikhand/puranachi poli

Nag Panchami (The Snake Festival): Dinde, sweet khandavi, modak

Narali Purnima (The Full Moon of the Coconut): Narali bhat/ karanji, modak

Ganesh Chaturthi (The Elephant God Festival): Steamed/fried modak, karanji

Gauri: Ghavan ghatlé, vadé, ghargé

Dussehra (Ten Day Celebration): Shrikhand, sakhar bhat, haldichya panatle patolé

Kojagiri Purnima: Masala milk, cardamom-scented coffee

Satyanarayana Puja: Satyanarayanacha shira, cardamom-scented coffee

Diwali (The Festival of Lights): Special sweet and snack platter (pharal): Shankarpali, anarsé, chakli, ladu, chivda, kadboli, shev, chiroté, etc.

Diwali (Padva): Shrikhand

Diwali (Bhau Beej—Brother-Sister Celebration): Basundi, jilebi, pakatli puri

Sankranti (Winter Solstice): Gulachi poli, tilaché ladu, til gul

Rang Panchami (The Festival of Colour): Sakhar bhat

Holi (The Second Day of the Festival of Colour): Puranachi poli.

Desserts: Fruit & Vegetable Delights

AMRAS
Mango Purée with Black Pepper
Serves: 4-6   Time: 30 minutes
Special equipment: churning stick

Marathi people are partial to the hapus (Alphonso mango) for eating sliced, but they also enjoy juice-mangoes that are softened and pulped into amras to eat with hot purya. Black pepper and tup on top neutralize the 'heat-causing' effect of mangoes and help digestion.

4 large ripe mangoes, washed and dried
Up to 25 ml milk
Sugar to taste (optional)
3-4 green cardamoms, powdered

Garnish:
Black pepper
Tup (ghee)

- Clean carefully around the mango stem to remove residual resin. Hold each mango firmly with your thumb on the stem and fingers underneath. Soften by squeezing gently, turning it occasionally to evenly loosen the flesh. Gently prise out the stem.

- Hold the mango stem-side down over a bowl. Squeeze gently from above to extract the softened flesh and stone. Press juice out thoroughly; then turn skin inside out to squeeze out remaining juice. Place the skin in another bowl. Pulp all the mangoes.

- Squeeze the flesh off each stone by holding it in one hand and pulling downward. Place stones in the bowl containing the skins and add milk. Rub them to extract more juice. Churn the milk.

- Mash the pulp and stir in the milk.

- Check the sweetness and stir in sugar and cardamom.

- Serve immediately or chill for 1 hour. Garnish individual servings with pepper and tup.

DUDHI HALWA
Wedding Pudding
Serves: 6-8   Time: 2-4 hours

Dudhi halwa is memorable for Sanjiv and me because it was served at our wedding in 1991. Sanjiv often tells the story of how he offered to lend my mother a hand mixing it some days before the wedding, and found himself stirring one of the gigantic thickening pots for hours and hours! Hard labour!

2 cups grated bottle gourd (lauki/ghia)
2 tsp tup (ghee)
340-395 gms sugar
950 ml full-fat milk or more as needed, boiled and cooled
10-12 cashew nuts, slivered or almonds, blanched, peeled and slivered
15-20 seedless raisins (kishmish)
5-6 green cardamoms, powdered
A few saffron strands

- Squeeze out the liquid from the grated gourd before measuring the gratings.

- Heat tup in a deep, heavy-bottomed pan. Sauté gourd over medium heat for 7-10 minutes, till translucent.

- Add sugar and milk. Slow-cook gourd over low heat for 1-1½ hours, till the liquid evaporates and only milk solids are left. Stir occasionally, adding more milk if the gourd is drying out too quickly. The pudding is done when it is moist but not runny.

- Stir in nuts, raisins, cardamom and saffron.

- Serve halwa hot or cold, by itself or with purya. For very special occasions, garnish with edible silver leaf (varq).

KELYACHA SHIRA

Cardamom-Scented Bananas
Serves: 4   Time: 15 minutes

This is a great snack for people who are fasting. It can be made with different varieties of ripe, firm bananas (Rajali, yellow, red, or velchi) or with sweet potato.

> 6-8 Rajali or yellow bananas or 1-2 large red bananas
> 4 tbsp tup (ghee)
> 1-2 cloves (optional)
> 115-170 gms sugar
> A pinch of salt
> 2-3 green cardamoms, powdered

- Slice bananas into 1" thick rounds.

- Heat tup in a skillet. Add cloves (if used).

- Stir in the bananas gently to avoid mashing them. Cook covered for 2-3 minutes (4-5 minutes for Rajali).

- After 2 minutes (4 for Rajali), stir in sugar and salt. Continue cooking for 2-5 minutes, till the sugar bubbles and the banana is tender.

- Add cardamom. Serve hot.

Variation: Use 3-4 peeled, grated or thinly sliced sweet potatoes. Sauté them in tup for 2-3 minutes. Cook covered for 5-7 minutes, stirring in sugar and salt after about 6 minutes. Mix in cardamom and serve hot.

Kheer (Milk Pudding)

A kheer consists of a grain, grain product (like semolina or pasta), lentil, vegetable (like bottle gourd) or fruit (like jackfruit) cooked in a large quantity of milk, or cooked and then added to the milk, and sweetened with sugar or jaggery. The milk might be flavoured with cardamom, saffron or nutmeg and sometimes with nuts and raisins.

Kheer is usually the consistency of soup, with milk in far greater proportion than other ingredients. Sometimes it is slightly thicker, like porridge, depending on its ingredients, the proportion of milk and personal preference.

Kheers are especially made for festivals and for the ritual daily offering to gods (naivedya). One particular kheer made with cooked rice is, at least in my father's 'tribe', only prepared for funeral rites. Some, like sabudanyachi kheer (sago pudding), are considered light, nourishing foods for invalids. One kheer is even made with onions, thought to be cooling, for persons recovering from typhoid.

Most kheers are quick and easy to prepare. Traditionally served warm or at room temperature, they may be eaten with puri or poli. Today they are sometimes served chilled as desserts.

GAVHLYACHI KHEER

'Little Stick' Pasta Pudding
Serves: 4   Time: 30 minutes
Contributor: Sudhakar Marathe

Gavhlé, small, home-made, whole-wheat pasta-sticks, are used in this kheer, prepared for any auspicious occasion or naivedya. In Maharashtra, they are now available commercially. Orzo or rice-shaped pasta, make a good substitute for gavhlé.

500 ml full-fat milk
1½ tbsp tup (ghee)
½ cup gavhlé (p. 40) or cooked orzo pasta
85-110 gms sugar
3-4 green cardamoms, finely powdered
2-3 saffron strands

- Bring milk to a boil on low heat over 10 minutes. Reduce it slightly by simmering for 15-20 minutes, stirring often and scraping the bottom of the pan. When it is thick and golden, turn off the heat.

- Heat tup in a medium pan. Briefly sauté the gavhlé or orzo for 2-4 minutes.

- Reduce heat and mix in milk, sugar, cardamom and saffron.

- Serve hot or at room temperature.

SAROLYACHI KHEER

Home-Made Pasta-Twist Pudding

Serves: 4-6   Time: 1 day for sarolya + 20 minutes for the kheer
Special equipment: foot-long turathi sticks/bamboo skewers
Contributor: Uma Dadegaonkar

An unusual kheer from north-eastern Maharashtra is traditionally served with amras (p. 305).

'Most housewives in the region make hand-fashioned vermicelli (shevaya). But women of unleisured Maratha or Kunbi households do not indulge in this "fine" exercise. They make sarolya (thicker and more rustic than shevaya). Being different from the usual kheer pasta, they are somewhat difficult to negotiate while eating, so sarolyachi kheer is used as a sort of test of how smart a prospective bridegroom is!'

Wheat is soaked and crushed to a powder. This 'rava' is soaked again for 4-5 hours, gathered into a lump with a touch of oil, and thoroughly pounded. The dough is wound around turathi sticks (p. 59), creating thin, long, spirals and thoroughly sun-dried on cloth spread across cots in the yard. They are then stored.

Make sarolya or use thick, long, twisted pasta (fusili lunghi or whole-wheat spaghetti, cooked according to package directions).

> 1 tbsp vegetable oil
> 20-25 sarolya
> 1 litre full-fat milk
> 4 tbsp sugar or to taste
> Mango pulp or amras (optional, p. 305)

- Bring 1 litre water to a boil in a large pan, as for pasta. Add oil, slide in the sarolya and turn off the heat. After 5 minutes, drain sarolya into a colander and rinse in cool water to stop the cooking.

- Bring milk and sugar to a boil in another pan, on low heat over 10-12 minutes. As soon as it bubbles, add the sarolya. Turn off the heat.

- Cool kheer before serving (do not refrigerate). Serve at room temperature topped with some amras, if you like.

SHEVAYACHI KHEER
Roasted Vermicelli Pudding
Serves: 7-8   Time: 1 hour
Contributor: Aditi Bhide

This one's a classic!

2 litres full-fat or low fat milk
½-1 tbsp tup (ghee – optional)
50-70 gms vermicelli
200 gms sugar
8-10 cashew nuts, slivered
3-4 pinches powdered green cardamom
4-5 saffron strands

- Boil milk in a heavy-bottomed pan over medium-low heat for 15-20 minutes.

- Heat tup (if used) in a skillet. Roast vermicelli for 4-5 minutes till golden.

- Add the vermicelli to the milk. Bring it back to a boil. Simmer for 5-10 minutes.

- Stir in sugar, cashew nuts, cardamom and saffron. Cook for 12-15 minutes, stirring occasionally, till the milk is golden and slightly thickened.

- Serve hot or cold.

GAVHACHI KHEER

Wheat-Jaggery Pudding

Serves: 4-6   Time: 2 hours soaking + 1-1¼ hours cooking
Contributors: Ashwini Marathe & Aditi Bhide

When I lived with my father's sister, Kunda Joshi, in Pune for a year, I had my first real taste of life in Maharashtra; education, music, theatre, food. Kunda Atya cooked wonderful, traditional Konkanastha food. I particularly enjoyed her gavhachi kheer: crunchy-chewy wheat, sumptuous coconut milk, sweet, fragrant jaggery. Atya passed away in 1995. Her daughters shared this recipe in her memory.

170 gms broken wheat (dalia)
600 ml full-fat or low-fat milk
365-370 gms fresh or dried coconut (kopra), grated
365-370 gms jaggery, grated
15 cashew nuts, raw or roasted, finely chopped
¼ tsp powdered green cardamom
50 ml thick coconut milk (p. 29)
½ tsp tup (ghee – optional)

- Soak wheat in 500 ml warm water for 1 hour, till it puffs up. Pressure-cook with 250 ml water (6 whistles) or cook covered for 45-60 minutes in a heavy-bottomed pan, till tender.

- Transfer the wheat from the pressure cooker to a heavy-bottomed pan. Add milk and coconut and simmer partially covered for 5-7 minutes. Stir occasionally to prevent the milk boiling over. Remove from heat and cool for about 15 minutes. Stir in jaggery and set aside for about 10 minutes, till it dissolves.

- Stir in cashew nuts, cardamom, coconut milk and tup (if used). Warm through once but do not boil.

- Serve kheer hot, at room temperature or chilled. Refrigerate for up to 1 week. Gently reheat before serving.

TANDULACHI KHEER

Rice Pudding
Serves: 1   Time: 10-15 minutes
Contributor: Meera Marathe

Here are four simple kheers served for breakfast, as young children's meals or for invalids. The recipes serve one but can be easily increased.

½ tbsp rice grains
175 ml full-fat milk
1½-2 tsp sugar
Powdered green cardamom or freshly grated nutmeg to taste

- Rinse rice briefly in water. Cook in a small pan over low heat with milk and sugar for 10 minutes, till tender.

- Add cardamom or nutmeg.

- Serve hot or cold.

POHYACHI KHEER

Beaten Rice Pudding
Serves: 1   Time: 10-15 minutes

2 level tbsp thick beaten rice (pohé), briskly rinsed
175 ml full-fat or low fat milk
1½-2 tsp sugar

- Rest rinsed beaten rice in a colander for 5 minutes.

- Scald milk and sugar in a small pan for 4-5 minutes.

- Add beaten rice, bring to a boil and cook for 5 minutes.

- Serve hot or cold.

RAVYACHI KHEER

Semolina Pudding
Serves: 1   Time: 10-15 minutes

1 tsp tup
1 tbsp scmolina (sooji/rava)
175 ml full-fat or low fat milk
1½-2 tsp sugar
A sprinkling of green cardamom or freshly grated nutmeg

- Heat tup in a small pan. Roast semolina for 1-2 minutes, till pink. Add milk and sugar.

- Bring to a boil over low heat over 2-3 minutes, stirring continuously. Cook for 1-2 minutes.

- Sprinkle with cardamom or nutmeg.

- Serve hot or cold.

SABUDANYACHI KHEER

Sago Pudding
Serves: 1   Time: 10-15 minutes

1 tbsp sago (sabudana)
1½-2 tsp sugar
175 ml full-fat or low fat milk
A drop of vanilla essence (optional)

- Soak sago in 3 tbsp water for 5 minutes. Add milk and sugar. Bring to a slow boil over 3-4 minutes, stirring occasionally. Cook for about 7 minutes. The kheer is ready when it begins to thicken.

- Serve hot or cold.

Sweet Rice

KESHRI BHAT AND NARALI BHAT
Saffron Rice and Coconut Rice
Serves: 2-4   Time: 25-40 minutes

Sakhar-bhat (sugar-rice, also made with jaggery) is made in many forms by several methods. Different flavourings—cardamom, coconut, saffron, lime, nuts—alter its flavour. I include keshri and narali bhat because they are served at festivals and feasts.

Narali Bhat is especially made in Shravan for Narali (coconut) Pornima, an important festival for fisher folk who pray to the ocean to keep them safe, and for Rakhi, celebrated the same day, to honour the bond between brothers and sisters.

Use the exact quantity of water listed or the rice will get mushy.

1 cup rice, preferably long-grained
2 tbsp tup (ghee) + extra for serving
4 cloves
4 green cardamoms
1 bay leaf (tej patta)
1 cup sugar
8-10 saffron strands
A few blanched, peeled and slivered almonds, chopped cashew nuts
and seedless raisins (kishmish)
2-4 lime wedges

- Rinse and drain the rice 15 minutes before cooking.

- Heat tup in a deep pan. Stir in cloves, cardamoms and bay leaf. Add rice and sauté for 6-8 minutes, till pinkish brown.

- Top with 2 cups water. Cook covered over low heat for 8-10 minutes.

- Stir in sugar, saffron, nuts and raisins. Cook covered for 10-15 minutes, till the rice is tender but the grains are distinct. Stir once if necessary with a long handled fork to prevent grains from breaking.

- Serve hot with a squeeze of lime juice and tup.

Variation: **Narali Bhat (Coconut Rice):** Make keshri bhat, adding ½ cup grated fresh coconut with the sugar. Serve narali bhat with tup but not lime juice.

Assorted Sweet Dishes

BASUNDI
Thick Saffron Milk with Nuts
Serves: 4-6   Time: 1 hour

Basundi, rich, spiced milk traditionally served on Akshaya Truteeya, is best made the day before serving, so flavours have time to blend. Serve garnished with nuts and edible silver leaf as a dessert, beverage or to scoop up with purya.

1½ litres full-fat milk
110 gms sugar or to taste
8-10 cashew nuts, slivered
6-7 almonds, blanched, peeled and slivered
2 tsp charolya (chironji)
6-7 green cardamoms, powdered
3-4 saffron strands

- Boil milk in a heavy-bottomed pan over very low heat for 12-15 minutes. Occasionally, stir the cream that rises, back into the milk and scrape the bottom of the pan.

- Cook for 20-25 minutes more, stirring frequently, till the milk is reduced by half. As it cooks, it will thicken and smell sweet.

- Add sugar. Cook for 15-20 minutes till basundi begins to coat the spoon like heavy cream. Stir in nuts, cardamom and saffron.

- Cool covered till serving time.

BOL MARIE

East Indian Coconut Pie

Makes: Two 9" pies or 6 'thalis' (small pies)
Time: 1 hour   Special equipment: pastry blender, pie tins
Contributors: The D'Penha family

Bol Marie is typical of the influences on the East Indian community of Bassein: native coconut meets European piecrust in a truly Anglo-Indian dessert. The pie is traditionally served at Christmas, christenings or other celebrations.

Filling:

400 gms sugar
6 eggs, well beaten
600 gms grated fresh coconut
250 gms unsweetened khava (mava) or ricotta cheese
1 tsp vanilla essence

Pastry:

800 gms + ½ cup sifted refined flour (maida)
100 gms powdered sugar
A pinch of salt
400 gms shortening or butter + extra for greasing tins

Filling:

- Add sugar to the eggs in a bowl. Beat till frothy. Stir in coconut, khava or cheese and vanilla.

Pastry:

- Combine 800 gms flour with sugar and salt in a bowl. Cut the shortening or butter into the flour with a pastry blender or your hands, till it resembles small beads.

- Gradually add up to 1½ cups cold water to bind the ingredients into a dough. Turn it on to a floured rolling board and gently knead just till it sticks together. Divide dough into 2 portions (for small pies, cut it into 6 equal portions).

Assembling and baking the pies:

- Preheat the oven to 180°C (350°F). Grease pie tins with a little shortening or butter.

- Sprinkle a little flour on the board. Gently roll a ball of dough into a 9" circle (or to fit the smaller tins), turning occasionally to roll evenly and prevent sticking.

- Gently place the crust in the first tin, fitting it into the sides, pressing it in place and crimping its edges.

- Spoon in filling to come halfway up the sides of the crust. Prepare all the pies this way.

- Using a knife or cookie cutter, make decorative shapes (leaves, stars, etc.) with the leftover dough. Decorate pies before baking.

- Bake for 20-30 minutes or till the filling sets and the crust is golden-brown.

- Cool on racks before serving.

GUP-CHUP
Blink-of-an-Eye Cake

Serves: 6-8   Time: 1 hour resting + 1¼ hours cooking
Special equipment: 9" cake tin
Contributor: Anuradha Samant

'My mother called it "ravaicha cake"! My mother-in-law called it "gup-chup" (hush-hush)! It was only when I saw it that I realized it was the same cake I had grown up with! It is called "hush-hush" because it is so easy to make that it's ready in the blink-of-an-eye before anyone realizes it!'

2 cups coarse semolina (sooji/rava)
1½ cups sugar
2 cups naturally sweet yogurt
100 ml milk
1 tsp tup (ghee)
A pinch of powdered green cardamom
4-5 cashew nuts, chopped or almonds, blanched, peeled and slivered
A pinch of saffron strands (optional)
¼ tsp sodium bicarbonate

- Mix semolina, sugar, yogurt and milk into a smooth batter. Set aside for 1 hour.

- Preheat the oven to 180°C (350°F). Grease the cake tin lightly with tup.

- Stir cardamom, nuts, saffron and sodium bicarbonate into the batter. Pour it into the tin.

- Bake for about 1 hour till golden and firm to the touch.

- Cool on a rack before cutting into wedges or squares.

- Serve with whipped cream and jam if you like.

MUGACHÉ KADHAN
Konkan Lentil-Coconut Pudding
Serves: 4-6   Time: 45 minutes
Contributor: Anuradha Samant

You can make mugaché kadhan ahead of time and serve it reheated or chilled.

250 gms split, husked green mung (mung dal)
250 gms jaggery, grated
½ fresh coconut, grated and finely ground
½ tsp powdered green cardamom
A pinch of salt

- Roast the dal lightly on a dry griddle for 4-5 minutes, till it begins to turn golden.

- Transfer to a medium pan and pour in 4 cups water. Cook for 10-15 minutes, till a kernel breaks in half between your fingers.

- Stir in jaggery. Bring kadhan to a boil over 4-5 minutes. Add coconut, cardamom and salt. Cook over low heat for 12-15 minutes, stirring occasionally, till it is as thick as desired.

- Serve hot or chilled.

SHRIKHAND
Rich Saffron Yogurt
Serves: 6-10   Time: 30 minutes

To me, shrikhand is the 'ultimate' Marathi dessert, exemplifying Marathi cuisine (and personality) in every contradictory bite: sweet, tart, simple, complex. Smoothly satisfying, no wonder it is called 'the sweet of the gods'.

My paternal grandfather, Srikrishna Marathe (Appa) was small and slight. But he would easily 'polish off' a pound of shrikhand at one sitting. Perhaps he shared something with his namesake, the dairy-loving god, Krishna! When Appa was done, his plate was wiped so clean, it looked as if it had been washed! Set the yogurt two days before you want to serve shrikhand.

3 litres full-fat milk, boiled + extra if required
1-2 tbsp yogurt
250-300 gms sugar
6 saffron strands soaked in 2 tsp warm milk
10 gms charolya (chironji – optional) + extra for garnish
Freshly grated nutmeg to taste

- When the milk has cooled to room temperature, stir the cream that would have risen to the top back into it. Add 1-2 tbsp yogurt to the milk as a starter to set yogurt (p. 31).

- The next day, when the yogurt is thick and firm (rest it longer if needed), drain it to make yogurt cheese (p. 34).

- Beat cheese smooth in a large bowl. Whisk or stir in sugar.

- Mix saffron-milk into the shrikhand. Add charolya (if used) and nutmeg. Stir till smooth, adding 1 tsp milk if needed.

- Garnish with more charolya and nutmeg.

- Serve at room temperature or cool.

Variation: **Amrakhand (Rich Mango Yogurt):** Using the above method, make very thick shrikhand with 200 gms sugar. Pulp 2-3 ripe Alphonso or other good quality, non-fibrous, ripe mangoes (p. 305). Do not add milk. Try canned pulp (1-2 cups) but remember it is thinner than the home-made kind. Fold only as much pulp into the shrikhand as it can take without thinning out. It should look orange and remain firm. Add more sugar if needed. Mix well. Cool covered for 1-2 hours. Serve with purya or as a pudding. Garnish with edible silver leaf (varq).

SOJI
Semolina-Coconut Pudding
Serves: 4-6   Time: 30 minutes
Contributor: Anuradha Samant

2 tsp tup (ghee)
1 cup coarse semolina (sooji/rava)
1 cup thick milk + 1 cup thin milk from ½ a fresh coconut (p. 29)
1 cup grated jaggery
A pinch of powdered green cardamom

- Heat tup in a medium pan. Lightly roast semolina for 5-7 minutes till aromatic and golden.

- Add 2 cups hot water, stirring continuously to prevent lumps. Cook covered over low heat for 4-5 minutes.

- When the semolina increases slightly in volume, stir in the thin coconut milk. Cook over low heat for about 5 minutes, stirring continuously, till homogenous.

- Add jaggery, thick coconut milk and cardamom. Cook for 4-5 minutes till jaggery melts and soji is smooth and thick.

- Serve cold.

Single Serving Sweets

ANARSÉ
Deep-fried Rice Flour-Jaggery Cakes
Serves: 6-10   Time: 2 weeks preparation & fermentation +
35 minutes frying
Special equipment: banana leaf/waxed paper/plastic sheet,
paper-lined platter

If I had to pick a favourite sweet, anarsé would be it. Rich jaggery
blends with delicate rice flour and poppy seeds in a slightly elastic,
delightful Diwali bread. It all but melts in your mouth! However,
anarsé are tough to make at home, their success depending on the
cook's skill and on the quality and texture of the ingredients.
Even my mother who makes everything from scratch describes
anarsé as tedious!

Here are her tips for light, non-greasy anarsé:

* The dough is delicate so fry one anarsa at a time.

* If the first one breaks, knead the dough again with a little
more tup.

* Fry each anarsa for 1-2 minutes or less, depending on the
temperature of the tup.

* Fry anarsa only on one side. Do not flip it over or fry it
poppy seed side down.

* Because the dough is porous, anarsé suck up tup. Drain each
fried anarsa between two slotted spoons into another clean,
dry pan. Reuse this tup for frying.

3 cups rice
3 cups grated jaggery
½ cup + 2 cups tup (ghee)
¼ cup poppy seeds (khus-khus)

Dough:

- Wash the rice well. Soak it in water for 3 days. Drain out extra water. Spread rice on a sheet to dry in the shade for several hours. It should be just short of bone dry. Grind fine to make washed-rice flour.

- Pound jaggery soft in a large mortar.

- Rub jaggery and ½ cup tup into the rice flour in a large parat or mixing platter, till homogenous and smooth. Ferment the dough, covered in a cool, dark place (do not refrigerate) for 2 weeks. This dough lasts several months.

Frying:

- To make anarsé, take out as much dough as you require. Knead it to the consistency and feel of puri dough.

- Roll a chunk into a lime-sized ball. Place a banana leaf, waxed paper or plastic sheet on a rolling board.

- Sprinkle ¾-1 tsp poppy seeds on it and place the dough on top. Pat it flat gently over the seeds into a 3" disc. Make all the anarsé before frying, setting them aside on a tray.

- Heat ¼-½ cup tup (just short of covering an anarsa) in a small wok till smoking hot. Reduce heat and gently lower in one anarsa, poppy seed side up.

- Spread hot tup over it. It will swell up and turn golden brown. Fry for 1-2 minutes for soft anarsé (golden brown), longer for a crisp texture (dark brown). Drain well and place on the paper-lined platter.

- Serve immediately or at room temperature.

KARANJI AND MODAK
Sweet Coconut Crescents and 'Figs'
Makes: 15-20   Time: 2 hours
Special equipment: pastry crimper, paper-lined platter

Karanjis (crescents) and modaks (figs) are flaky pastry around
rich, sweetened coconut, traditionally made for Ganpati and
Diwali. The filling uses fresh or dried coconut while the pastry
dough is made from wheat, rice flour or even beaten rice, depending
on the community. The pastries can be fried, steamed or baked!

Pastry:
200 gms sifted refined flour (maida)
3 tbsp vegetable oil or tup (ghee)
A pinch of salt

Filling:
1 cup grated fresh or dried coconut (kopra)
1 cup sugar
400-500 ml full-fat milk
2-3 green cardamoms, powdered
A handful of chopped almonds and seedless raisins (kishmish)
1-1½ tbsp roasted semolina, if required
1 tbsp poppy seeds (khus-khus – optional)
Tup (ghee) for deep-frying

Pastry:
- Use the above quantities to make karanji dough, using up to
  1 cup water (p. 91).

Filling:
- Combine coconut, sugar and milk in a pan. Cook over

medium-low heat for 35-45 minutes stirring occasionally till the milk evaporates, creating a soft filling.

- Add cardamoms. If the filling seems too soft, add semolina. Cook for 5-10 minutes more.
- Add poppy seeds if dried coconut is used.
- Stir and cool completely.

Forming and frying the modaks or karanjis:

- To form modaks, see ukdiché modak (p. 331).
- To form karanjis, and to deep-fry both pastries, see matarchi karanji (p. 91).
- If possible, fry pastries in tup instead of vegetable oil.
- Serve them hot or at room temperature. Store in an airtight container for up to 4-5 days, or refrigerate up to 10 days.

PATHARÉ PRABHU 'BAKED' KARANJIS
Patharé Prabhu Baked Crescents
Makes: about 50   Time: 1½-2 hours
Special equipment: pastry crimper, baking sheets
Contributor: Ujwal Mankar

'Our karanjis were traditionally baked in a bhatti, a copper-coated bronze box with hot coals below it and on the lid.'

Pastry:
50 ml + 50 ml vegetable oil
500 gms sifted refined flour (maida)
A pinch of salt
150 gms rice flour
250 gms refrigerated tup (ghee)

Filling:
2 tsp tup (ghee)
2 fresh coconuts, grated
750 gms + 250 gms sugar
10 green cardamoms, powdered
100 gms seedless raisins (kishmish)
100 gms almonds, blanched, peeled and slivered
A pinch of saffron strands dissolved in 2 tsp hot milk

Pastry:

- Heat 50 ml oil till very hot but not boiling.

- Place refined flour in a bowl. Gradually add hot oil, stirring continuously till thoroughly incorporated.

- Knead into a firm dough with salt and up to 2 cups cold water.

- Set aside, wrapped in damp cheesecloth for at least 30 minutes.

Filling:

- Heat tup in a large pan. Stir in, but do not brown, the coconut. Cook for about 5 minutes, stirring continuously.

- Add 750 gms sugar. Cook for 10-12 minutes, stirring till melted. Cook for 10-15 minutes more till the filling can be shaped into soft balls.

- Check the sweetness. Add up to 250 gms sugar and cook for 10 minutes more.

- Stir in cardamoms, raisins, almonds and saffron.

- Cool to room temperature.

Forming and baking the karanjis:

- Measure rice flour into a bowl. In a parat or mixing platter, using a rotating movement of your palm, break down the

Desserts & Sweets
329

cold tup and slowly add it to the flour, kneading till the flour is incorporated into the tup. Pour cold water into a medium bowl and float the flour mix in it.

- Heat 50 ml oil in a pan.

- Divide the wheat dough into 6 equal parts. Roll one out into a 12" disc and place on a large, flat surface.

- Spread the rice flour-tup mix over it as if generously 'buttering toast'. Sprinkle this with hot oil.

- Roll out another ball of dough. Place it over the first. Apply the rice-tup mix and sprinkle with oil again. Repeat.

- Tightly roll the three layers into a jam roll-like cylinder.

- Repeat the process with the remaining three balls of dough. Cut each cylinder into 1" discs and place under a damp cloth.

- Roll each disc into a 4" oval. Put 1-1½ tsp cooled filling on its centre.

- Fold one side of the pastry over the other to form a crescent. Press the edges together tight and trim with a crimper. Form all the pastries.

- Meanwhile, preheat the oven to 95°C (200°F).

- Arrange pastries on one or two large baking sheets. Bake for 15-20 minutes or till golden brown.

- Cool on racks and store in an airtight container.

Note: Freeze leftover sweet filling up to 2 weeks for later use. Patharé Prabhu karanji dough is great for baked ground meat karanjis too.

UKDICHÉ MODAK
Steamed Coconut 'Figs'
Serves: 6-8   Time: 1½ hours
Special equipment: steamer, cheesecloth/banana leaf/
parchment paper

Hot steamed modaks are served at Ganpati, drizzled with tup.
Prepare the filling up to a week in advance. Steam the sweets just
before serving.

Pastry:
¼ tsp unsalted butter
A pinch of salt
250 gms rice flour

Filling:
1 fresh coconut, grated
2-3 green cardamoms, powdered
¼ cup grated jaggery

Dough:

- Bring 1 cup of water to a boil in a medium pan. Reduce heat
  to low and stir in butter and salt.

- Add flour slowly in a steady stream, stirring continuously to
  prevent lumps. Cook for 5-7 minutes, stirring continuously,
  till it comes together and looks as clear as glass. When steam
  rises from the flour, it is cooked.

- Turn the lump on to a clean surface. It cools quickly so knead
  it immediately and vigorously for 5-7 minutes into a smooth,
  pliable dough.

- Divide dough into 1½" balls. Using a rolling pin or your
  fingers, shape or pat the dough balls into very thin, even

3"-5" discs. Make them as thin as possible or they will taste doughy.

Filling:

- Combine coconut, cardamom and jaggery in a small pan. Cook over low heat for 12-20 minutes, till the liquid evaporates but the filling is still moist.

- If pre-cooked, bring it to room temperature before filling it in the pastry.

Forming and steaming the modaks:

- Prepare a steamer's cooking chamber with cheesecloth, banana leaf or parchment paper.

- Put 1-1½ tsp filling in the centre of each dough disc. Fold up the edges to create a pursed, fluted, inverted cone on top of the mound of filling. Press the ends tight so they don't open up during cooking. The dumplings resemble figs in shape. Prepare all of them this way.

- Before steaming, very quickly dip each in water. They cook better and stay moist.

- Place 6-8 modaks in the steamer and steam for 3-6 minutes. They are done when the pastry looks glassy.

BATATYACHI VADI

Mom's Potato Fudgies
Makes: 25-30 vadya   Time: 2 hours

½ cup tup (ghee)
1 kg potatoes, boiled, peeled and mashed
1 kg sugar
1 tsp powdered green cardamom

- Grease 1-2 platters well with 2 tsp of the measured tup.

- Heat remaining tup in a heavy-bottomed pan. Sauté potatoes for about 10 minutes, till golden.

- Add sugar and cook over medium-low heat for about 1 hour, stirring frequently, till the fudge thickens and leaves the sides of the pan, converging in the middle. It is ready when it forms a ball.

- Quickly spread it on to platters in ¾"-1" thick layers. Sprinkle with cardamom.

- When set and completely cool, after about 30 minutes, it will be firm and dry. Cut into squares or diamonds.

- Store in an airtight container for up to 2 weeks.

BESANACHI VADI

Gram Flour Squares

Makes: 30-32 vadya   Time: 45-55 minutes

1 tsp + 6 tbsp tup (ghee)
1 cup gram flour (besan)
1 cup sugar
2 green cardamoms, powdered
4-5 cashew nuts or almonds, blanched, peeled and slivered

- Grease a platter liberally with 1 tsp tup.

- Roast gram flour in a dry frying pan for 10-15 minutes, stirring often.

- Add 2 tbsp tup and sauté for 3-5 minutes.

- Cook sugar with ½ cup water for 8-10 minutes over low-medium heat till it forms a thick syrup.

- Reduce heat. Stir in 2 tbsp tup.

- Pour in gram flour in a steady stream, stirring till smooth. Slowly add the remaining tup.

- Cook for 4-7 minutes, stirring often, till the fudge thickens and leaves the sides of the pan, converging in the middle and frothing into a lump (for softer vadya, cook slightly less).

- Pour the mixture immediately on to the platter. Spread evenly and cut into squares. Sprinkle with cardamom and nuts.

- The vadya set immediately. Do not lift them out for at least 10 minutes, till completely cool.

- Store in an airtight container for up to 2 weeks.

KHOBRYACHI VADI

Vahini Aji's Coconut Fudge
Makes: 25-50 vadya   Time: 2 hours

We grew up eating these addictive sweets!

1 tsp tup (ghee)
2 fresh coconuts, grated
2 litres full-fat milk + 3 times the volume of coconut
The same volume of sugar as coconut
100 gms ground or chopped cashew nuts
1 tsp powdered green cardamom

- Grease a platter liberally with tup.

- Cook coconut and milk in a heavy-bottomed pan over low heat for 45-60 minutes, stirring frequently, till reduced to half its volume. Stir in sugar, nuts and cardamom.

- Cook for 15-25 minutes, stirring frequently. The fudge is ready when it begins to leave the sides of the pan. Put a spoonful on the platter. If it is runny, it needs to cook more. If it sticks together, it is done.

- Spread it in the platter to a ¾" thickness. Cool completely, for 45-60 minutes.

- When it does not look and feel wet, it is set. Cut it into squares or diamonds. Flip the vadi to let the underside dry out.

- Store in an airtight container for up to 2 weeks.

TILACHI VADI

Sankranti Sesame Treats
Makes: 25-50 vadya   Time: 2 hours
Contributor: Aruna Karande

Sesame-jaggery sweets (tilachi vadi or til gul) are traditionally served at Sankranti.

1½ tsp tup (ghee)
100 gms white sesame seeds (til)
100 gms jaggery, grated

- Grease the underside of a parat or mixing platter well with ½ tsp tup.

- On a griddle, over low heat, roast sesame for 7-10 minutes, till golden. Stir often.

- Heat jaggery with 1 tbsp water in a heavy-bottomed pan over very low heat for 4-7 minutes, stirring occasionally, till syrupy. Put a drop on a plate: if it pops, it is ready.

- Stir in the remaining tup, mix in sesame and remove immediately from the heat. Stir till ingredients are well combined.

- Spread on to the parat to a ½" thickness, with a rolling pin.

- Apply some tup to a knife blade. Cut the brittle into ½"-1" squares while warm. Do not separate the squares till dry.

- Store in an airtight container for up to 10 days.

Ladus (Sweet Balls)

Maharashtra's beloved ladu is made from virtually any flour or combinations of flours (rava, besan, rava-besan ladus), fried batter beads (bundiché ladu, motichuraché ladu), or ingredients like whole grains, peanuts, coconut, milk solids, even crunchy fried puris, mixed with powdered sugar or a sugar syrup, often with tup added. It is flavoured with cardamom or sweetmeats before being bound into firm balls.

Popular varieties include rava, besan and policha ladu, made with day-old polya (p. 103). Bundiché and motichuraché ladu are served at special events like weddings.

Traditionally, ladu ingredients are measured by volume and since the thickness of many flours is variable, most quantities are given in cup measures here. Recipes are precise but the cook's judgement (when adding tup, sugar, etc.) is critical in achieving the right sweetness, texture and consistency.

Tips for making ladus:
- For syrup-based ladus, the main ingredients are generally added to hot syrup, a little at a time. Stir between additions, pressing out lumps. Stop when the mixture seems firm enough to bind.

- For flour ladus, if the mixture seems too loose or sticky, add a little dry-roasted gram flour, mixing well between additions till firm enough to bind. If it seems too dry, sprinkle a little milk over small portions of it to help bind it.

- Ladus are usually bound while the mixture is still fairly warm (except for semolina ladus). Stir well and watch your hands. Wet your palms lightly if necessary. If the mixture is too hot to handle, wait briefly but stir it occasionally to prevent it from firming up too quickly.

- Place the mixture in the palm of one hand. Squeezing with the palm of the other hand, gently shape and smoothen it in a firm, even ball.

- To prevent breakage, place bound ladus on a platter in a single layer.

- Store when cool (in a single layer for soft ladus) in a flat, airtight container, in a cool place. Consume ladus containing coconut within 1-2 days and refrigerate.

BESNACHÉ LADU
Gram Flour Balls
Makes: 25 small ladus   Time: 60 minutes

¾ cup + 1 cup tup (ghee)
4 cups gram flour (besan)
½ cup milk
1¾ cups powdered sugar
¾ tsp powdered green cardamom
¼ cup seedless raisins (kishmish – optional)

- Heat ¾ cup tup in a large skillet for 2-3 minutes. Toast gram flour in it for 10-12 minutes, till pinkish golden and aromatic. Stir in the remaining tup and cook for 3-5 minutes.

- Mix in milk. The gram flour will froth. Add sugar and cook for 2-3 minutes more. Stir in cardamom and turn off the heat.

- Mix in raisins and bind ladus as soon as you can handle the mixture, kneading and then rolling it into 1"-1½" balls.

- They crush easily. Store carefully for up to 10 days.

Note: If powdered sugar is unavailable, powder granulated sugar at home.

RAVA-BESAN LADU

Semolina-Gram Flour Balls
Makes: 25 small ladus   Time: 60 minutes

2 cups semolina (sooji/ rava)
2 cups gram flour (besan)
¾ cup + ¾ cup + ¼ cup tup (ghee)
1¾ cups powdered sugar
½ cup milk
¼ cup seedless raisins (kishmish – optional)
¾ tsp powdered green cardamom

- Toast the semolina and gram flour separately using ¾ cup tup for each.

- Then combine them in a pan with the remaining tup and follow the method for besnaché ladu, opposite.

CHURMA LADU

Great Grandma's Crunchy Treat
Makes: 28-30 medium ladus   Time: 2 hours

Mom learnt this recipe for crisp, long-lasting ladus from her grandmother. 'My Ai Aji was an excellent cook. We would all sit around her as she cooked. If we asked for a taste, she always obliged and was happy to see our smiles.'

500 gms sifted refined flour (maida)
110 gms tup (ghee) or butter
A pinch of salt
1 litre vegetable oil
250 gms sugar
1 cup chopped cashew nuts, almonds or pistachio nuts
A handful of seedless raisins (kishmish)

- Place flour in a parat or mixing platter. Rub in tup or butter and salt. Adding up to ½ cup of cold water, knead a firm dough. Rest covered for 1 hour.

- Roll into 2"-2½" puris and fry in hot oil till crisp and golden (p. 108). Cool puris to room temperature.

- In a large pan, cook sugar and ½ cup water to make a syrup. Cook for 5-9 minutes, till it froths and a drop of syrup put into water immediately becomes a firm ball.

- Meanwhile, crush puris into small, even crumbs.

- Remove the syrup from the heat and stir in puri crumbs, nuts and raisins.

- Before the sugar hardens, quickly bind into medium ladus.

GULPAPDICHÉ LADU
Sweet-Crunchy Flour Balls
Makes: 25-30 ladus   Time: 1½ hours
Special equipment: paper-lined platter

2 cups grated dried coconut (kopra)
1½ cups vegetable oil
1 cup thick beaten rice (pohé)
3 cups tup (ghee)
6 cups sifted wholewheat flour (atta)
6 cups grated or chopped jaggery
¼ cup poppy seeds (khus-khus), toasted and powdered
4-5 green cardamoms, powdered
¼ nutmeg, freshly grated

- Toast coconut for 5-8 minutes on a hot griddle, stirring often, till golden.

- Heat oil in a medium wok. When bubbles rise to the top,

carefully add and deep-fry the beaten rice for 1-2 minutes, turning occasionally, till crisp and golden. Reduce heat if it is cooking too fast. Drain well and remove quickly, placing it on the paper-lined platter. When cool, crush it to a fine powder between your palms.

- Heat tup in a large wok. Toast flour for 15-20 minutes, till golden brown and aromatic.

- Mix in coconut, beaten rice, jaggery, poppy seeds, cardamom and nutmeg and stir till the jaggery dissolves.

- Form 'gul papdi' into small balls, placing them on a platter.

- Store cool, firm ladus in an airtight container.

Variation: **Gulpapdichi Vadi (Sweet-Crunchy Flour Squares)**: Make vadya (squares) with the above mixture, using only 2¼ cups tup. Prepare as for batatyachi vadi (p. 333).

RAVYACHÉ LADU

Semolina Balls

Makes: 30-32 medium ladus   Time: 1-1½ hours

My brother, Sameer is very fond of ravyaché ladu. When we were kids, he would pop them into his mouth whenever he was hungry.

4 cups semolina (sooji/rava)
2-3 tbsp tup (ghee)
2 cups sugar
½ cup milk
3-4 tbsp cashew nuts or blanched, peeled almonds, finely chopped
2-3 tbsp seedless raisins (kishmish)
3-4 green cardamoms, powdered

- Roast semolina for 7-12 minutes in a hot skillet. Add tup and sauté for 5-7 minutes, till aromatic.

- In a large pan, cook sugar and 1½ cups water for 7-10 minutes over medium-low heat to make a syrup.

- Sprinkle milk over the semolina. Stir well. Fold in nuts, rasins and cardamoms. Stir semolina into the syrup.

- Rest for 30 minutes to 4 hours till the liquid is absorbed. Mix well and bind the semolina into 1½" balls.

TANDULACHYA PITHACHÉ LADU
Rice Flour Balls
Makes: 12-15 small ladus   Time: 15 minutes
Contributor: Meera Marathe

2 cups rice flour
1½ cups powdered sugar
½-¾ cup or more tup (ghee)

- Combine rice flour and sugar, pressing out lumps.

- Melt tup over low heat for 2-3 minutes. Add it in a steady stream into the flour, stirring continuously.

- Shape into small ladus. If too soft or crumbly, add some more tup, a little at a time, till ladus hold together when pressed tightly in the palm.

- Store in an airtight container.

Sweet Breads

BHOPLYACHI PURI
Tasty Fried Pumpkin Bread
Makes: 15-20 purya   Time: 30 minutes
Special equipment: pastry blender
Contributor: Meera Marathe

Make these fruity snacks soft or crisp like cookies. Traditionally they contain pumpkin. You could also use apples, pears, ripe peaches, plums or almost overripe bananas.

1 cup grated red pumpkin (kaddu)
500 ml vegetable oil
2-4 tbsp sugar or jaggery
2 cups sifted wholewheat flour (atta)
4 tbsp butter

- Sauté pumpkin briefly in 1 tsp oil. Cover pan and steam-cook for 5-6 minutes, till tender. Mash further if needed. Transfer pumpkin to a bowl. Add sweetener.

- In a separate bowl, combine flour and butter. Using a pastry blender, cut butter into the flour till it forms small beads.

- Use the pumpkin to bind the dough. Knead well.

- Divide dough into 1" flattened discs. Roll each disc into a 3" wide, ¼" thick puri.

- Heat oil in a wok. When bubbles rise to the top, reduce the heat slightly. Fry 2-3 purya at a time (p. 108). These dense purya are unlikely to really puff up.

Note: Bhoplyachya purya last for up to 10 days—more in dry weather. If exposed to dry air, they go hard. Use up other fruit purya within a week.

PAKATLI PURI

Deep-Fried Rounds in Lemony Syrup
Makes: 8-10 purya   Time: 60 minutes

Ai Aji made puris-in-syrup for my father's birthday when he was a child. They are excellent fresh and warm but Dad says they improve with time. He likes them stale, with an extra squeeze of lime juice or thick yogurt, which is how many Marathis eat jilebis as well!

Puri:
1 cup sifted refined or wholewheat flour (maida or atta)
2 tbsp moderately tart to very tart yogurt
A pinch of salt
1 tbsp vegetable oil

Syrup:
¾ cup sugar
Juice of ½-1 lime
A few saffron strands
3 green cardamoms, powdered

500 ml vegetable oil

Puri:

- Make a firm puri dough with the these ingredients and cool water (p. 108). Rest covered for 1-2 hours.

Syrup:

- Heat sugar and with ¾ cup water in a medium pan over low heat, stirring occasionally till the sugar dissolves. Raise the heat. Bring the syrup to a boil and simmer for 5-7 minutes, till thickened.

- Stir in lime juice, saffron and cardamom.

To fry:

- Roll and deep fry purya (p. 108). Cool completely.

- Arrange purya in a deep, flat serving dish. Cover completely with all but ½ cup syrup. Soak for at least 3 hours before serving.

- Pour the reserved syrup over the purya, if needed.

SHINDI DASHMI
Crunchy Marathi Cookies
Makes: 4 cookies   Time: 30 minutes
Contributor: Sushama Marathe

My aunt learnt this recipe from her mother, Sushila Divekar.

¾ cup sifted wholewheat flour (atta)
¾ cup powdered sugar
¼ tsp freshly grated nutmeg

2-2½ tbsp tup (ghee)
4-5 tbsp milk + extra

- Combine all ingredients except milk in a bowl. Slowly adding milk, knead a firm dough.

- Divide it into 2" balls. Dip your fingers in milk and pat each ball into a flat disc, turning to make it evenly round.

- Heat a griddle well. Roast dashmis on each side for 1-2 minutes, till dark brown.

- Serve hot.

GULACHI POLI

Sesame-Jaggery Winter Bread
Makes: 6-8 polya   Time: 90 minutes
Contributor: Meera Marathe

Crisp thin Sankranti breads are stuffed with jaggery and sesame seeds. Serve them with fresh tup.

Dough:
1 cup sifted refined flour (maida)
¼ cup gram flour (besan)
2 tbsp vegetable oil
A pinch of salt

Filling:
2 tsp vegetable oil
½ cup gram flour (besan)
1 cup crushed and softened jaggery
2 tbsp sesame seeds (til)

Dough:

- Combine flours in a parat or mixing platter. Make a well in the centre and add oil and salt. Rub them into the flour. Slowly adding up to ¾ cup of water bind the flour into an elastic dough. Knead very thoroughly for 3-5 minutes. Rest covered for at least 30 minutes.

Filling:

- Heat oil on a griddle. Roast gram flour for 3-5 minutes, till aromatic and light brown. Knead it into a ball with jaggery and sesame. Rest covered for 15 minutes.

Forming and roasting the poli:

- Divide dough and filling into 8-10 equal-sized balls.

- Stretch a dough ball slightly in one palm with the fingers of the other hand. Place filling into it and fold the dough over to cover completely.

- Gently roll out the stuffed ball on a lightly floured board till about ¹/₁₆" thick. Ensure that no stuffing leaks out. It will burn.

- Heat a griddle well. Gently place the poli on it and roast once on each side for 2-4 minutes, till golden brown. Cool the polya on a platter.

- Roll the next poli while one roasts. Scrape burnt bits off the griddle between roastings. Stack and wrap cooled polya in a clean muslin cloth.

- Store in an airtight container.

KHAVYACHI POLI
Rich Milk-filled Sweet Bread
Serves: 8-10   Time: 90 minutes
Contributor: Medha Marathe

Make these rich, milk-solid stuffed breads in advance. Lightly reheat to serve.

Dough:

500 gms sifted refined flour (maida)
A pinch of salt

Filling:

500 gms khava (mava) or ricotta cheese
½ cup semolina (sooji/rava)
500 gms powdered sugar
2 green cardamoms, powdered
½ tsp freshly grated nutmeg
A few saffron strands
1-2 tsp rice flour, if required

1½ cups tup (ghee)

Dough:

- Place flour in a bowl. Make a well in the centre. Add salt and oil, rubbing them into the flour. Slowly adding up to 1¼ cups water, make a firm dough. Knead it smooth. Rest covered for 30 minutes.

Filling:

- Sauté khava in a skillet over low heat for 3-4 minutes, till grainy and dry. Set aside.

- Toast semolina in the same skillet for 4-5 minutes, till aromatic and starting to turn golden. Reduce heat and mix in khava. Turn off the heat.

- Stir in sugar and spices. The filling should be as firm as the dough. If it is too soft, mix in rice flour.

- Shape equal-sized balls of dough and filling that fit in your palm. Roll out a large enough disc of dough so that when the filling is placed in the centre, there is enough dough to fold around it. Seal the filling completely within the dough. Flatten the filled ball gently. Carefully roll it into a 6"-8" disc. Prepare all the polya this way.

- Heat a griddle over medium heat. Spread a thin layer of tup. Roast a poli in it for 1-2 minutes, till golden (for soft polya, cook to the colour of yellow cream). Flip over and roast for just under a minute.

- Store in an airtight container when cool.

SHIRYACHI POLI
Sweet Semolina-Filled Bread
Makes: 4 polya   Time: 30 minutes

- Make poli dough (p. 103) and gode shira (p. 69).

- Fill each ball of dough with 1 tbsp shira.

- Roast as for khavyachi poli (opposite page).

PURAN POLI

Festival Sweet Bread

Makes: 15-20 polya   Time: 2-3 hours over 2 days
Special equipment: puran yantra, muslin cloth
Contributor: Meera Marathe

Sweetened mashed Bengal gram in silky dough make the quintessential Marathi dessert, puran poli. Widely believed to be difficult to make successfully, there is a special word for someone who can do so: sugran (a competent housewife). Eat puran polya hot, with hot or cold tup, or cold with warm milk or thick cream! Then use the leftover puran, stuck to the sides of the pan, to make katachi amti (p. 352).

Filling:
2 cups split, husked Bengal gram (chana dal)
1½ cups sugar or 1 cup sugar + ½ cup thoroughly crushed jaggery
3 green cardamoms, powdered
A few saffron strands
¼ tsp freshly grated nutmeg

Dough:
2 cups sifted refined flour (maida) + extra for rolling
¼ cup vegetable oil + extra for coating dough
A pinch of salt
A few saffron strands soaked in ½ tsp warm milk

Filling:

- Prepare the filling a day earlier. Pressure-cook gram in 5 cups water for 10-15 minutes after cooker reaches full pressure (3-4 whistles) or on the stove top for 45-60 minutes, till tender.

- Drain gram and reserve the water for katachi amti (p. 352).

- Grind gram into a thick paste. Mix in sweetener and spices.

- Cook paste in a heavy-bottomed pan for 40-60 minutes, stirring often, till moist but thick enough to form a ball.

- Cool thoroughly. Shape into 1½" balls (15-20 balls) for immediate use. (Refrigerate for later use for up to 2-3 days. Bring puran to room temperature before proceeding.)

- Reserve the pan unwashed, to make katachi amti.

Dough:

- Place flour in a parat or mixing platter. Make a well in the centre. Add ¼ cup oil and salt. Rub them into the flour thoroughly. Add saffron and its soaking liquid.

- Adding up to ¾ cup water very slowly, make a soft, white, very elastic dough. Knead very thoroughly for 5-7 minutes.

- Spread oil liberally over it and rest covered for at least 30 minutes.

To make the polya:

- Make as many even-sized balls of dough as there are balls of filling.

- Stretch out dough, patting it with the fingers of one hand into the palm of the other. Place the filling in the centre and gently seal it completely within the dough. Make sure there are no gaps or the filling will squeeze out.

- Form all the balls similarly, keeping them covered with a slightly damp cloth to prevent drying.

- Lightly flour a rolling board. Gently and uniformly roll a stuffed dough ball into a thin 8" disc. Rolling out this pliable dough, made even more delicate by the filling, is more demanding than rolling out other polya. Use flour sparingly and make sure no filling oozes out as you roll.

- Meanwhile heat a griddle well. Reduce heat slightly. Gently place the poli on it, roasting for 2-4 minutes on each side, till golden.

- Roll and roast all polya this way.

- Cool them in the parat before stacking and wrapping them in a muslin cloth.

- Store in an airtight container for up to 10 days.

KATACHI AMTI
Pan Edge Lentils
Serves: 4-6   Time: 30 minutes

Filling left over in the pan after making puran poli (p. 350)
25 gms grated dried coconut (kopra)
1 tsp cumin seeds
3 tbsp tamarind pulp (p. 27)
1-2 tsp salt
1½ tsp red chilli powder
1 tsp goda masala (p. 48)
3-4 tsp finely grated jaggery or 4-6 tsp sugar

Seasoning:
2 tbsp vegetable oil
4-5 x 1" sticks cinnamon
4-5 cloves
2-3 bay leaves (tej patta)
10-12 curry leaves

- Add 4 cups water to the pan in which the filling for the puran poli was made. Scrape the gram off the sides and bottom of the pan.

- Add 4-6 tbsp more dal paste if the mixture looks too thin.

- Meanwhile, roast coconut on a hot griddle till golden and aromatic. Grind it with cumin into a powder.

- Heat oil for seasoning in a large pan. Stir in cinnamon, cloves and bay leaves. Add curry leaves, a ladleful of reserved gram water (while making puran poli) and tamarind. Stir briskly.

- Bring to a boil over low heat. Add salt, chilli powder and goda masala. Simmer for 5-7 minutes. Add sweetener and the remaining gram water. Bring to a boil again.

- Add the coconut-cumin powder. Boil for 5-7 minutes.

- Serve hot or cold with rice or with pieces of plain or puranachya polya dipped or soaked in it.

Candy & Simple Pleasures

Candy

This chapter is not about lollipops or chocolate bars but about goodies that mothers and grandmothers lovingly make for their families. Many such 'candies' are made in Marathi homes like shrikhandachi vadi or alyachi vadi (shrikhand or ginger candy), while fresh chunks of sugarcane, raisins, bits of jaggery or rock sugar are also special treats, occasionally eaten with peanuts as a wholesome snack. Here are a few favourites.

CASHEW ROCK
East Indian Cashew Nut Brittle
Makes: 50 pieces   Time: 40 minutes

East Indians make this brittle for Christmas.

250 gms raw cashew nuts
1 tsp + 2 tsp tup (ghee)
300 gms sugar
1 tsp rose essence
A few drops of red food colouring (optional)

- Grind cashew in batches into a coarse but even powder. Grease a platter with 1 tsp tup.

- In a large pan, bring sugar and ½ cup water to a boil.

- Stir in nuts. Cook for about 10 minutes, till thickened. Test by holding up a spoonful of syrup. If it does not drop off easily, it is ready. Mix in 2 tsp tup, rose essence and food colouring (if used).

- Evenly spread brittle on the platter. Cut into diamonds while hot. Cool completely before removing from the platter.

- Store in an airtight container for up to a month.

LONAVLA CHIKKI
Peanut Brittle
Serves: 10   Time: 30 minutes
Contributor: Usha Marathe

About 90 kms from Mumbai, the train stops at the hill station of Lonavala. Passengers poke their heads out to see if chikki vendors are hopping on to the train to sell chikki, a great 'time-pass'. Try my aunt's easy recipe at home. This chikki is delicious with almonds or cashews too.

¾ cup raw or roasted peanuts
2 tbsp tup (ghee)
1 cup grated jaggery or sugar

- Use whole nuts or grind them coarse and chunky. Grease a platter liberally with tup. Sprinkle the nuts across it.

- Heat sweetener for 3-5 minutes in a pan over medium heat, stirring occasionally till syrupy and frothy. Drop a little syrup into a bowl of water. It should ball up immediately. Press it between your fingers. If it is so sticky that it is difficult to pull your fingers apart, the syrup is done.

- Pour it immediately over the nuts and spread evenly across the platter. Cool for 2-3 minutes. Cut into squares or diamonds. Cool completely before removing the pieces.

- Store in an airtight container.

Simple Pleasures

As an occasional treat, a mother might serve her children a sweet condiment with their meal: jam and tup or even a mashed banana sprinkled with sugar, to scoop up in poli or bhakri, or a sweet, warm, concoction with milk and bread for a soothing supper.

DUDH-BHAKRI
Bhakri-Milk Mush
Serves: 1   Time: 5 minutes

Keya loves this mush when she is tired and hungry.

1 bhakri
Sugar to taste
½ -1 cup hot or cold milk

• Shred bhakri into a bowl. Sprinkle with sugar. Stir in milk. Mash thoroughly.

Variation: **Dudh-Poli (Chapatti-Milk Mush)**: Use 1-2 polya instead of bhakri. Or try white bread!

GUL-CHUN
Jaggery-Coconut Relish
Serves: 1-2   Time: 5 minutes

Reserve some coconut for gul-chun when you are scraping it for another dish.

½ cup grated fresh coconut
3-6 tsp slightly softened grated jaggery
1 tsp or more tup (ghee)

• Mix coconut with jaggery. (Briefly place jaggery by the stove if needed, to soften it.)

• Mix solid or warm tup into the chun.

Variation: **Gul-Tup (Jaggery and Clarified Butter)**: Grate or mash jaggery and serve it with fresh polya. Spoon cold or warm tup over individual servings. Mash it with your fingers as you eat.

KELYACHI SHIKRAN
Fresh Banana Pudding
Serves: 1   Time: 10 minutes

Shikran can be made in two ways, with a distinct flavour difference.

1 banana, sliced or diced
1 tsp sugar (optional)
½ cup milk at room temperature

- Combine the ingredients in a bowl. Stir to dissolve the sugar.
- Serve at room temperature or chilled.

Variation: Mash the bananas instead of slicing or dicing them.

TUP-KELA
Clarified Butter with Bananas
Serves: 1   Time: 5 minutes

1 tbsp tup (ghee)
1 banana, peeled
Sugar to taste (optional)

- Put tup on a peeled banana. Mash the banana into the tup while eating or eat chunks with a dab of tup alongside.
- Or sprinkle a little sugar over the banana, or briefly sauté it in tup before serving, to caramelize it slightly.

TUP-SAKHAR
Clarified Butter and Sugar
Serves: 1

½ tsp or more sugar
1 tsp solid or warm tup

- Spoon sugar on a plate. Add tup. Mix well and eat with poli or bhakri.
- Try this with jam and tup too.

Drinks

Drinks

Here are some of the beverages Marathi people enjoy. They also relish sipping or drinking during a meal: spiced buttermilk (phodnicha tak, mattha), gravied vegetables (patal bhaji) and lentils (amti, kadhi), etc. Traditionally, the only other drink at mealtime would be water.

Many medicinal drinks (kadha) are made elaborately from herbs and spices but these belong to a whole other realm of cookery. Here I include only tulshicha chaha, sacred basil-black tea brew.

Dairy Drinks

HALDICHA DUDH
Milk with Turmeric
Serves: 1   Time: 5 minutes

Warm milk foments, and turmeric soothes a sore throat. Drink it as hot as you can, twice a day.

1 cup milk
Sugar to taste
½-1 tsp turmeric powder

- Bring milk to a rolling boil in a small pan. Briskly stir in sugar and turmeric.

- Serve immediately.

MASALYACHA DUDH

Spiced Sweet Milk

Serves: 4   Time: 30-40 minutes

Kojagiri Purnima is the full moon night celebrated in Ashwin (September-October). It is also known as Kaumudi Purnima because it is a celebration of the moon (Kaumudi means moonlight). People stay awake all night, singing songs and playing games in honour of the goddess of wealth, Lakshmi. They sip masalycha dudh.

1½ litres full-fat milk
100 gms sugar
6 cashew nuts, chopped
5 almonds, blanched, peeled and chopped
5 pistachio nuts, chopped (optional)
4-5 saffron strands
1 tsp charolya (chironji – optional)
5-6 green cardamoms, powdered

- Boil milk in a heavy-bottomed, deep pan over low heat for 10-15 minutes. Stir the cream that rises to the surface back into the milk occasionally.

- Reduce milk for 15-20 minutes, stirring frequently. When golden and thick but of a drinkable consistency, turn off the heat.

- Add the remaining ingredients.

- Chill or cool in a parat or mixing platter filled with water.

GODE TAK

Sweetened Buttermilk

Serves: 2   Time: 10 minutes
Special equipment: churning stick/whisk

Though buttermilk (a by-product of churning butter) is delicious drunk fresh and pure, sweetened buttermilk is refreshing too. Gode tak, mattha and even lemonade are accepted drinks for fast days (except on those days when tart or white foods are forbidden).

3 cups churned buttermilk or 1 cup yogurt + 2 cups water
2-3 tbsp sugar
A pinch of powdered green cardamom (optional)

- Whisk liquefied yogurt (if used) till smooth. Stir sugar and cardamom into the buttermilk or liquefied yogurt.

- Serve at room temperature or refrigerate covered for 2-3 hours and serve chilled. Stir before serving.

PHODNICHA TAK

Buttermilk with Seasoning

Serves: 2   Time: 10 minutes

500 ml buttermilk or 1 cup yogurt + 400 ml water
½ tsp ginger paste
½ tsp sugar
½-1 tsp salt

Seasoning:
1 tsp tup (ghee)
½ tsp cumin seeds

- If using tart buttermilk, dilute it with up to ½ cup water and whisk till smooth. Whisk liquefied yogurt (if used) till smooth.

- Add ginger, sugar and salt.

- Heat tup in a small wok. Add cumin seeds and let them pop.

- Pour seasoning over the drink, stir well and serve.

MATTHA
Buttermilk with Coriander and Green Chillies
Serves: 2   Time: 10 minutes

Mattha is made from yogurt and is slightly thicker than phodnicha tak (previous page). It can also be made from 500 ml not-too-tart buttermilk.

200 gms yogurt + 300 ml water
½ tsp sugar

Spice paste:
1 tbsp coriander leaves
1" piece of ginger
1 small green chilli
½ tsp cumin seeds
½-1 tsp salt
1 tsp tup (ghee)

- Whisk liquefied yogurt till smooth. Grind spice paste ingredients fine.

- To serve, stir sugar and spice paste into the yogurt.

- If you like, season the drink as for phodnicha tak (previous page).

Fruit Drinks

Serve fruit beverages at room temperature or chilled, plain or over ice.

AMSULACHA SARBAT
Tart-Sweet Kokum Cooler
Serves: 4   Time: 60 minutes soaking + 15 minutes preparation

Amsul helps fight nausea resulting from stomach problems and migraines.

½ cup kokum (amsul)
½ cup sugar
½ tsp salt

- Soak kokum in 1 cup warm water for 1 hour. Add 3 cups water and squeeze and rub the kokum to express more juice. Discard (or munch) the skins. Strain.

- Briskly stir in sugar and salt before serving.

AVLYACHA SARBAT

Indian Gooseberry Cooler

Serves: 4-6   Time: 1 hour preparation + 8-12 hours soaking +
45 minutes cooking

250 gms Indian gooseberries (avla/amla), washed, wiped dry and
pricked with a fork
¼ tsp edible lime (chunam)
750 gms sugar
1-2 drops green food colouring (optional)
A pinch of powdered green cardamom per serving
A pinch of salt per serving

- Soak avlas overnight with edible lime in 2 cups water. Drain and rinse well.

- Pressure-cook for 5 minutes after cooker reaches full pressure (2 whistles) or steam for 15-20 minutes, till very soft. Cool, remove seeds and grind avlas to a paste.

- Using the same container, measure equal parts by volume of sugar and water into a large pan. Cook into a simple syrup over low-medium heat for 10-15 minutes. Carefully press a drop of syrup between thumb and index finger. When you pull your fingers apart, it should stretch to a thin strand. If watery, cook slightly longer, if too thick, add a little water, heat briefly and test again.

- Remove syrup from heat and stir in the avla pulp. Cool completely. Add food colouring (if used).

- Refrigerate concentrate in an airtight jar for up to 1 week (freeze for up to 2 months).

- To serve, briskly stir 1 tsp concentrate into 1 cup of water with a pinch each of cardamom and salt.

CHINCHECHA SARBAT

Thirst-Quenching Tamarind Cooler
Serves: 6-8   Time: 1 hour soaking + 10 minutes mixing

This summer drink from the 'Desh' replenishes essential salts and sugars, and tastes great!

250 gms tamarind
A pinch of salt
1-3 tbsp sugar per serving

* Heat 1 litre water almost to boiling. Soak tamarind in it for at least 1 hour. Strain and mash the pulp through a sieve into a bowl. Add salt.

* To serve, combine 1-2 tbsp pulp with 1 cup water and sugar in a glass.

KAIRICHA PANHA

Steamed Green Mango Juice
Serves: 4-6   Time: 30 minutes

My mother makes panha, a refreshing green mango drink, every summer and freezes some to serve after summer has faded away.

4 medium-large green mangoes, washed
1 cup sugar or jaggery
4 green cardamoms, powdered
A pinch of saffron strands, powdered
½-¾ tsp salt

- Place mangoes in a large pan three-quarters filled with water. Cover and bring to a boil over medium heat. Simmer for 20-25 minutes, till the mango flesh is soft and the skins are loose and yellowy. Turn off the heat.

- Drain off the water, cool the mangoes, skin them and put the pulpy flesh into a bowl. Squeeze the pulp off the stones and place stones in another bowl.

- Add a little warm water to the stones and extract more pulp. Combine this with the thick pulp.

- Add sweetener and mash till smooth.

- Stir in cardamom, saffron and salt. Carefully remove any fibres (blend if you like).

- Refrigerate panha in a glass jar for up to 1 week. For later use, freeze it in ice trays.

- To serve, spoon a ladleful or 1-2 pulp cubes into a glass. Briskly stir in water.

LIMBACHA SARBAT

Marathi Lemonade
Serves: 1   Time: 5-7 minutes

Marathi lemonade is delicious and refreshing.

1 tbsp lime or lemon juice
1½ tbsp sugar
A pinch of salt
A pinch of powdered green cardamom

To serve, briskly stir the ingredients together with 120-150 ml water, till the sugar dissolves.

Tea & Coffee

CHAHA

Marathi Tea for Two and Three Variations
Serves: 2   Time: 5-7 minutes
Contributor: Padmavati Marathe

Add a pinch of powdered cardamom or nutmeg or 1 cinnamon stick to flavour the tea. The variations below also serve two and take 5-7 minutes.

2 cups water
2 tsp sugar or to taste
2 tsp good quality Indian black tea leaves
Full-fat milk to taste

- Combine water with the sugar in a pan and bring to a rolling boil.

- Add tea leaves. Turn off the heat. Steep tea covered for about 2 minutes.

- Meanwhile, heat milk to boiling.

- Strain tea into cups, add milk and serve hot.

Note: A pan with a lip is more efficient for pouring out tea through a strainer. To cool tea quickly, add cold milk or cream.

GULACHA CHAHA

Jaggery Tea
Serves: 2   Time: 5-7 minutes

Till recently, tea was sweetened with jaggery in Maharashtra. Gulacha chaha is still drunk in rural parts.

½ cup milk
1½ cups water
4 tsp grated jaggery
2 tsp good quality Indian black tea leaves
½ tsp grated ginger or a pinch of cardamom (optional)

- Combine all ingredients in a small pan. Bring to a rolling boil over high heat for 2-3 minutes.

- Reduce heat and simmer for 1-2 minutes. Turn off the heat.

- Steep tea covered for about 2 minutes, strain and serve hot.

ALYACHA CHAHA

Ginger Tea
Serves: 2   Time: 5-7 minutes

I use this tea often in the winter, when coughs and colds inhabit the house.

1 cup milk
1 cup water
2 tsp sugar or to taste
2 tsp good quality Indian black tea leaves
½ tsp ground dried ginger (saunth) or ½ tsp grated fresh ginger

- Make tea as given for chaha (previous page), adding ginger only after the milk and water have boiled.

SPEED-OF-LIGHT GINGER TEA FOR ONE

While the tea water boils, crush a small piece of ginger. Add it to a mug with a teabag of good quality Indian tea. Pour boiling water over and steep covered for 2-3 minutes.

Remove tea bag and ginger, add sugar and milk, and drink as hot as possible!

BADSHAHI CHAHA

Tea Fit for a King
Serves: 4   Time: 10-15 minutes
Contributor: Meera Marathe

This is a lovely rich brew.

700 ml full-fat milk
9-10 tsp sugar or to taste
4-5 tsp good quality Indian black tea leaves
½-¾ tsp powdered cardamom
½-¾ tsp freshly grated nutmeg

* Boil all ingredients in a pan for 7-10 minutes, till the milk turns a nice pinkish brown.

* Steep tea covered for 1-2 minutes, strain and serve hot.

KONKANI CHAHA

Coastal Tea

Serves: 4   Time: 10-15 minutes

Contributor: Anuradha Samant

In the Konkan, Badshahi chaha is sometimes deliciously made with coconut milk.

4-8 tsp sugar
6 tsp good quality Indian black tea leaves
2 cups water
½ tsp powdered cardamom (optional)
½ tsp grated nutmeg (optional)
2 cups thick coconut milk

• Make tea as as given for chaha (p. 373), but add coconut milk *after* the water has boiled and the heat is reduced. Warm but do not boil the tea once the milk is added.

• Steep tea covered for about 2 minutes, strain and serve hot.

TULSHICHA CHAHA

Sacred Basil-Peppercorn Tea

Serves: 1   Time: 5-7 minutes

Contributor: Sudhakar Marathe

½ cup milk
½ cup water
1½ tsp sugar
1 tsp good quality Indian black tea leaves
5-6 large sacred basil leaves (tulsi), washed
2-3 peppercorns, crushed

- Boil all ingredients in a small pan. Turn off the heat.
- Steep tea covered for about 2 minutes. Strain and serve hot.

HALDI-KUNKU COFFEE
Party Coffee with Cardamom
Serves: 2   Time: 10 minutes
Contributor: Ashwini Marathe

This delicious coffee is often served at haldi-kunkus.

200 ml whole or low-fat milk
200 ml water
3 level tsp or more sugar
1½ level tsp ground coffee
A pinch of grated nutmeg
A pinch of powdered green cardamom or 2-3 cardamoms, with peel,
crushed

- Combine all ingredients in a pan and bring to a rolling boil for 5-7 minutes over medium heat. Stir occasionally. Turn off the heat.
- Brew covered for 2-3 minutes, till the coffee grounds settle. Strain and serve piping hot.

Note: Ashwini uses an equal mix of Peaberry and plantation beans with 10 per cent chicory.

Glossary

ENGLISH	MARATHI	HINDI
Ajwain/carum	Ova	Ajwain
Almond	Badam	Badam
Amaranth	Lal math	Cholai bhaji
Apple	Safarchand	Seb
Asafoetida	Hinga	Hing
Aubergine/brinjal/eggplant	Vanga	Baingan
Banana	Kela	Kela
–Flower	Kelphul	Mocha
–Leaf	Kelyachi pana	Kela ka patta
Bay leaf	Tamal patri	Tej patta
Beetroot	Beet	Chukander
Bengal gram		
–Flour	Besan	Besan
–Gram flour strings	Shev	Sev
–Green (fresh)	Harbhara	Hara chana
–Husked, split	Harbaryachi/ chanyachi dal	Chana dal
–Roasted	Phutané	Bhuna chana
–Roasted, split	Chivda dal	–
–Whole	Harbhara	Kala chana
Bitter beans	Val	–
Bitter gourd	Karla	Karela
Black beans/gram		
–Husked, split	Udid dal	Urad dal
–Whole	Udid	Sabut urad
Black pepper	Kali miri	Kali mirch
Bottle gourd	Dudhi bhopla	Ghia/lauki
Bread	Pav/bread	Double roti
Brown mung	Mutki	Mutki/moth
Butter	Loni	Makkhan
–Clarified	Tup	Ghee
Buttermilk	Tak	Chhaas

ENGLISH	MARATHI	HINDI
Cabbage	Kobi	Bandgobhi
Capsicum	Bhopli/ bhongi mirchi	Shimla mirch
Cardamom		
–Black	Veldoda	Badi elaichi
–Green	Veldoda	Hari/chhoti elaichi
Carrot	Gaajar	Gaajar
Cashew nut	Kaju	Kaju
Cauliflower	Phulkobi	Phoolgobhi
Chemical lime (edible)	Khaycha chuna	Chunam
Chicken	Kombdi	Murgh
Chilli	Mirchi/Mirchya	Mirchi
–dried red	Mirchya	Sookhi mirch
–Green	Hirvya mirchya	Hari mirch
–Red	Lal mirchya	Lal mirch
Cinnamon	Dalchini	Dalchini
–fruit	Nagkesar	Nagkesar
Clove	Lavang	Laung
Cluster beans	Gavar	Gwar ki phalli
Coconut		
–Copra (dry)	Suka khobra	Kopra
–Fresh	Naral	Nariyal
–Milk	Naralacha kol	Nariyal ka doodh
Colocasia	Alu	Arbi
–Leaf	Aluchi pana	Arbi patta
Colostrum	Chik	Khees/navdugdh
Coriander		
–Fresh	Kothimbir/sambar	Hara dhania
–whole seeds	Dhanay	Sabut dhania
Corn	Maka	Makkai
Cream	Saay	Malai
Cubeb pepper	Kankol	Kabab cheeni
Cucumber	Kakdi	Kheera/kakdi
Cumin seeds	Jira	Jeera
–Black/royal cumin	Shah jira	Kala/shah jeera
Curry leaf	Kadhilimbachi pana	Kari patta
Drumsticks	Shevgyachya shenga	Surjan ki phalli

ENGLISH	MARATHI	HINDI
Duck	Badak	Badak
Egg	Andi/anda	Anda
Egyptian/brown lentils		
–Husked, split	Masur dal	Masur dal
–Whole	Masur	Sabut masur
Elephant's Foot Yam	Suran	Zimikand
Fennel seeds	Badishep	Badi saunf
Fenugreek		
–Fresh leaves	Methi	Methi bhaji
–Whole seeds	Methi	Methi dana
Fish	Maasa/maase /maasali	Machchi /machchli
French beans	Shravan ghevda	Fransbin
Garlic	Lassun	Lassun
Ginger		
–Dry	Suntha	Saunth
–Fresh	Ala	Adrak
Goa spiceberry	Triphala	Triphala/tirphal
Green mung beans		
–Husked, split	Mugachi dal	Mung dal
–Whole	Mug	Sabut mung
Green peas	Matar	Matar
–Dried	Vatana	Sookhé mattar
Horse gram/vetch	Kulthacha pith	Kulthi ka dal
Indian gooseberry	Rai avla/ dongri avla	Amla
Ivy gourd	Tondli	Tendli
Jackfruit	Phanas	Kathal
Jaggery	Gul	Gur
Kingfish/seer	Surmai	Surmai
Lettuce	Salad	Salad ke patté
Lichen	Dagad phul	Dagad phul
Lime	Limbu	Limbu/nimbu
Liver	Kaleji	Kaleji
Mace	Jaipatri	Javitri
Mackerel	Bangda	Bangda
Mango	Kairi	Aam
–Powder	Amchur	Amchur
–Ripe	Amba	Aam
Milk	Dudh	Doodh

ENGLISH	MARATHI	HINDI
Millet		
–Hill	Vari	–
–Pearl	Bajri	Bajra
–Pearl millet flour	Bajricha peeth	Bajra ka atta
Minced meat	Khima	Keema
Mint	Pudina	Pudina
Mustard		
–Oil	Mohricha tel	Sarson ka tael
–Black/brown seeds	Mohri	Sarson/rai
–Yellow seeds	Mohri	Peeli sarson
Mutton	Mutton	Gosht
–Baby goat's meat	Mendhicha mutton	Kid
Nutmeg	Jaiphal	Jaiphal
Oil	Tel	Tael
Okra/ladies fingers	Bhendi	Bhindi
Onion	Kanda	Pyaaz
Peanut	Shengdana	Mungphali
–Powder	Danyacha kut	–
Pigeon peas/yellow lentils	Turichi dal	Arhar/toover
– stalks	Turathi	
Pineapple	Annanas	Annanas
Pistachio nuts	Pista	Pista
Pomfret	Poplet	Chhamna/paplet
Poppy seeds	Khaskhas	Khus-khus
Pork	Dukrachey mutton	Suvar ka gosht
Potato	Batata	Alu
Pumpkin		
–Red/yellow	Lal bhopla/bhopla	Kaddu
Radish		
–Ma-in	Ma-in mula	–
–White	Mula	Safaid mooli
Raisin		
–seedless	Kismis	Kishmish
Rice	Tandul	Chaval
–Beaten/flattened/pound	Pohé	Poha
–Flour	Tandulacha peeth	Chaval ka atta
–Puffed	Churmura	Murmurra
Rose water	Gulab jal	Gulab jal
Safflower Oil	Kardai	–

ENGLISH	MARATHI	HINDI
Saffron	Keshar	Kesar/zafran
Sago	Sabudana	Sabudana
Salt	Meeth	Namak
Semolina	Rava	Sooji/rava
Sesame seeds	Til	Til
Shrimp	Kolambi	Jhinga
–Dried	Sodé	Sukha jhinga
Silver leaf	Varkha	Varq
Snake gourd	Padval	Chirchinda
Sorghum	Jwari	Jowar
–Flour	Jwaricha peeth	Jowar atta
Sodium bicarbonate	Soda	Meetha soda
Spinach	Palak	Palak
Sugar	Saakhar	Cheeni/shakkar
Sweet potato	Ratala	Sakarkand
Tamarind	Chincha	Imli
Tea leaves	Chahachi pud	Chai patti
Tomato	Tamatar	Tamatar
Turmeric	Halad	Haldi
Vermicelli	Shevaya	Sevian
Vinegar	Shirka	Sirka
Wheat	Gahu	Gehun
–Broken/cracked/burgul /bulghur	Gahu	Dalia
–Plain/refined flour	Kanik	Maida
–Wholewheat flour	Kanik	Atta
Yogurt	Dahi	Dahi
–Cheese	Chakka	–

Bibliography

ENGLISH TITLES

Achaya, K.T. *A Historical Dictionary of Indian Food.* New Delhi: Oxford University Press, 2003.

Jaffrey, Madhur. *A Taste of India.* New York: Macmillan, 1988.

Jaffrey, Madhur. *An Invitation to Indian Cooking.* New York: Alfred A. Knopf, 1973.

Marathé, Kaumudi. *Maharastrian Food: A Family Treasury.* Mumbai: Zaika, BPI, 1999.

Marks, Copeland. *Sephardic Cooking: 600 Recipes Created in Exotic Sephardic Kitchens from Morocco to India.* New York: Plume, 1994.

Patnaik, Naveen. *The Garden of Life: An Introduction to the Healing Plants of India.* New York: Doubleday, 1993.

Solomon, Charmaine. *Encyclopedia of Asian Food.* Boston: Periplus Editions, 1998.

MARATHI TITLES

Aurangabadkar, Anuradha. *Laduch Ladu.* Pune: Indrayani Sahitya Prakashan, 2005.

Barve, Mangala. *Annapurna.* Mumbai: Majestic Prakashan, 1978.

Dalvi, Lata. *Lajjatdar Malvani.* Mumbai: Rohan Prakashan, 2006.

Godbole, Kamla. *Maharashtriya Khaas Padartha: Puran Poli te Masalyachi Supari.* Pune: Sathe Prakashan, 2004.

Gupte, Bhanumati. *CKP Khasiyat.* Mumbai: Rohan Prakashan, 2005.

Marathe, Sangeeta. *Masta Malvani.* Pune: Indrayani Sahitya Prakashan, nd.

Nadkarni, Shalini. *Saraswat Swayampak* ati Prakashan, 2001.

Ogale, Kamlabai. *Ruchira.* Pune: Sa ss, 1970.

Purohit, Usha (compiler). *Sugrani ala.* Pune: Rohan Prakashan, 2005.

Vaidya, Laxmibai. *Pakasiddhi.* Pune: Utkarsh Prakashan, 1969.

Endnotes

1   Marathé, Kaumudi. *Maharashtrian Food: A Family Treasury*. Mumbai: Zaika, BPI, 1999.

2   I wrote an essay about 'forgotten foods' for the 'Mumbai Buzz with Mumbai Mirror' (*The Times of India Sunday Magazine*, Mumbai). The essay (published 25 February-3 March 2006), was the seed for this introduction.

3   A women's socio-religio-cultural event.

4   Vaidya, Lakshmibai. *Pakasiddhi*. Pune: Utkarsh Prakashan, 1969.

5   Ogale, Kamlabai. *Ruchira*. Pune: Sangam Press, 1970.

6   For a list of Marathi-language cookbooks, see bibliography on p. 381.

7   *CKP Khasiyat, Lajjatdar Malvani, Laduch Ladu*, etc. Publication details in bibliography, p. 381.

8   Fisher, M.F.K. *The Gastronomical Me*. New York: North Point Press, 2001, Reprint. Originally published: New York: Duell, Sloan & Pearce, © 1943.

9   About 308,000 sq kms; 35 districts.

10 Over 96 million people, according to the 2001 census.

11 Centre for Monitoring Indian Economy (CMIE), http://www.cmie.com/database/?service=database-products/regional-monitoring-service/maharashtra.htm, October 2006.

12 Encyclopaedia Britannica. 'Maharashtra', Britannica Online. http://www.eb.com: 180/cgi-bin/g?DocF=micro/368/6.html, January 1998.

13 Fisher folk of Konkani origin.

14 '. . .Coconut milk, hot chilli, cardamom, cinnamon, turmeric, ginger, cumin, coriander . . . are standard flavourings . . .'. Marks, Copeland. *Sephardic Cooking: 600 Recipes Created in Exotic Sephardic Kitchens from Morocco to India*. New York: Plume, 1994.

15   Maharashtra State Gazetteer, Government of Maharashtra, Mumbai, Directorate of Government Printing, Stationery and Publications, Maharashtra State, 1963, pp.185-241.

16   BAIF, www.baif.com, March 2006.

17   Patnaik, Naveen. *The Garden of Life: An Introduction to the Healing Plants of India.* New York: Doubleday, 1993.

18   http://dev.gramene.org/triticum/triticum_nutrition.html, October 2006.

19   Ibid.

20   The endosperm sifted out of durum wheat (hard wheat) is used to make pastas.

21   From *Charmaine Solomon's Encyclopedia of Asian Food*, Periplus Editions, 1998, supplied courtesy of New Holland Publishers (Australia).http://www.asiafood.org/glossary_1.cfm?alpha=S&wordid=2631&startno=27&endno=51, October 2006.

22   http://www.fao.org/rice2004/en/p6.htm, October 2006.

23   Nutrition Data.com: http://www.nutritiondata.com/facts-B00001-01c21US.html October 2006.

24   http://dev.gramene.org/species/pennisetum/pearlmillet_nutrition.html October 2006.

25   Ibid, November 2006.

26   I have referred extensively to Gernot Katzer's Spice Pages online: http://www.uni-graz.at/~katzer/engl/.

27   Achaya, K.T. *A Historical Dictionary of Indian Food.* New Delhi: Oxford University Press, 2003, chunam, p.45.

28   http://www.askoxford.com/concise_oed/chutney?view=uk, Compact Oxford English Dictionary definition 20 December 2006.

29   Achaya, K.T. *A Historical Dictionary of Indian Food.* New Delhi: Oxford University Press, 2003, chatni, p.45.

30   Ibid.

Index

Index   387

Dudh-poli (Chapati-milk mush) 359
Gul-chun (Jaggery-coconut relish) 360
Gul-tup (Jaggery and clarified butter) 360
Kelyachi shikran (Fresh banana pudding) 360
Lonavla chikki (Peanut brittle) 358
Tup-kela (Clarified butter with bananas) 361
Tup-sakhar (Clarified butter and sugar) 361

CHUTNEY PASTES
Aruna's kharda (Green chilli-garlic chutney) 277
Bhoplyachya salachi chutney (Red pumpkin rind chutney) 274
Coriander-onion chutney 278
Coriander-tomato chutney 278
Kandyachi chutney (Mouth-watering onion chutney) 275
Khobryachi chutney – I (Meera's coconut chutney) 279
Khobryachi chutney – II (Anuradha's coconut chutney) 280
Kolhapuri kharda (Chilli-onion-tomato chutney) 276
Kothimbirichi chutney (Meera's coriander chutney trio) 277
Lasnichi oli chutney (Vahini Aji's super moist garlic
    chutney) 278
Thecha (Pounded chilli & lime chutney) 281

CHUTNEY POWDERS
Danyachi chutney (Peanut chutney) 270
Kadhilimbachi chutney (Curry leaf chutney) 271
Karlyachi chutney (Bitter gourd chutney) 272
Khevda (Garlic-Peanut Chutney) 273
Lasnichi chutney (Garlic chutney) 273

DESSERTS & SWEETS
Amrakhand (Rich mango yogurt) 324
Amras (Mango purée with black pepper) 305
Anarsé (Deep-fried rice flour-jaggery cakes) 325
Basundi (Thick saffron milk with nuts) 318
Batatyachi vadi (Mom's potato fudgies) 333
Besanachi vadi (Gram flour squares) 334

- Tandulachya pithachi bhakri (Hand-flattened rice flour bread) 107

Sorghum
- Bhakri (Hand-flattened millet or sorghum bread) 102
- Ukad shengulé (Sorghum pasta) 120

Sweet Breads
- Bhoplyachi puri (Tasty fried pumpkin bread) 343
- Gulachi poli (Sesame-jaggery winter bread) 346
- Khavyachi poli (Rich milk-filled sweet bread) 348
- Pakatli puri (Deep-fried rounds in lemony syrup) 344
- Policha ladu (Chapatti-jaggery balls) 106
- Puran poli (Festival sweet bread) 350
- Sakhar poli (Simply sweet bread) 105
- Shindi dashmi (Crunchy Marathi cookies) 345
- Shiryachi poli (Sweet semolina-filled bread) 349

Wheat
- Fugia (East Indian fried bread) 110
- Ghadichi poli (Layered wholewheat bread) 103
- Phulka (Puffed wholewheat bread) 106
- Policha ladu (Chapatti-jaggery balls) 106
- Puri (Airy fried bread) 108
- Satyanarayanacha shira (Heavenly semolina) 71
- Shankarpali (Savoury flaky pastry squares) 84
- Shira, tikhat (Steamed semolina with vegetables) 71
- Tikhatamithachi puri (Spicy fried bread) 111

LEGUMES
Ambat varan (CKP sour lentils) 208
Bajricha khichadi (Millet-Lentil 'rice') 118
Chanchyachi dal ghalun bhajya (Vegetables with Bengal gram) 172
Dal-methi (Fenugreek lentils) 209
Dudhacha pithla (Gram flour topping cooked in milk) 228
Ghavari/papdichi bhaji (Green beans with Marathi spice) 174
Gole sambar/golyachi amti (Bengal gram dumplings in gravy) 210

Index

Sodyaché kanda pohé (CKP beaten rice with dried shrimp) 90
Vada-pav 88
Vatli dal (Tangy Bengal gram hash) 96

VEGETABLES
Aubergine
- Bharli vangi (Aubergine stuffed with coconut and tamarind) 168
- Bharli vangi, sode ghalun (Aubergine and potato stuffed with
    dried shrimp) 170

Banana
- Kelphulachi bhaji (Banana blossom stir-fry) 178

Beans
- Gavari/papdichi bhaji (Green beans with Marathi spice) 174

Cabbage
- Wafola (Baba's savoury cabbage cake) 162

Colocasia
- Aluchi vadi (Sanjiv's favourite leafy roll) 154

Cucumber
- Kakdichi amti (Gravied cucumber) 190

Drumsticks
- Shevgyachya shengancha rassa (Divine drumsticks) 195

Green peas
- Konkanastha matarchi usal (Konkanastha green peas) 222
- Matarchi karanji (Savoury green pea-filled crescents) 91

Gourds
- Dudhi-kajuchi Sonari amti (Goldsmith's bottle gourd and cashew
    sauce) 189
- Lal bhoplyachi bhaji (Fenugreek-scented pumpkin) 179